The
Compassionate
Beast

The Compassionate Beast

WHAT SCIENCE IS DISCOVERING ABOUT THE HUMANE SIDE OF HUMANKIND

Morton Hunt

WILLIAM MORROW AND COMPANY, INC.
NEW YORK

Recognizing the importance of preserving what has been written, it is the policy of William Morrow and Company, Inc., and its imprints and affiliates to have the books it publishes printed on acid-free paper, and we exert our best efforts to that end.

Library of Congress Cataloging-in-Publication Data

Hunt, Morton M., 1920-
    The compassionate beast : what science is discovering about the humane side of humankind / by Morton Hunt.
        p.   cm.
    Includes bibliographical references.
    ISBN 0–688–07577–0
    1. Altruism.   2. Helping behavior.   I. Title
BF637.H4H86   1990
155.2'32—dc20   89-38546
                                                            CIP

Printed in the United States of America

First Edition

1 2 3 4 5 6 7 8 9 10

BOOK DESIGN BY BERNARD SCHLEIFER

To my son Jeffrey

CONTENTS

The
Compassionate
Beast

CHAPTER ONE

Strange Behavior

THE MYSTERY OF ALTRUISM

He seemed a rather ordinary man, a balding, middle-aged bank examiner with a grizzled moustache and small beard; those who knew Arland Williams, Jr., were as astonished as the rest of the world at his behavior one January afternoon in 1982.

It was nearly dark in foggy, bitter-cold Washington that day as homeward-bound cars choked the Fourteenth Street Bridge over the Potomac. Suddenly there was the growing roar of a large jet approaching, laboring—and then it burst into sight, slammed across the bridge with a deafening crash, and plunged into the icy river in a cascade of water, shattered parts, and flying bodies.

Seventy-nine of the eighty-five people aboard the Air Florida plane either died instantly or within a few seconds of being thrown into the frigid river. But the crew of a police rescue helicopter, arriving moments later, saw three women and two men clinging to the broken-off tail section, which remained afloat, and another man treading water nearby.

The helicopter, hovering overhead, lowered a rope to the man treading water and hauled him off to safety. Then it came back and lowered the rope to the group hanging onto the tail section. A balding man with a small beard caught it, but before the rescuers could pull him up, he handed the rope to Kelly Duncan, a cabin attendant, and the helicopter took her away.

When it returned, he caught the rope again, and again handed it to someone else. Arland Williams, forty-six years old and a sedentary worker, must have known that he was no better equipped than the others to endure the ordeal and that

*his chances of survival were slipping away fast. And he had a lot to live for;
divorced some time earlier, he had recently fallen in love and become engaged. Yet
the third time and possibly a fourth time (eye-witness accounts vary) that he caught
the rope, he gave it to another person.*

When the helicopter returned one last time, for him, he was gone.

How admirable—and how incomprehensible.

We are awed by such behavior, yet it mystifies and disturbs us.
Although we believe that helping someone else in distress is good
and right, we also feel that helping someone else, especially a stranger, at the cost of one's own life is unnatural. Acts of this kind baffle
and trouble us, for they run counter to the primal urge to do whatever increases one's chance of staying alive and to avoid doing
whatever has the opposite effect.

What is far more important, we may feel somewhat the same
mixture of respect and uneasiness about all sorts of relatively ordinary and undramatic acts of kindness, helpfulness, or generosity to
strangers or outsiders. Such behavior always costs the giver something, sometimes a great deal, in time, effort, and money; when it
involves no expectation of repayment or reward—when it is what
we call altruism—we find it especially praiseworthy, but puzzling
and even troubling.

It is easier for us to understand selfish, aggressive, or brutal acts,
for they almost always benefit, or are meant to benefit, the one who
so acts. But altruistic acts seem so contrary to the fundamental drive
toward self-preservation that we tend to look for hidden payoffs,
bizarre neuroses, or other dark ways of explaining them. Even as we
may secretly wonder what Arland Williams's "real" reasons were
for giving the rope to others, we may wonder about the secret
motives of anyone who operates a soup kitchen for the homeless,
spends time playing with abandoned children in hospital wards, or
merely stops to pick up a stranded motorist by the roadside.

The perplexity that altruistic behavior arouses in us emanates
from a dour view of human nature that has been dominant, at least
in Western cultures, since the time of the Greeks. While a few sages
have argued that humankind is essentially good, or at least potentially so, the great majority of thinkers have echoed Plautus's dismal
view that "man is a wolf to man," a selfish, brutal, and vicious
beast—more savage, indeed, toward its own kind than any other
beast. In our era, with its unparalleled record of massacres, vast
wars, and genocide, such misanthropy is the preferred, the smart,

the supposedly realistic view; any more positive view of human nature is widely regarded as naive or Panglossian.

Yet such realism arises from a strongly biased body of information. We are very apt to judge the sum total of human benevolence as trifling compared with the sum total of human bestiality because history and the news media record chiefly the latter and rarely consider the former worth mentioning. Moreover, most of us, even though we may aver that humankind is beastly, expect human beings to be generally decent and helpful to each other—a basic assumption taught to almost all children—and hardly notice most such behavior; like the air around us, it is the unperceived atmosphere of our daily lives. But we notice its opposite—muggings, murders, rapes, child abuse, race riots, wars, genocide—precisely because these behaviors are *not* what we really expect of our fellow human beings. As altruism researchers Harriet L. Rheingold and Gena N. Emery of the University of North Carolina ruefully comment, "Such is the orientation of the world . . . that disruptive behaviors command attention while the overwhelmingly more common prosocial behaviors go largely unremarked." And so we may easily believe that the human being is not only a beast but the most vicious of beasts.

In our own time, however, and for the first time in history, statistics are routinely gathered that give some hint of the dimensions of human altruism. For instance:

- Each year about nine million Americans give one or more pints of their blood for the benefit of people they do not know, although they will never receive the thanks of those in whose bodies their blood will circulate or even learn whether the gift of blood sustained life in them.
- Nearly half of all American adults, according to a 1988 Gallup survey, did volunteer work in 1987, some of them for their clubs and neighborhoods, but others for the benefit of people they did not know and who, in many cases, lived in remote parts of the nation or the world. The average volunteer spent nearly five hours a week (the national total was 19.5 billion hours) pushing the ill in wheelchairs in hospitals, tending the dying at home, answering hot lines for the frightened and suicidal, raising funds for AIDS research, and so on and on.
- People in seven out of ten American households contributed

to charities of one sort or another in 1988, most of them to benefit strangers they did not know or had no direct connection with. Despite recent unfavorable changes in tax law, individual donors gave nearly $87 *billion,* a 7.3 percent increase over the previous year, more than two thirds of it purely voluntary and outside the relatively obligatory channel of religious donations.

But more emotionally compelling than such data is the evidence of our own everyday experiences of altruism, most of which we take for granted and overlook when making generalizations about human nature, such as:

- the innumerable tiny kindnesses we render many people to whom we have no close bonds—neighbors, fellow passengers on the bus or train, strangers in the street—without weighing what we may get in return (typically, for example, nearly all of us, seeing a car in a restaurant parking lot with its headlights left on, will try to turn them off or make some effort to find the owner inside);
- the physical help nearly all of us unthinkingly and instantly offer someone who has slipped and fallen, dropped something, or looks lost and bewildered;
- the pocket change we give to blind beggars and Salvation Army Santa Clauses, or drop in good-cause collection jars of all sorts;
- the calls we make to fire companies or the police on behalf of others, often strangers, even though our own interests are not threatened;
- the help many of us automatically offer people who have been driven out of their homes by fire, flood, or explosion; the donations many of us make when we read how an earthquake has destroyed the homes of a distant, alien people or see photographs of swollen-bellied, stick-legged children dying of starvation in some African nation we know nothing about.

Such responses to other people's needs rarely make the news. But those that do, however, because there is something dramatic or noteworthy about them, are typically not examples of the superhuman behavior of extraordinary people but of the normal responses of ordinary people to a stranger in pain or danger. A few recent examples:

- When television newscasts reported, in 1987, that seven-year-old Ronald DeSillers, Jr., had already rejected one transplanted liver and would soon die if he could not get another—which his mother could not afford—people all over the country, unbidden, sent in contributions ranging from the very small to the substantial and totaling $690,000.
- In Riverhead, New York, Joan and Roger Metcalf, Charles West, and Donna Lee spent every Saturday, during much of 1988, building a house, not for themselves but for Classie Kelly, a black woman with five children who could not otherwise have afforded it. The four weekend builders, all members of the Mount Sinai Congregational Church, are part of Habitat for Humanity, an international group with branches in twenty-five countries; its members put in unpaid time as laborers on housing for low-income families. (In the United States alone some 280 projects are currently under way.) The recipients work along with the volunteers and pay the costs of materials and land; Mrs. Kelly, a school custodian, got her house for about forty thousand dollars. Why do the volunteers choose this arduous and demanding form of giving? Mrs. Metcalf's explanation is as good as any: "I like to help people and I don't like to sit in meetings. I like to see something happening."
- In December 1982, twenty-nine-year-old Reginald Andrews, a black man, then unemployed and deeply in debt, was standing on a subway platform in Manhattan, mulling over his inability to do much about Christmas for his eight children. The train pulled in. In front of Andrews, David Schnair, an elderly, blind white man, felt around with his cane, mistook the space between two cars for a door, and fell onto the track. Andrews instantly jumped down under the train, dragged Schnair to a cubbyhole beneath the platform, out of the way of the wheels, and held him there until the train, which had started moving, was stopped and the two could be hoisted to safety. Asked later why he had done it, Andrews said simply, "I knew what I had to do." (His altruism had a consequence that he never reckoned on when saving Schnair's life: Three days later, someone who had read about

the rescue in a newspaper and chose not to be identified sent Andrews a three-thousand-dollar check with which to wipe out his debts.)

One could compile a huge dossier of such evidence of the ubiquity of altruism, but a single pervasive, easily overlooked fact proves that although we often behave abominably to our fellow human beings, we are also routinely and spontaneously caring and benevolent to them. That proof: *We endure.* Our emotional and physical makeup requires that we live in contact with other people, but we could not survive social life if we were primarily cruel and selfish.

Nor is our benevolence toward each other merely a matter of cooperation. Helping others in order to benefit ourselves is necessary but insufficient for communal living; by itself it yields a social life something like an armed truce. Helping others without any expectation of personal benefit, or even at some cost to ourselves, is very different; this is what binds individuals together and makes a society of them. No society could exist, the great sociologist Émile Durkheim hypothesized, in which people did not continually make self-sacrifices for each other.

But while Durkheim's hypothesis holds that altruism is essential to human survival, it does not solve its central mystery: how such behavior can arise in conflict with the drive to self-preservation.

Scientists are usually intrigued by any phenomenon that is a mystery, but until a couple of decades ago they virtually ignored the subject of altruism. Psychologists and other behavioral and social scientists felt uncomfortable about the subject and mistrusted the evidence of it since it clearly contradicts the most basic rule of learned behavior, *the law of reinforcement,* which states that creatures learn to act in those ways that reward them or that enable them to avoid unpleasant experiences. From the pigeon in a Skinner box learning to peck the red button for a bit of food to the senator running for reelection, the behavior of sentient creatures is shaped by gain and pain.

But since altruism yields neither apparent reward nor escape from pain, and is usually costly to a lesser or greater degree, how do we acquire such behavior and why do we engage in it? As long ago as 1883, Lester Ward, the first American sociologist, termed this "the altruism paradox." Until recently, most social and behavioral scientists preferred to think that altruism was only an illusion—that it had some hidden selfish or self-serving motive—rather than suppose that it was a reality that called in question the very foundation of behavioral science.

Of course, perhaps altruism is not learned but instinctual. Yet this, too, makes no sense: Any instinct that serves to decrease a creature's well-being, and thus its chances of enduring and of perpetuating its kind, should be weeded out by the struggle of the fittest to survive. Thus, again, altruism is a paradox; and again, it is tempting to suppose it only a disguised form of self-interest.

Today, although more than two decades of research have produced a vast amount of knowledge about altruism, many scientists still see it as something of a paradox and seemingly incompatible with the basic laws of psychology and life. The more generous any act, the more unnatural and suspect some people find it. Not many years ago, a study reported that most physicians seriously doubted the altruism of people who volunteered as living organ donors; they felt that such persons, if related to the recipient, had yielded to family pressure, and if unrelated to the recipient, were mentally ill.

But another view is now possible: The accumulating evidence of altruism research has not only gone far to dispel the mystery and explain the paradox but given us reason to think better of human nature than we have in the past. And reason, too, to hope that some day, perhaps soon, we may find ways to build a better, less hostile, more humane world; for if we knew enough about what engenders altruism to be able to cultivate it—and the evidence suggests that we already do—we could vastly improve family life, community life, the life of our society, and perhaps even relations among the peoples of the world.

WHAT DO WE MEAN BY ALTRUISM?

Before we look at that scientific evidence, we had better pause briefly to define more precisely what it is that we are talking about.

The word altruism is sometimes used as if it meant any and all behavior intended to benefit others in any way: Psychotherapists and social workers, for instance, are sometimes said to practice altruistic professions. But the practice of their professions benefits them as well as others; so do teamwork activities in which we seek our own good as well as that of our teammates, kindnesses we know will elicit the same in return (watering a neighbor's plants while he is out of town so that he will do the same for you), and acts that benefit us by avoiding penalties (sweeping our sidewalk, lowering our headlights when a car is approaching). There is nothing mysterious or contrary to self-interest about such behavior; it is socially valuable, but it is not altruistic.

Altruism is also often equated with helping, or helping with altruism. That's somewhat closer to the mark, but still too broad. Altruism almost always involves helping someone who needs it, but not all helping is altruistic. Much of it is cooperative (again, meant to benefit the helper as well as the helped); some of it is forced, not freely given; and some is intended to win prestige or other rewards and thus is self-serving.

All the above socially beneficial acts are part of what social scientists call *prosocial behavior*. Altruism is one form of prosocial behavior—but the only one that appears to violate the law of reinforcement and run counter to self-interest.

How then shall we define it? Of the many definitions proposed by social scientists, the one offered some years ago by psychologists Jacqueline R. Macaulay and Leonard Berkowitz appears to be the most widely accepted: "Behavior carried out to benefit another without anticipation of rewards from external sources."

That nicely excludes most acts that simulate altruism but are not genuinely altruistic. A biology professor I know recently told me that when she was a teenager in Poland in 1944 and 1945, during the time of the Final Solution, she and nearly a dozen other Jews spent half a year huddled in a stinking, muddy pit under the floor of a chicken shed, half-frozen and choking in the fetid, used-up air; the whole pitiful band of them subsisted on one bucket of boiled potatoes per day. Was the peasant an altruist who, risking his life, hid them from the Nazis and fed them? Hardly. Despising them as much as any Nazi, he hid them for pay, treated them far worse than his chickens, bullied and badgered them for extra money, and, whenever they asked for more food and better ventilation, threatened to turn them in. No, though he saved their lives, he did it to benefit himself; he was no altruist.

The Macaulay-Berkowitz definition also excludes such self-serving acts of generosity as the "potlatch," the curious folkway of the Kwakiutl Indians of the Pacific Northwest that so impressed early explorers. At a ceremonial feast, the host would distribute to his guests great quantities of food and valuable property, leaving himself virtually a pauper. Anthropologists who studied this custom recognized that while it seemed to embody boundless generosity, its real purpose was to maintain or increase the giver's status in the community; the giving was highly competitive and self-seeking rather than altruistic.

Much the same is true of certain acts of benevolence in our own society. The money-raising efforts of well-to-do urbanites on behalf of the arts and medical research are a case in point. Those who exert themselves in such philanthropic causes serve good ends, but for a major payoff: Their activities are a way of "making it" in society. Such money-raising is altruistic only when the social payoff is not the primary and crucial motive, but from all accounts, that is rarely the case; if there were no public acclaim, if the money-raising had to be done secretly, the people who carry out the good work would do something else altogether. Their work is socially useful and praiseworthy, but there is neither paradox nor mystery in it; to say it is not real altruism is not to denigrate it but merely to classify it correctly.

A little more difficult is the case of well-to-do persons whose donations and contributions earn them a substantial tax saving. Such giving is usually thought of as altruistic, but the givers often have mixed motives; humanitarianism is one of them, but to the extent that, save for the tax benefit, the giver would give less or nothing, it is a hybrid form of altruism or perhaps a form of pseudoaltruism. Similarly, doctors and lawyers who put in a few hours per week of free service to the poor are, for the most part, living up to the ethical expectations of their fellow professionals; sociologist Robert K. Merton calls this "institutional altruism," to distinguish it from behavior motivated by a desire to help another without an external reward in mind. It is altruism of an adulterated sort—socially valuable and estimable, but not what we should put under the microscope if we are trying to understand the phenomenon.

Several levels of pseudoaltruism coexist in the operations of Samaritania, a company in Grafton, Massachusetts, that operates vans manned by "Samaritans" who cruise busy highways looking for motorists in need of help. The company is financed by corporate sponsors who, in return for their donations, have their names displayed on the side of the vans; the drivers are paid from $15,000 to $25,000 a year. Who are the altruists in this operation? The proprietors of Samaritania? Hardly; they're in it to earn money by doing a socially useful thing. The sponsors? They're in it partly to render service but in larger part to earn good will for their companies. The drivers? The pay beclouds the issue, although because it's far from munificent, only those who like doing good take such a job; it would be more accurate to call what they do paid prosocial behavior. We will come to understand altruism better if we look at less ambiguous examples.

The Macaulay-Berkowitz definition is thus excellent, as far as it goes; it focuses our attention on the uniqueness of the altruistic phenomenon—the intent to benefit another without the expectation of external reward. (Internal reward such as a sense of satisfaction or pleasure at doing good is another matter; we'll come to that a little later.)

In one respect, however, the definition is too rigorous: One may be primarily motivated by the desire to do good to others, yet realize that he or she will probably reap some kind of reward. Still, if the selfless motivation is not only stronger but sufficient to make the altruist act, the additional existence of a selfish motive does not mean the act is not altruistic. My friend William J. Goode, a distinguished sociologist, after asking me what I meant to include in this book, wrote me a concerned letter in which he urged me not to try to distinguish between "true" altruism and lesser varieties:

> I worry that you are embracing a Platonic notion of altruism, and thus a false dichotomy. The skeptic can say: Prove to me that the person really sought nothing else but did the altruistic deed for no gain at all. There are so many levels of gain. When someone gives generously to the museum, one may be quite sincerely aiming at half a dozen purely disinterested goals, including helping humankind. But one may also be aware that one will get social approval for it, esteem, possibly an invitation to a prestigious cocktail party.

His point is well taken, yet the example he gives seems to me not to invalidate the notion of true altruism. If the donor to a museum would have given anyway without the rewards, then giving for others' sake *plus* his own is still altruistic; if he would not have given except for the self-benefit—if, that is, self-benefit is his primary and essential motive—his giving is not altruistic even though it benefits others.

Finally, the Macaulay-Berkowitz definition makes no mention

of one important component: the *cost* of altruism to the altruist—often its central mystery. Did you give a quarter to a blind beggar? Your act cost you very little in cash and nothing whatever in time or effort; still, it was a measurable cost. At the other end of the spectrum, each year the Carnegie Hero Fund Commission honors a number of men and women (and even a few children) for deeds such as rushing into a burning building or leaping into an icy pond to save some stranger's life, often suffering serious injuries or even death as a consequence. That is far harder to account for than the giving of a quarter; yet no matter how small or large the cost, any kind of cost has some deterrent effect and is therefore an essential component of the mystery of altruism.

My own working definition is thus: "Behavior carried out to benefit another at some sacrifice to oneself, and without, or not primarily because of, the expectation of rewards from external sources."

DOES "REAL" ALTRUISM EXIST?

The definition is ideally exemplified by one of the best-known of all acts of altruism: the rescue, by a passerby, of a stranger who had been robbed, wounded, and left bleeding by the roadside. I refer, of course, to the parable of the Good Samaritan; it is worth rereading here, since we will have several occasions to allude to it.

A disputatious lawyer, to whom Jesus said, "Thou shalt love thy neighbor as thyself," asked, "And who is my neighbor?" Jesus replied:

> A certain man went down from Jerusalem to Jericho, and fell among thieves, which stripped him of his raiment, and wounded him, and departed, leaving him half dead. And by chance there came a certain priest that way: and when he saw him, he passed by on the other side. And likewise a Levite, when he was at the place, came and looked on him, and passed by on the other side.
>
> But a certain Samaritan, as he journeyed, came where he was: and when he saw him, he had compassion on him, and went to him, and bound up his wounds, pouring in oil and wine, and set him on his own beast, and brought him to an inn, and took care of him. And on the morrow when he departed,

he took out two pence, and gave them to the host, and said unto him, Take care of him; and whatsoever thou spendest more, when I come again, I will repay thee.

Which now of these three, thinkest thou, was neighbor to him that fell among the thieves?

And he said, He that shewed mercy on him. Then said Jesus unto him, Go, and do thou likewise.

The priest should have helped the victim because it was his duty, the Levite because he was a fellow Judean, but neither did so. The Samaritan, however, although he was a stranger and a member of a people who had poor relations with Judeans, saw the victim as a "neighbor"—a fellowman—and treated him as one, at some cost to himself in time, effort, and money, and without any apparent reward or expectation of future reward. His act is the very model of altruism.

But, one may reasonably say, it is only a parable; Christ was teaching how people *should* behave, not how they *do* behave. Why would anyone help a stranger when doing so offers him nothing in return, not even the sense of fulfilling an obligation to a kinsman or compatriot, and, furthermore, costs him time, effort, and money? If our behavior is governed by the law of reinforcement and if self-interest is the most fundamental of motivations, why would anyone act like the Samaritan?

Many of those who have believed that human beings are essentially selfish have flatly said that there is no such thing as "real," "true," or "pure" altruism. What looks like selfless benevolence has hidden rewards; what altruists do for others serves their own ends. From Lucretius to John Stuart Mill, those philosophers who have considered pleasure the prime mover of behavior have said that we benefit others only to increase our inner satisfactions; even when an altruistic act causes us pain, we do it in the expectation of a higher or greater pleasure later on.

As the seventeenth-century cleric and author, the Archbishop Fénelon—himself a good and kind person—wrote to Madame de Maintenon, "All generosity, all natural affection, is only self-love of a specially subtle, delusive, and diabolical quality." Others have argued that often we do good to avoid feeling bad: The eighteenth-century satirist Bernard de Mandeville said that if we have seen an infant about to fall into the fire and rescued it, "we only obliged ourselves, for to have seen it fall, and not striven to have hindered it, would have caused a pain which self-preservation compelled us to prevent."

Most contemporary psychologists offer much the same explanation of altruism and back it up by experiments showing that benevolent behavior, however noble in appearance, is primarily motivated by self-interest of some kind. It is the dominant view in contemporary psychology, as it has long been in Western philosophy.

Some altruism researchers claim, for instance, that all altruists seek or expect such overt rewards as return favors or public esteem. Others say that even when there is no such external payoff, the altruist acts chiefly for internal rewards, particularly feelings of worth and self-esteem. Julie Leirich, a Los Angeles supermarket clerk who salvages thrown-out food and gives it to homeless people on the Santa Monica beach, told a reporter for *People* that doing so gives her "goose bumps." Mrs. Esther Taylor, a retired nurse in Southampton, New York, spends several half-days a week as a hospice volunteer, giving aid, comfort, and personal service to people dying at home; when I asked her what moves her to do so, she said, simply, "I *enjoy* helping others. I have many beautiful moments and experiences with my patients."

Other researchers maintain that the primary goal of altruism is a rather different kind of internal reward: the relief of the discomfort we feel when we witness distress in someone else. Psychologist C. Daniel Batson, though he vigorously contests this view, likes to cite a charming anecdote about Abraham Lincoln that purports to exemplify it. According to an item in the Springfield (Illinois) *Monitor*, Lincoln told a fellow passenger in a coach that all men, when they do good, are motivated by selfishness. Just then, crossing a bridge, they heard a sow on the bank making a terrible noise because her piglets had fallen into the water. Lincoln asked the driver to stop, jumped out, lifted the piglets out of the water, and placed them on the bank. When he returned, his fellow passenger said, "Now Abe, where does selfishness come in on this little episode?"

"Why, bless your soul, Ed," said Lincoln, "that was the very essence of selfishness. I should have had no peace of mind all day had I gone on and left that suffering old sow worrying over those pigs. I did it to get peace of mind, don't you see?"

We can't know whether Lincoln was serious, or pulling Ed's leg, or simply hiding his genuine feelings; many who are moved to acts of altruism fear to be laughed at or thought somewhat peculiar.

But the question of whether an altruist is primarily trying to ease another's pain or his own need not exclude acts such as Lincoln's from the realm of altruism. There are many motives for altruistic behavior and many shades of moral value to altruistic acts; only when the primary motive is external reward, and is clearly more powerful than the desire to help the other person, is the beneficial act not one of altruism.

Here is a handful of examples of compassion or benevolence in each of which we can either see or easily imagine some personal reward, some egoistic motivation. Yet each so clearly benefited the recipient more than the donor, and two were so costly to the donors, that it seems reasonable to classify them as instances of true altruism. (The examples range from a trifling good deed to total self-sacrifice, but even trifling examples may be enlightening.)

- Cyrus Segal, a bassoonist with the New York City Opera and the American Ballet Theater, was waiting for a bus at Lincoln Center in Manhattan not long ago when his prized $12,000 bassoon, on the sidewalk at his feet in a large black canvas case, was stolen. Segal had owned it for twenty-five years, and although it was insured, he was deeply upset. "Bassoons have different personalities," he said. "I would never have found another one just like it." A vagrant brought the bassoon into a nearby store, Olga's Luggage and Gifts, and offered it to storekeeper Mark Mavris for ten dollars. Mavris, who comes from a musical family and knew what the owner must be feeling, immediately decided to buy it; he bargained the vagrant down to three dollars and a pack of cigarettes, and once in possession, began asking musicians who came into his store if they knew of anyone whose bassoon had been stolen. Within four days word had reached Segal, who came in and identified his beloved instrument. Marvis asked for no reward and even refused to accept the return of the three dollars and the cost of the cigarettes.
- Georgia Advocacy is a group that finds friends and counselors for the mentally handicapped and other needy people. In 1986, Irene Cissel, a mildly retarded woman of sixty-three, had medical problems requiring hospitalization and was going to have to send her two retarded adult children, who could not fend for themselves, to a mental institution. Alice Smith, fifty-six, a retired medical clerk, volunteered through

Georgia Advocacy to help: She took full care of Cissel's children until Cissel got out of the hospital, and since then has continued to stop by regularly to see to the family's needs and to spend time with them.

- In New York City, volunteers man the telephone hotlines, day and night, of The Samaritans of New York, Inc., where they compassionately listen to suicidal callers and try to help them find reason and strength to go on. (There are some seventy volunteers in all; each puts in at least three four-hour shifts a month.) The nondenominational organization is one of 126 branches of the Samaritans in 26 countries. At the New York center, according to director June Mann, an average of seventy depressed and potentially suicidal people call in each day. Listening to them and trying to help them is emotionally wearing and sometimes deeply depressing, since, as Ms. Mann says, "Not everyone who calls us makes it. We know some of them die." But the belief that many do make it who might have died without help motivates the volunteers to continue.

- In 1963, Paul Theroux, a young man destined to become a celebrated author, went to Malawi as a Peace Corps volunteer, where, living in primitive conditions, he worked hard for two years at various projects. Theroux, a maverick, detested the bureaucracy of the Corps and had his difficulties with it, but his feelings about what he did in Malawi—teaching school, running a literacy program, coaching sports, planting trees, helping build a road—reflect those of the majority of Peace Corps volunteers as revealed by psychological evaluations: "I felt I belonged there, I was happy, I was committed. I was having a good time as well as doing something worthwhile—what could have been better?"

- After German forces moved into Italy in 1943 and Jews were being arrested and shipped off to concentration camps, an Italian priest was asked by the Archbishop of Florence to head a committee to hide them in convents, garages, and private homes.* Because the Jews would need money for food and clothing, the priest got 720,000 lire—a very large sum at that time—from a wealthy philanthropist and for a

---

*He remains anonymous, as do all the rescuers of Jews interviewed by a team led by sociologist Samuel Oliner, whose study will be described in Chapter Seven.

while distributed funds to a number of them. But then the committee was betrayed and its members, including the priest, were imprisoned. He expected to be executed but, thanks to the intervention of a powerful friend, was eventually released. By then, all the others had been sent to Germany, and no one knew he still had 400,000 lire. Despite his being a known rescuer, he told a few Jews to pass the word that every morning he would be on the Ponte Vecchio and every afternoon in the cathedral; Jews in need could find him in those places. Risking his life day after day, he parceled out funds to those who sought him out until the fortune was all gone.

• Sixty-three of the 207 Medals of Honor awarded for service in Vietnam went to soldiers who used their own bodies to shield others from exploding devices—in most cases by throwing themselves on live hand grenades. (Fifty-nine of the sixty-three died). Sociologist Joseph A. Blake of Virginia Polytechnic Institute and State University studied the phenomenon and found that the more cohesive a combat group was, the greater the likelihood that it would produce such acts; those who committed them had sacrificed themselves not for their group's military goals but for the other men in it. Accordingly, Blake classifies their acts as "altruistic suicide," a phenomenon first identified in 1897 by Durkheim.

THE SCIENTIFIC STUDY OF ALTRUISM

Altruism, so named in 1851 by Auguste Comte, the first sociologist, was long known by other names—benevolence, pity, compassion, generosity, and so on—and often mentioned by holy men and philosophers, but only within the past generation has it been investigated scientifically. Until then, what was known—or, rather, believed—about it was the product of moralizing and armchair philosophizing.

Religious sages praised altruism as an ethical ideal and urged it on their listeners. Philosophers were of two minds about it: Many, as already noted, peremptorily dismissed it as nothing more than disguised self-interest; others, among them Plato, Aristotle, and Spinoza, believed that it did exist but made no effort to explain it except in the most general terms. Spinoza, for instance, had little to say about benevolence other than that it stems from a natural tendency in human beings to pity those in adversity and envy those who are in prosperity. Adam Smith, similarly sure that real altruism exists, was similarly uninformative about its psychological origins:

> How selfish soever man be supposed, there are evidently some principles in his nature, which interest him in the fortunes of others, and render their happiness necessary to him, though he derives nothing from it, except the pleasure of seeing it. Of this kind is pity or compassion.

Comte, too, regarded the existence of altruism—in his view the highest of virtues—as self-evident, and although he was a social scientist rather than a philosopher he made no effort to verify its existence empirically or to conduct experiments to discover how it arises.

Nor, for various reasons, did other behavioral or social scientists take any interest in it until more than a century after Comte had named it.

Sociologists were concerned with more purely social phenomena, such as how societies are organized and how social change comes about; in their eyes, the study of altruism belonged to psychology. The notable exception was the Harvard sociologist Pitirim Sorokin, who in the 1940s and 1950s wrote about "altruistic love," which he regarded as the only force that could reform the world. But his approach to the subject was mystical, spiritual, and hortatory, and his views on it had no empirical basis and offered no scientific explanation of it.

Psychologists, meanwhile, sought from the birth of their science to investigate individual psychological phenomena, but not interpersonal ones such as altruism. One of the two major schools of psychology in the late nineteenth century was that founded by Wilhelm Wundt, a German physiologist who, at the University of Leipzig in 1879, established the first laboratory for psychological experimentation. He and his followers were interested primarily in elementary psychological processes, amenable to study by means of simple experiments, such as the speed and accuracy with which people respond to visual or auditory signals under different conditions; altruism, obviously, lay outside their purview.

The other major school of psychology in that era was founded at about the same time by William James at Harvard; unlike Wundt, he and his followers were interested in exploring, chiefly through introspection (volunteers' reports of their thoughts and feelings under experimental conditions), such internal mental phenomena as habit formation, consciousness, the self, imagination, reasoning, and will. But like the Wundtians, their subject matter was the psychology of the individual; altruism, which is as much a social as a psychological phenomenon, was outside their area of interest.

Nor did altruism seem a suitable research topic to the members of most of the schools and subspecialties of psychology that sprang up during the first half of the present century. The trend in psychological research was toward ever smaller and more specific topics. This was only natural; every new science goes through a period of microinvestigations before it can turn to larger phenomena and overarching theories. Moreover, during most of those years psychological research in America was dominated by behaviorism, which looked only at observable, objective behavior and ignored internal, subjective processes such as reasoning and emotions, which its adherents considered unobservable and unverifiable.

For such reasons, most psychological research during much of the present century dealt with small, objective phenomena such as how animals or people can be conditioned or trained to respond in various ways, how these responses can be unlearned or replaced, and how natural or spontaneous responses can be inhibited.

But social psychology, a new specialty developing in the 1920s, deals with just such interpersonal and subjective phenomena as altruism. It is the study of how we perceive or misperceive others, respond to them, and are affected by them in social situations; its territory lies between individual psychology and sociology, and somewhat overlaps each.

At first, however, most social psychologists, influenced by behaviorism, limited themselves to small topics and to experiments yielding behavioral data—such questions as whether people perform tasks better when alone or when others are present, and whether an individual's perception of the length of a line can be swayed by the opinions of other people (and thus what conditions tend to produce conformity). Almost no one in social psychology was interested in, nor was the methodology of the discipline capable of, the investigation of so subtle and complex a phenomenon as altruism.

And by the time it was, World War II had turned the attention of social psychologists in the opposite direction, to the study of aggression, violence, and genocide. Not until the 1960s did social psychologists and, to a lesser extent, other behavioral and social scientists, begin to investigate the nature of altruism.

By then, two other trends in psychology had created conditions favoring its study. One was the displacement of behaviorism by a more holistic view of psychology, that of cognitive science, which saw it as possible—and essential—to study internal mental processes. The other was the rise of developmental psychology: The Swiss child psychologist Jean Piaget and his many American followers, observing children from shortly after birth to near maturity, were discovering how mental functions and their expression in behavior are assembled step by step by experience interacting with innate tendencies.

But while these two developments made it more feasible than formerly to investigate altruism and other aspects of prosocial behavior, what actually motivated social psychologists and others to do so was, according to many altruism researchers, the mood and the social changes of the 1960s. As Israeli social psychologist Daniel Bar-Tal, who spent many years in this country and has himself conducted many altruism studies, explains the burgeoning of research interest in the subject in the 1960s and especially in the 1970s:

> The study of helping seems to have emerged as a consequence of a social *Zeitgeist.* . . . Interest in the study of helping behavior has developed not only because of the scientific merit of the problem, but mainly as a consequence of the nature of the social problems that have preoccupied America in the last decade. In the way that the rise of fascism influenced the study of authoritarian personality, the events of the Second World War stimulated research into aggression, and the pressures of McCarthyism provoked the study of conformity, so the interest in helping behavior [arose] in a period when American society was looking for a better way of life—for ways of improving the quality of interpersonal relations.

It was a time when President Kennedy's ringing call—"Ask not what your country can do for you; ask what you can do for your country"—touched off an explosion of idealism; a time when civil rights, aid to the poor, and other humanitarian issues were high on the national agenda; a time when much of American youth was revolted by the war in Vietnam and passionately devoted to peace, cooperative endeavors, and good causes.

First a handful, then dozens, then hundreds of behavioral and social scientists began conducting laboratory experiments and field studies on cooperation, sharing, reciprocity, donating, helping in emergencies, and the like. On altruism alone, by 1970 some 150 studies had appeared in psychology-related journals; by 1982 the total had swelled to 1,050; and today the figure is estimated at 1,200. Scores or possibly hundreds of other studies of altruism have been made within other disciplines and published in other journals.

What sort of people have been doing all this work? Most are nearing or in early middle age (they were graduate students when altruism studies first became popular), but some are young graduate students and others are graying senior professors. They have diverse reasons for their interest in the subject: Some are still motivated by an idealism that had its roots in the 1960s; others are merely working in what they see as a valuable and reasonably "hot" area of research; a few come from religious backgrounds that gave them an abiding interest in ethical behavior; and a few are Holocaust survivors who were rescued by altruistic non-Jews and have a deep personal interest in understanding and promoting helping behavior. About the only trait altruism researchers have in common is one they share with all researchers in the behavioral and social sciences: the adult version of the child's insatiable curiosity about why other people behave as they do.

In short, there is no such thing as a typical altruism researcher. Any small sample of the people in the field would be unlikely to include two of a kind—any kind. Here, for instance, is a random selection of thumbnail sketches of half a dozen leading altruism researchers:

- Robert Cialdini, a social psychologist and professor at Arizona State University, is forty-three but boyish-looking— lots of straight brown hair, somewhat pug-nosed, quick to grin, enthusiastic. He traces his interest in altruism research back to his graduate student days when, although rather knowledgeable about psychology, he was puzzled and intrigued by his own susceptibility to door-to-door solicitors for charities (it wasn't that he felt he *wanted* to give but that they somehow made him feel *obliged* to). From then—1971—

until now, he has been devising and running laboratory experiments in which unsuspecting volunteers are asked, under varying conditions, to help someone in need, in an effort to ascertain to what extent the motives for generosity are selfish rather than unselfish.

- Carolyn Zahn-Waxler, a developmental psychologist and researcher at the National Institute of Mental Health in Bethesda, Maryland, is fiftyish, soft-spoken, and motherly-looking. She sees her interest in altruism as having deep-seated emotional sources: Her own mother had had severe emotional problems and frequently been hospitalized, and the daughter felt that as a result her own emotional development had been far from ideal. As an undergraduate at the University of Wisconsin she got "hooked on psychology," she says, in large part looking for self-understanding. What she found led her to devote her working life to studying the influences of the emotional milieux of home and school on child development, in particular which styles and techniques of parenting and teaching promote the development of altruism in children and which inhibit it.

- J. Philippe Rushton, a social psychologist and professor at the University of Western Ontario, is forty-five, dark-haired, good-looking, and voluble. Formerly British and something of a 1960s maverick in dress and manner, he is now Canadian and conventional in appearance—but not in psychological viewpoint. After a decade of studying the emotional and social influences that make children altruistic, he began reading zoologists' descriptions of animal altruism and was captivated by the notion that human altruism might be partly an inherited, biologically determined trait, even though—or perhaps because—this contradicted the weight of opinion in his own field. In recent years he has been studying twins in an effort to show the degree to which altruism is genetically determined, and publishing research findings that infuriate most other psychologists, a fact that seems to delight him.

- Nancy Eisenberg, a developmental psychologist and professor at Arizona State University, is tiny, slim, intense, and in her late thirties. A nonstop worker, in less than fifteen years she has published over a hundred research articles and reviews, a dozen chapters in books, and five books (two coedited with colleagues) on altruism and allied topics. She traces her interest in the subject back to her undergraduate years, when, in the spirit of that time (the 1960s), she wanted to study how people develop liberal and humanitarian political attitudes. But after immersing herself in the psychological literature, she concluded that the real, and more definable, issue was how they develop helping and altruistic attitudes. Ever since, she has been doing research on how children of different ages think about moral problems, such as what to do if someone needs help but giving it would be inconvenient or unpleasant. She sees adult altruism as the final stage in an unfolding process of emotional and intellectual growth.

- C. Daniel Batson, a social psychologist and professor at the University of Kansas, is forty-five, lean and balding, quiet and relaxed in body style, and possesses a deep, mellifluous voice and a warm, serious manner that would befit a minister. And, in fact, he started out to be a clergyman and earned two degrees in religious education at Princeton Theological Seminary, where his major interest was ethical behavior. But what theology had to say about how people should behave failed to explain why they actually behave as they do. Psychology, he decided, might provide answers to that more vital question. He therefore undertook the graduate study of psychology at Princeton, earned a doctorate, and since then has been conducting experiments in most of which volunteers come across people in need of help. His main goal is to test his hypothesis that some people help others out of the purest of motives; he is the leading spokesman in social psychology for the view that "true" altruism can and does exist.

- Ervin Staub, originally a personality and clinical psychologist, and now a personality-social psychologist and professor at the University of Massachusetts at Amherst, is a small, bald, handsome man of fifty; warm and outgoing, he often smiles enchantingly as he speaks with fervor about altruism, the subject that has dominated his professional life. He has good reason to care deeply about it: In Budapest in 1944, when he was six and when the Nazis were seeking to exterminate the city's Jews, he and his sister were placed in a "protected house," thanks to the Swedish diplomat Raoul Wallenberg, who almost single-handedly saved the lives of many thousands of Hungarian Jews. There, the Staub children were sheltered and cared for by Gentiles; later, their parents joined them. (Many other members of the family perished in the Nazi camps.) As an assistant professor of psychology at Harvard, Staub became interested in children's sharing and helping behavior, and studied both topics for years without asking himself why they interested him. Then he looked deep within himself, recognized the link with his own past, and realized that children's helping and sharing were only part of the larger and immensely important subject of prosocial and, in particular, altruistic behavior. He is a prodigiously productive experimenter and theoretician, and to date has written or coauthored six major books and some sixty articles and book chapters on the personality traits and social influences making for altruism.

These six and hundreds of other researchers have been assiduously exploring a broad array of factors they believe either foster or inhibit altruistic behavior and trying to assemble their disjoined findings into one coherent and comprehensive explanation. In their search for hard data, they have concocted a wide variety of hypotheses and devised a great many methods of putting them to the test.*

Some have conducted experiments to see whether animals ever act altruistically (which would suggest that altruism is, at least in part, instinctual). Among other things, they have:

- Hoisted a laboratory rat up on a platform, squealing in fear, to see whether another rat, which could lower the first one by pressing a bar, would do so to relieve its distress.
- Placed two cages side by side in each of which was a hungry chimpanzee, then given one of them a little food, to see whether it would give any to the other.

Other researchers have sought to discover whether altruism in human beings is, at least in part, hereditary and instinctive rather than learned. In two approaches to this goal, they have:

- Located sets of identical and fraternal twins, had them fill out questionnaires measuring their tendency to be altruistic, and then mathematically analyzed the data to see to what extent altruism is related to genetic similarity. (If identical twins are

*The findings of the following experiments will be discussed in later chapters.

more alike than fraternal twins in their tendency toward altruism or selfishness, altruism would appear to be at least partly an inherited trait.)
- Enlisted mothers of toddlers in an experiment in which the mothers would pretend they had hurt themselves, in order to see at what age and developmental level children begin spontaneously trying to comfort someone else in pain and to what extent these first efforts represent innate rather than learned behavior.

Other investigators have focused on the social settings in which people either help others in trouble or fail to do so, on the assumption that in some social situations most of us feel impelled to help but in others inhibited from helping. They have, for instance:

- Created what appeared to be accidents of various kinds in an adjoining room—usually the sound of someone falling off a ladder, then crying out in pain for help—to see whether people will help more readily when they are alone or when they are with others who make no move to help.
- Had assistants (confederates) fall down in a subway car and struggle unsuccessfully to rise, varying this scenario in a number of ways to see what conditions elicit the helping impulse and what ones repress it.
- Stationed a young female assistant next to a car with a flat tire, sometimes alongside a busy highway and sometimes alongside a quiet country road, to see when people were more likely to stop and offer help. Ran the same kind of experiment, this time with another female with a flat tire further back on the road being helped by someone, to see if the good example would induce more people to stop and help.

Still other researchers have been interested in the personality and social status of people who help as compared with those of people who do not. In two such studies the investigators:

- Dropped wallets, each containing a small amount of cash, an identification card, and personal items such as pictures, near the entrance to a paperback bookstore and to a bookstore specializing in pornography, both in downtown Seattle;

noted the clothing of those who picked them up; and by means of code numbers in the wallets, identified the clothing category (apparent social class) and bookstore choice of those who did, and those who did not, return the wallets.

- Went into both squatter communities and better neighborhoods in Istanbul and Ankara, asked passersby for favors— to make change, and to fill out a short questionnaire—and later dropped the top box of an awkward load and attempted clumsily to retrieve it, to see in which kind of community people would be more helpful to a stranger.

A number of other researchers have been interested in the extent to which generosity or helpfulness is a result of one's mood or emotional state. In experiments typical of this genre, investigators have:

- Solicited donations for a well-known charity from people who had just seen a sad movie and from others who had just seen a movie neutral in mood.
- Had half of a group of volunteers imagine they were enjoying a wonderful vacation in Hawaii, the other half that they were making arrangements of geometrically shaped pieces of paper (an emotionally neutral task), then asked each if they'd be willing to help a psychology researcher by filling out a boring questionnaire.

Finally, some researchers have sought to identify the social characteristics, personal traits, and major life experiences of people who have been notably altruistic. In one of the most ambitious of such projects, investigators gathered personal histories from people who had rescued Jews from the Nazis, and similar histories from people of comparable age, class, economic level, and region who had not done so; they then computer-analyzed the data to see how the upbringing and life experiences of the two groups had differed prior to the Nazi era, and which factors were related to their altruism or lack of altruism.

What emerges from all these varied approaches is a persuasive and satisfying explanation of this strange and wonderful phenomenon. But it is an intricate explanation, for like all complex behaviors, altruistic acts are the end product of varied combinations of many interacting causes. Everything from one's genetic inheritance and childhood experiences to the trivial events of the moment and their influence on mood plays a part in determining whether or not one acts altruistically in any situation. As Pope jested in his *Moral Essays:*

Who does a kindness is not therefore kind;
Perhaps prosperity becalm'd his breast;
Perhaps the wind just shifted from the East.

I hope, however, that as you see first one, then another, explanation of altruism, it will become apparent from the sequence in which they appear that they do fit together in one coherent and interdependent whole.

AN ALTRUISM QUIZ

All this will seem more immediate and personally meaningful if you test your own tendency to be or not be altruistic in various situations. Here is a quiz, adapted from the Helping-Orientation Questionnaire recently created by psychologists Daniel Romer, Charles L. Gruder, and Terri Lizzadro of the University of Illinois.* It consists of a dozen real-life situations with a set of responses that people often make. The original questionnaire contains twenty-three situations; I omit a number that apply primarily to college students.

Romer et al. validated their questionnaire—that is, made sure it actually measures altruism—by comparing the scores that a group of undergraduate men and women at the University of Illinois at Chicago got on it with scores the same people got on several well-authenticated tests of personality and altruistic tendencies and with their behavior in a real-life helping situation. My abbreviated version may not be quite as valid as the original, but I think it will be a stimulus to self-knowledge.

Imagine yourself in each of these situations and choose the action that most nearly describes what you would do. (In some cases you might prefer another action to any of those listed, but choose the one that comes closest.) Since no one but you

*Daniel Romer, Charles L. Gruder, and Terri Lizzadro, "A Person-Situation Approach to Altruistic Behavior," *Journal of Personality and Social Psychology*, 51,5:1001–1012, (1986). Copyright 1986 by the American Psychological Association; adapted by permission of the publisher and Dr. Romer.

will know how you answer the questions, try not to make yourself seem more virtuous than you really are.

Instructions on evaluating your answers, and a table by means of which you can compare yourself to Romer et al.'s sample, follow the quiz.

1. You have come across a lost wallet with a large sum of money in it as well as identification of the owner. You:
   A. return the wallet without letting the owner know who you are.
   B. return the wallet in hopes of receiving a reward.
   C. keep the wallet and the money.
   D. leave the wallet where you found it.
2. A child riding his or her tricycle past your house appears to be lost. You:
   A. ignore the child so as to avoid potential entanglements and misunderstanding.
   B. figure the child can find his or her own way home.
   C. ask the child where he or she lives and take him or her home.
   D. take the child into your home and notify the police.
3. A man who confronts you in Chicago's Loop [a sleazy area] does not speak English but appears to need directions. You:
   A. keep on walking so you won't be late.
   B. pretend you don't hear him.
   C. decide what to do on the basis of his appearance.
   D. help him in any way you can.
4. When it comes to cooperation when I would rather not, I usually:
   A. cooperate if it is helpful to others.
   B. cooperate if it is helpful to me.
   C. refuse to get involved.
   D. avoid situations where I might be asked to cooperate.
5. A friend asks to borrow an article of clothing. You:
   A. say you don't like to lend clothing.
   B. say no.
   C. lend the article if you may borrow something in return on another occasion.
   D. lend the article if you know the person really wants it.
6. A neighbor calls you and asks for a ride to a store that is six blocks away. You:
   A. refuse, thinking you will never need a favor from him.

    B. explain that you are too busy at the moment.

    C. immediately give the ride and wait while the neighbor shops.

    D. consent if the neighbor is a good friend.

7. Alone in your home, you hear a woman outside calling for help. You:

    A. go to her aid.

    B. call the police and join them at the scene.

    C. are afraid to intervene directly, so you take no action.

    D. are sure someone else has heard her so you wait.

8. An elderly lady standing on a street corner appears to be lost. You:

    A. go and help her.

    B. help her only if she is dressed nicely.

    C. assume someone else will help her.

    D. leave her alone, fearing she may think you are a purse snatcher.

9. A hitchhiker is thumbing for a ride late in the evening. It is raining and few cars are on the road. You:

    A. offer a ride if the person looks like someone you want to talk to.

    B. drive by, fearing for your safety.

    C. drive by and avoid the person.

    D. stop and offer a ride.

10. You are in a waiting room with another person. If you heard a scream in the adjoining room and the other person failed to respond, you would:

    A. help the screaming person whether the other person helps or not.

    B. help the screaming person only if the other person does too.

    C. wait to see if the screaming continues.

    D. leave the room.

11. A poorly dressed person confronts you on a deserted street and asks for a dime. You:

    A. ignore him.

    B. ask him what the money is for.

    C. give him the dime without asking any questions.

    D. refuse him the dime because it's just too much trouble.

12. When asked to volunteer for a needy cause for which you will receive pay, you:

A. volunteer but don't accept the pay.
B. volunteer and accept the pay.
C. do not volunteer.
D. volunteer if you are certain of getting paid and if the work is not demanding.

Interpreting Your Answers

The quiz distinguishes among three kinds of people: (1) the *altruistic;* (2) the *helpful but not altruistic* (those who help but want something in return); and (3) the *unhelpful* (Romer et al. specify two kinds—those who want others to help them, and those who neither help nor want anything from others—but for our purposes we can lump them together).

The following table shows which answers rate as altruistic, helpful, and unhelpful; it also shows what percentages of people in the sample gave each answer (the percentages sometimes add up to more than one hundred because of rounding). By comparing your answers to those of the sample, you can judge whether you are average, above average, or below average in altruism.

A caveat: The figures indicate what the people in this sample *thought* they'd do, but empirical studies have shown that such imagined behavior is apt to be somewhat more admirable than actual behavior. Of course, the same may be true of you.

It's clear enough that altruism isn't an across-the-board trait; people are much more likely to be (or think they'll be) altruistic in some situations than in others. Even if imagined behavior isn't

Altruistic	Helpful But Not Altruistic	Unhelpful
1. A (38%)	B (47%)	C, D (15%)
2. C (79%)	D (9%)	A, B (13%)
3. D (59%)	C (32%)	A, B (9%)
4. A (61%)	B (20%)	C, D (19%)
5. D (69%)	C (13%)	A, B (18%)
6. C (33%)	D (56%)	A, B (11%)
7. A (44%)	B (49%)	C, D (7%)
8. A (76%)	B (7%)	C, D (17%)
9. D (10%)	A (6%)	B, C (84%)
10. A (50%)	B (10%)	C, D (40%)
11. C (45%)	B (16%)	A, D (40%)
12. A (20%)	B (62%)	C, D (19%)

wholly matched by actual behavior, the quiz should have given you some idea of your own leaning toward—or away from—altruistic acts in a variety of situations.

The quiz has answered one question: "How altruistic am I?" You may want to come back to it after reading this book to see whether, having learned more about what makes people altruistic or selfish, you would respond differently to any of the situations.

But I hope that answers to a number of other questions of larger importance will be suggested by the research investigations and findings to be presented here. Among those questions:

- What inhibits altruism in us? What promotes it?
- What child-rearing techniques will foster the development of kindness and generosity in children?
- Can altruism be taught, or at least encouraged, in schools?
- What kinds of behavior on our own part will promote kindness and generosity in those with whom we interact?
- How can the general level of altruism be increased within a community?
- What government policies might raise the level of altruism throughout our society?
- Could our present knowledge of altruism be used to diminish hostility and tension among nations?

I cannot promise that this book will definitively answer all these formidable questions. But it will, I trust, show that we already know enough about altruism to be able to devise child-rearing techniques, educational methods, and social policies that could go a long way toward making us a more humane species, and this a more humane world.

CHAPTER TWO

In Accordance with Nature

GREATER AND LESSER ALTRUISTS

Recently, those who take a dark view of human nature have found in zoological studies new data to support their misanthropy. Ethologists' observations of animal behavior, they say, show that altruism is not uniquely human and, in fact, that we are only niggardly altruists compared to many other creatures. Consider this evidence:

- The scene: a broad green lawn in front of a suburban colonial house on a sunny spring morning. A plump-breasted robin is hopping across the grass, cocking its eye this way and that as it looks for a worm; nearby, several others are doing the same thing. Suddenly the robin sees the ominous wide-winged silhouette of a hawk glide into view, and crouches low, whistling piercingly. The other robins fly off toward the trees, while the hawk, alerted by the warning cry, dives. In an instant, the hawk is flapping heavily away, the robin, its beak agape in agony, clutched in its talons.

  Robins and birds of certain other species, such as thrushes and titmice, utter a distinctive warning cry at the approach of a hawk or other predator. The warning enables the sentinel's fellows to hide or take flight, but the sentinel, in calling out, attracts the predator's attention and often pays for its good deed with its life.

• The scene: a plain deep in tall grass, somewhere in eastern Africa, toward evening. Near the edge of the forest, a score of vervet monkeys are idly grooming each other, munching on food, or playing. Abruptly one of them, hearing a sound, stands up and looks toward it, sees the feared shape of a leopard crouching in the grass, and frantically utters a series of loud short cries. All the monkeys scramble toward the trees, but the leopard, guided by the cries of the one who called out, bounds across the grass and has him in an instant, the powerful jaws swiftly cutting short his screams.

Like robins, vervet monkeys and various other mammals that live in bands or troops warn their fellows of the approach of a predator. The vervets, more sophisticated than birds, make any one of four different sounds—one for flying enemies, another for animals on the ground, a third for tree-climbing enemies, and a fourth for snakes—thereby enabling the others to know from whence the threat is coming and which way to go to be safe. But as with a bird that warns its fellows, the vervet that issues the alarm advertises its whereabouts and is more likely than the others to lose its life.

• Some creatures are even more self-sacrificing. The robin and monkey at least have some chance of surviving, but there is none for the soldiers of an ant colony; unlike human soldiers, they never take flight, no matter how hopeless their situation, but fight to the death, if necessary. The battle technique of warriors of the African termite *Globitermes sulfureus* is inevitably suicidal; for the good of the colony, the termite spits out a stream of yellow stuff that congeals in the air, permanently trapping the antagonist (usually an ant)—and itself. Worker bees, too, die to defend their hive from human beings or other marauders: The bee's stinger remains stuck in the flesh of the enemy and, when the bee is knocked off, tears its body apart and causes its death.

And we? Such self-sacrifice, to save fellow human beings, is so rare that, as with the grenade suicides mentioned earlier, it is considered worthy of the highest honors.

• As if all this were not bad enough, even a single-celled animal can outdo us in altruism (in the ethologists' broad sense of that term—self sacrifice for another's benefit, even if not consciously motivated). The amoeba *Dictyostelium discoideum,* a slime mold, lives independently in the watery medium of its soil habitat, feeding on bacteria and procreating by fission. But when food grows scarce and the amoeba population overlarge, the amoebas aggregate; some form themselves into a spherical mass and produce spores that become the new generation, while others, "altruistically" denying themselves the chance to reproduce, form the thin stalk needed to support the sphere.

Which of us is as noble as the slime mold?

Such is the biological evidence cited for the view—actually an ancient one—that altruism is not natural to us as it is to many lower creatures but is forced upon us against our natural inclinations by civilization. As Thomas Hobbes grimly wrote in *Leviathan* three centuries ago, "Such gentler virtues as justice, equity, mercy, and, in sum, *doing to others as we would be done to,* without the terror of some power to cause them to be observed, are contrary to our natural passions." In more modern times, Freud expressed much the same opinion in *Civilization and Its Discontents,* and we often hear something similar today from various sources, among them those ethologists and sociobiologists who argue that we are more beastly than other beasts, and people who find animals more loving and lovable than human beings.

But if we are less self-sacrificing than the social insects, robins, and vervet monkeys, there is a vast difference between their kind of altruism and ours. When we are altruistic, it is because we mean to be; when animals are, with a few exceptions they are acting instinctively and without any such intention.

That, however, in the opinion of some hard-headed naturalists, does not make animal altruism any the less altruistic. Zoologists Mark Ridley and Richard Dawkins of Oxford University, for instance, maintain that intentionality is irrelevant and that altruism is to be measured by results alone:

Zoologists do not concern themselves with questions of subjective motive. If we use words like altruism at all, we define them by their effects and do not speculate about the animal's intentions. It follows that an indubitably unconscious entity such as a plant, or a gene, is in principle capable of displaying "altruism."

But what Ridley and Dawkins are talking about is not really altruism, even though many ethologists like to call it that. It has nothing to do with compassion, benevolence, or the desire to benefit another; it is, rather, instinctive behavior selected by evolution because it maximizes the animal's chance of perpetuating its own genes.

That may seem an absurdity: How could self-sacrifice increase the creature's chance of propagating itself?

Among the social insects, the answer is that the soldier is sterile and cannot propagate, but its act of self-sacrifice protects the fertile members of the colony, who are very close to it in genetic structure but whose hormones inhibit the self-sacrificing tendencies. In such a system, altruism helps preserve the altruist's own genes through its fertile siblings. But the insect warrior doesn't know that or mean to achieve that end; it simply responds, in preprogrammed ways, to the smell, touch, and other stimuli of the enemy, and does battle as automatically as a heat-seeking "smart bomb."

Birds, though well up the evolutionary ladder from insects, and monkeys, which are much farther up, also are responding unthinkingly and unintentionally to stimuli when they utter warning calls. The robin will sound its alarm when it sees a hawk, whether or not any other robins are nearby; even robins that have been raised by scientists in complete isolation from other robins do so. It's just something they can't help doing when they see a hawk.

The vervet monkey, when young, calls out whenever it sees something flying, prowling, or slithering around; its repertoire of calls is built in. It does learn from observing adults to use its calls with precision and not to sound the flying enemy call when it sees a falling leaf, but essentially its brain is preprogrammed to produce specialized warnings at the sign of danger—not with the aim of protecting its fellows but simply as a gut reaction to the stimulus that, as it happens, is useful to the species.

But many naturalists and animal-lovers interpret such behavior as being closely akin to the intentional and benevolent altruism of human beings. Even animal psychologists sometimes make that assumption. In the previous chapter I mentioned experiments in which a rat was given the opportunity to free a fellow rat from a frightening situation (being hauled up on a platform) by pressing a bar. In some cases, though not all, the rat that could ease the other's anxiety did just that; the researchers took this as proof of the rat's concern for its brother. Later, another experimenter gave a rat an even better chance to demonstrate altruism: He taught it to press a bar to get food, then hooked things up so that pressing the bar would also give an electric shock to another rat. Astonishingly, the first rat held back, apparently denying itself a meal in order not to shock its fellow.

But Daniel Batson—the theological seminary graduate who became a psychologist and altruism researcher—wasn't convinced. He and one of his graduate students subjected two rats to a series of shocks and noises to sensitize them. Then they offered one rat a chance to get food by pressing a bar that sometimes would simultaneously shock the other rat and sometimes would turn on noise. The rat did indeed avoid seeking food when it would shock its fellow—but also when it would turn on noise; evidently, what motivated the rat to abstain from food was its dislike of any noise, including that made by a frightened fellow rat. The researchers' conclusion: "When laboratory rats help a distressed companion, it is not because of altruistic concern for the other; their concern is for themselves."

The same is true of various forms of cooperation and mutual aid among higher animals. Many grazing animals congregate in herds, partly for mutual defense; some predators hunt in packs and help each other kill large and dangerous prey; and many animals clean or groom each other's coats in order to be groomed in return. In every case, the behavior is self-serving.

Only among some of the higher vertebrates are there a few instances of what may be genuine altruism: conscious and voluntary efforts to benefit another at some cost, at least in the form of unrewarded effort, to the benefactor. The examples are very few and minor, but they do exist and may be evolutionary precursors of human altruism. For instance:

- Wolves, highly social animals—social to their own kind, that is—will sometimes adopt the offspring of other wolves that have been killed.
- When a young elephant is in trouble (stuck in the mud, for instance), adult animals other than its mother may offer it help.

Still, such examples involve helping behavior among closely related pack members or are hormonally driven instinctive responses to the needs of the young. The only animal that sometimes very clearly tries to benefit a nonrelative at some cost to itself, not instinctively but as a result of mental or emotional processes, is our closest relative, the chimpanzee, to wit:

- When a chimpanzee has killed a small animal and is holding a piece of meat, an unrelated hungry chimpanzee may come up and beg for some; if the suppliant looks at the owner pleadingly and reaches out a hand, the owner will often let the other tear off small pieces, or may even tear them off and hand them over.
- A chimpanzee may rescue an unrelated chimpanzee that is in danger. An example of this, related by the ethologist Jane Goodall in *The Chimpanzees of Gombe,* took place at a captive chimpanzee colony, where, because the apes can't swim and are afraid to enter water, they are sometimes kept on islands surrounded by water-filled moats. Ms. Goodall writes:

> Washoe spent some time at Norman, Oklahoma, on an island ringed with an electric fence. One day a three-year-old female, Cindy, somehow jumped this fence. She fell into the moat, splashed wildly, and sank. As she reappeared, Washoe leaped over the fence, landed on the narrow strip of ground at the water's edge, and, clinging tightly to a clump of grass, stepped into the water and managed to seize one of Cindy's arms as the infant surfaced again. [Yet] Washoe was not related to Cindy and had not known her for very long. At Lion Country Safaris in Florida a number of [similar] rescues or attempted rescues have been observed.

Several important conclusions can be drawn from all these examples.

First, innate, automatic, self-sacrificing altruism is common among social insects, certain birds, and a few social mammals such as the vervet monkey.

Second, a somewhat different form of altruism—cooperation and/or favor-swapping that is largely innate and largely unlearned—exists among predators that hunt together and among some herding mammals.

Third, both of these kinds of altruism have some resemblance to the human kind, but the differences between human and animal altruism (except for that of the chimpanzee and possibly one or two other species) are far greater than their similarities. Much or even most of human altruism is conscious, intentional, and knowingly performed even when it is against the altruist's own best interest; that is what makes it special.

This is not to say that animal and human altruism are wholly unrelated or that human altruism has no built-in biological basis. Since altruistic behavior of one kind or another is common among social animals, and since for them it has great survival value and was therefore selected by evolution, we must ask: Does human altruism too have a genetic basis, acquired through evolution because it has survival value? Is that the answer, or part of it, to the paradox of altruism?

No doubt it would be more flattering to think that our altruism is wholly the result of emotional and mental processes and owes nothing to automatic responses to certain stimuli. But from what we have seen, it seems likely that our altruism is the outgrowth of primitive biological tendencies, and that some innate mechanisms make us capable of reacting to others' distress in ways that can develop, through social experience, into full-fledged altruism.

An analogy: Human infants arrive in the world without language, and though after several months they begin to babble, they never generate language on their own; they learn it from those around them, as is obvious from the fact that they learn the language that is spoken to them. Since not even the most intensively tutored ape can do one percent as well, it must be, as linguist Noam Chomsky maintains, that the human brain has built-in neural networks for making sense out of words, interpreting sentence structure, and using those interpretations as the basis of its speech. But the speech itself is learned behavior. We are born with the hardware; experience is our software.

So too with human altruism. It is not an automatic and unlearned response to stimuli, does not have stereotyped patterns, and does not assume identical form in different persons or different societies, yet it does develop in nearly everyone and in all societies. The many forms it assumes in individuals and in varied settings suggest that it is largely learned, but its universality and the general similarity of those forms indicate that it is the outgrowth of a genetically created predisposition interacting with social experience.

Such is the hypothesis one can propose based on the animal data. Let us see if there is any hard evidence to confirm it.

IS THERE AN ALTRUISTIC GENE?

The title of this section may seem absurd: How could any single gene, out of the million each of us possesses, produce behavior as complex and subtle as altruism?

It couldn't, any more than a single gene could produce political ambition, religious fundamentalism, or romantic love. Only a few scraps of simple behavior are genetically preprogrammed in human beings—the startle response to a sudden noise, or babies' sucking, for instance—and even these are the results of complex interactions among many genes and the body systems they chemically direct. But the phrase "the altruistic gene" is used by many scientists as shorthand; it refers to those built-in neural and visceral reactions to distress in others that are the substructure of altruistic behavior.

What proof is there that the altruistic gene exists? Since the infant, from its first day of life, learns from its surroundings, how can we know whether any part of a child's or adult's behavior is based on innate predispositions? A behavioral scientist may isolate a laboratory rat from its fellows at birth in order to see whether, at maturity, it will automatically know how to fight, mate, care for its young, and so on, but doing so to a human infant would be unthinkable.

Such experiments have, however, been unintentionally conducted by a few psychotic parents and stepparents. Some years ago, Genie, a thirteen-year-old girl who had been locked away by her parents since birth, was discovered by Los Angeles authorities. She was mute, incontinent, crawled on all fours, and understood nothing that was said to her. Some people suspected that Genie was mentally defective, but within four years, in foster care, she had gained some language ability, many social skills, and the mental capacity of an eight-year-old. If a human child cannot develop simple language, bladder control, or upright walking on its own, behavior as complex as altruism surely cannot be specifically coded in the genes.

But the equipment creating the *proclivity* and *capacity* for altruism may be. The major evidence, as shown by recent research, is the fact that young children, long before they can comprehend so sophisticated a concept as altruism, are made unhappy by the sight of unhappiness or pain in others and may even make primitive attempts to alleviate it.

This runs counter to the view long held by most child psychologists that altruistic behavior does not exist before six or seven years of age. Until then, they said, children are egoistic and see things only from their own viewpoint; not until the school years are they able to take others' viewpoints. Most psychologists have therefore held that younger children are unable to empathize with another person (that is, imagine or vicariously feel what that other person is feeling), and hence have no inclination toward altruism.

But that view has been contradicted in recent years by a number of studies by developmental psychologists who have closely observed and analyzed young children's behavior toward each other in naturalistic situations. One who has done such studies is Dr. Carolyn Zahn-Waxler, the developmental psychologist we have already met who is a researcher at the National Institute of Mental Health's Laboratory of Developmental Psychology in Bethesda, Maryland. She described her findings when I visited her:

"In graduate school I learned the standard view," she told me. "Then I came here in 1967 and became a participant in a series of studies that changed my mind. Part of that series was an experiment to see if we could train children in the three-to-six-year-old age range to be altruistic. First we had to establish a baseline—the typical behavior of three-year-olds—in order to see if the training made any difference. But in doing so, we were intrigued by our finding that, contrary to the accepted view, some of the children were already clearly altruistic by age three. How could that be? We thought a lot about it, and it was our hunch that the origins of altruism had to be something unlearned that existed in the child even earlier.

"So in 1973, after the main experiment was concluded, we started looking at still younger children. Mothers would bring their preschoolers to our lab to play in groups, and we'd observe them to see at what age, and how often, they'd show signs of distress when another child was distressed, or try to be comforting, or lend help of some kind. Sometimes we would have an adult in the classroom drop an armful of materials to see if the children would help, or get under a desk to retrieve something and bump her head to see if they'd try to comfort her.

"We taught a number of mothers to observe and rate their infants' and toddlers' reactions at home whenever other people were upset by ordinary incidents. Also, we trained the mothers to simulate pain, fake a choking cough, act angry on the telephone, and to cry, to see how their children reacted. To verify their reports, staff people would visit the home and do some of those same things.

"In all this we kept seeing instances of care-giving by children at very early ages. They'd try to comfort the distressed mother or visitor, or ask them what was wrong, or bring them a toy or some other object to distract them. Even a one-year-old might look distressed when his mother cried and sometimes even make some comforting gesture. Of course, we couldn't be sure whether the one-year-old was *giving* reassurance or *seeking* it, or both. But in children only a few months older we'd see unmistakable expressions of concern for the other person. The floodgates of altruism open along with the development of language."

Dr. Zahn-Waxler led me to a small room containing video equipment and played a tape for me. In one scene after another, a young mother, sitting on the floor or a stool and playing with a child, would suddenly cry out, "Oh! *Ooo!* It hurts!," clutch her knee, and perhaps even pretend to cry. A one-year-old boy, clearly upset, stared at his crying mother and then turned and stumbled away from her. A girl of about the same age reached out to pat her mother but then burst into tears and hid her face in a pillow. But a boy of about a year and a half solicitously asked his crying mother, "Why? Why?" and stroked her knee. Another boy of the same age was banging the floor with a hammer; when his mother pretended he had hit her hand and cried out, he kissed her fingers and said again and again, "You okay? You okay now?"

Turning off the tape, Dr. Zahn-Waxler said, "It's clear that during the second year of life empathy emerges and begins to generate simple altruistic behavior. To be sure, there are wide differences among children. Some are altruistic sooner than others, and at every age some are more altruistic than others. One obvious reason is that they get different kinds of training at home—but as a developmental psychologist, I see altruism developing almost universally and showing up in predictable forms at relatively predictable stages and ages. That suggests to me that whatever part experience plays, the organism is 'hard-wired' with a tendency to respond empathetically and, based on that, to develop altruistic behavior."

Striking evidence of the hard-wiring is to be seen in newborns, whose behavior owes nothing to experience. Social psychologist Martin L. Hoffman of the City University of New York is one of several researchers who have reported that one-day-old and two-day-old infants cry when they hear another infant cry. It's not the noise that bothers them—they cry much less, if at all, when researchers experimentally play loud white noise. Nor is it any crying that bothers them: the crying of another newborn disturbs them far more than computer-generated crying or the tape-recorded sound of their own crying. This isn't due to altruism or even empathy, Hoffman says, but what he calls *empathic arousal*—a reflexive reaction to the signs of distress in another infant that is probably the innate response out of which empathy is later developed.

Several other kinds of evidence also point to the existence of neural and visceral mechanisms that predispose the human being to learn to be altruistic. Among them:

- Children and adults tend unthinkingly to imitate the facial expressions and body posture of persons they are in the presence of. Like the person they're with, they smile, frown, sit up straight or relax, and so on. This unconscious mimicry, says Hoffman, provides cues to their own emotional system, inducing something of the other person's feelings. (If you grin because someone you're looking at is grinning, you tend to feel amused or cheerful.)

- Studies show that young children from varied family backgrounds in countries as dissimilar as the United States, France, Israel, and the Ivory Coast of Africa show roughly comparable kinds of caretaking and comforting behavior at much the same ages. In view of the variety of social settings in these studies, it seems likely that innate mechanisms must be directing development along relatively similar paths.

- People often act instantly to help or rescue others in extreme emergency situations—a response that seems to be unthinking and automatic and, at least in part, the result of a biologically based reaction to the other's plight rather than a realistic evaluation of the risks involved. In August 1985, at Aberdeen, Washington, for example, a twelve-year-old boy named Patrick Miller fell off a dock into the Wishkah River; unable to swim, he screamed for help while struggling to stay afloat. Alfred LaMere, a man of sixty-four, retired and in poor health, ran from his nearby house and leaped into the river. Telling Patrick how to float, LaMere began pushing him toward the bank; en route, the boy panicked and dragged him under, but LaMere fought his way back up, continued to shove Patrick the rest of the way to safety, and made it to shore himself. Though suffering from hypothermia and exhaustion, LaMere was treated and survived. The Carnegie Hero Fund Commission, which awarded him a medal, annually gives a number of such awards for "outstanding acts of bravery"; almost all involve automatic, unhesitating efforts to rescue others in imminent peril. Daily newspapers, too, often report similar events, in which rescuers act within seconds of seeing or hearing another person in pain or danger.

• In experiments using simulated emergencies such as those referred to earlier—the faked accident in the next room, the man with a cane who falls in a subway car—those who respond do so in anywhere from five to ten seconds unless inhibiting conditions exist. That compares surprisingly well to response time in familiar emergencies for which people have been trained to render immediate help; a study made in Botswana, an African country in which mothers regard an infant's crying as an emergency and act as fast as they can, found the average response time was six seconds. One would expect the bystanders in the experimental emergencies to take time to appraise the unfamiliar situation, consider whether they could or should help, and decide what action to take. But apparently certain distress signals bypass all this and evoke responses from more basic levels of the nervous system.

NATURE CONDUCTS AN EXPERIMENT

Jim Lewis and Jim Springer, identical twins, were separated four weeks after birth in 1940 and grew up forty-five miles apart in Ohio in different families, with no knowledge of each other. In 1979, when they were thirty-nine years old, Professor Thomas Bouchard, director of the Minnesota Center for Twin and Adoption Research of the University of Minnesota, tracked them down and brought them together. No sci-fi author could have concocted a more bizarre script: Beyond the fact that, aside from their clothing, they were physically indistinguishable, both men had wives named Betty, drove Chevrolets, chain-smoked Salems, chewed their fingernails, and owned dogs named Toy.

Some of these coincidences could be due to pure chance, others to their living in the same part of the country. But Bouchard and his research team were looking for more significant similarities: They put the two men through a lengthy battery of personality tests that measured traits such as flexibility, self-control, and sociability, and found the twins' responses nearly identical.

Since the two men, being identical twins, have precisely the same million genes, one might conclude that their near identity of traits means that personality is very largely produced by the genes. But even though Bouchard's interest is in showing the hereditary contribution to personality, he doesn't go that far; the evidence doesn't warrant it. Over the past decade, he and his team have located and studied dozens of pairs of identical twins who grew up apart as well as others who grew up together and have found that many pairs, despite striking similarities, are less alike than the two Jims.

Twins are a kind of natural experiment by means of which behavioral scientists can calculate to what extent heredity determines personality. But only on the average, not in individual cases. They no longer try to answer the simplistic and outmoded question, "How much of So-and-so's personality is due to Nature, how much to Nurture?" because they know today that heredity and environment interact in somewhat different ways and proportions in each individual's case. What they *can* ask—and answer—is: How much of the "variance"—the range of differences among people in any trait—is due to heredity and how much to environment? The answer indicates to what extent, on the average, that trait is of genetic origin.

Twin studies can answer such questions because in identicals the effect of heredity is nailed down: Since their complement of genes is exactly the same, any differences between them can only be due to differences in environment. By comparing the differences in pairs of identical twins to the differences in pairs of fraternal twins, who have only about half the same genes—and differ more—statisticians can calculate how large a part heredity plays, generally speaking, in the development of any given trait.

In the case of height, for instance, an easily measured and unambiguous characteristic, the Minnesota researchers have calculated, from such comparisons, that 90 percent of the differences among human beings are due to genetic factors. But, cautions psychologist Nancy Segal, a member of the Bouchard team, "We're not saying that ninety percent of *your* height is influenced by genetic factors and the other ten percent by environmental factors. We're saying that ninety percent of the differences in height in the population can be explained by genes and ten percent by environment."

The extent to which personality traits are determined by the genes is studied by similar methods. The results of a number of such studies, according to a recent painstaking review of them, is that roughly 40 percent of variance in personality is of genetic origin, 60 percent of environmental origin.

These, however, were studies of twins who grew up together in the same homes; that weakens the argument, since it could be the sameness of the experiences of twins who grow up together, rather than their genes, that makes them so much alike. For that reason, identical twins reared apart are a far better natural experiment, since only their genes, not their environments, are identical. Identical twins reared apart and fraternal twins reared apart are few and hard to find but worth the trouble of tracking down; the comparison of such pairs is a virtual Rosetta stone of human nature.

Over a period of years the Minnesota Center for Twin and Adoption Research has located fifty-four pairs of identicals and twenty-four pairs of fraternals reared apart. Based on about fifty hours of study of each twin pair, the Center's latest conclusion is that heredity accounts for about 50 percent of the variance in personality traits in the population at large. As Bouchard recently said, "The evidence is now so overwhelming that it is [safe] to assume that traits, including social attitude, are significantly influenced by genetic factors . . . over the entire course of a life span."

What does this say about the genetic contribution to altruism? Unfortunately, empathy and altruism are not among the fourteen traits measured in the Minnesota Center's twin studies. But since these and other twin studies have found so many other personality traits to be in considerable part governed by heredity, the same is almost surely true of altruism. It would be reasonable, therefore, to guess that, like other personality traits, altruism is about 50 percent heritable. But we can do better than guess: A recent twin study by J. Philippe Rushton of the University of Western Ontario, the maverick psychologist-turned-psychogeneticist we met a while back, specifically examined the heritability of altruism and came to that very conclusion.

In 1970, when altruism was becoming a hot new topic in psychology, Rushton, with a brand-new Ph.D. in social psychology from the University of London, plunged into altruism research, guided by somewhat utopian views of the matter. "I believed then that everybody came into the world a blank slate and could be socialized to be altruistic," he told me. How on earth, I asked him, did he get from that position to a psychogenetic view? He chuckled.

"For ten years," he said, "I was a social learning theorist, doing research in how to teach children to be altruistic through good example, preaching, all that sort of thing. I did about a dozen experiments with children and wrote a whole book from that point of view. And all the while, I put off wrestling with two anomalies in the approach.

"One was that altruism appears to exist in animals. When I looked at the data, it untidied my world—there had to be an explanation different from that of pure social learning theory.

"The other was that according to social learning theorists, we don't have general traits of personality but simply act a certain way in a particular situation; if a person learns to be brave in one situation, that doesn't carry across to other situations. But that runs counter to real-life experience, so I read the research literature and concluded that traits of personality do exist and that it is possible to say that a person is basically honest, brave, and so on.

"Then I thought: If there are genes for altruism in animals—and traits of character in people—then might there not be genes that produce a general trait of altruism in people? I locked myself away in the library and read up on behavior genetics, and it was as though blinkers had been taken away from my eyes.

"I decided a twin study would be the best way to measure the heritability of altruism. I'd been in touch with Hans Eysenck [a distinguished research psychologist] at the University of London Institute of Psychiatry off and on since my graduate school days and I knew that he and his team had collected a huge register of twins over the years. So I wrote to him about it—I was living in the other London, the one in Ontario—and by 1982, when I got some grant money, he and his people agreed to go ahead with me on such a study.

"I worked up an altruism questionnaire made up of twenty questions such as, 'I have helped push a stranger's car out of the snow' and 'I have done volunteer work for a charity,' each with five possible answers ranging from 'Never' to 'Very often.' I included sets of questions measuring empathy and nurturance, and my English colleagues added one on aggression.

"They sent the thing out to their whole list of twins, and when the completed questionnaires had come in, I went over there to work with them on the data. We had answers from 573 pairs, about half identicals and half fraternals, half male and half female. David Fulker and Michael Neal of the Institute did the statistical analysis for me. We compared the degree of similarity in identical pairs with that in fraternal pairs, and from the differences between them we estimated, through statistical analysis, the heritability of altruism.

"I had thought it might be as high as thirty percent, but I was stunned when the computer results started looking more like fifty percent. The genetic influence in altruism was nearly twice as high as I had expected. It was alarming!"

Why alarming? I asked him. Shouldn't he have been exultant?

Rushton laughed heartily. "I realized that my findings were a message that neither parents nor most psychologists would welcome," he said. "Altruism is a trait parents would like to be able to socialize into their child. With some traits, like introversion, they'll accept it and say, 'That's just how my child is.' But if they have a child who's always getting into fights and is mean to other kids, they'll say, 'He's going to have to learn different behavior.' They don't like what I have found."

As for Rushton's fellow psychologists, he added, most of them have been less than enthusiastic about his results: "The old-style social learning psychologists prefer to ignore it. 'Ah, well,' they say, 'twin studies—they're all fraud anyway.' The behavior geneticists have more or less ignored it too. 'Old hat,' they say, 'we've done it for crime and delinquency all along.' The one group who do like the findings and pay attention to them are the sociobiologists, people like Edward O. Wilson."

I asked whether Rushton's new view had disheartened him, since he could no longer believe that all children could be trained to be altruistic. "Don't forget," he answered cheerfully, "it's still fifty-fifty. In the past, some people felt that human behavior was only ten percent a matter of genetics—you could do anything with a child—others that it was eighty percent genetic—you could do very little. Now we find out that it's fifty-fifty, and that's not so bad after all, now is it?"

THE DARWINIAN PUZZLE

But why wouldn't the human altruism gene have been eliminated rather than selected by evolution?

Every truly altruistic act diminishes to some extent the altruist's chances of thriving, surviving, and perpetuating his or her line. Whether you put a couple of dollars in Santa Claus's kettle, help a rival colleague rather than undercut him, or try to rescue a woman from an armed rapist, you lessen your advantages in the great struggle, especially if you have not yet completed the rearing of offspring. Other things being equal, the person who gives nothing, uses dirty tricks to get ahead of his rival, and stays out of the rape scene has it over you.

As Dennis Krebs, professor of psychology at Simon Fraser University (British Columbia) and long-time toiler in the altruism vineyards, puts it, "If altruism is defined as behavior that enhances the net fitness of another at a net reduction in the fitness of the helper, then it should not evolve according to Darwin's principle of natural selection."

Darwin himself felt that the altruism of the social insects created "one special difficulty, which at first seemed to me insuperable, and actually fatal to the whole theory [of natural selection]." But as we have seen, later discoveries in genetics showed that among ants and other social animals the altruistic gene is so widely disseminated that although the altruistic individual dies, the gene lives on.

Human beings, however, are nowhere near as alike as ants or bees, or even robins, in their genetic makeup, so the disadvantages of altruism should long ago have eliminated it from our species. How is it possible, then, for there to be any hereditary predisposition toward altruism in the human race? Scientists of various disciplines have offered three possible explanations of the Darwinian puzzle in recent years. They are, in brief:

Reciprocal Altruism

The grouper, a medium-size fish, opens its jaws wide to allow the wrasse, a tiny fish, to swim inside; there the wrasse cleans certain ectoparasites from the grouper's mouth and gills, and the grouper, which could eat the wrasse, allows it to do its work and leave. The result: The grouper is freed of its parasites and the wrasse gets a meal.

Some years ago the biologist Robert L. Trivers offered examples like that of the wrasse and grouper as evidence that reciprocal altruism has survival benefits and hence is favored by natural selection. Any grouper that happened to have an innate tendency to eat the wrasse would be less likely than a more benign one to remain healthy, live long, and reproduce.

The same principle, Trivers has recently argued, accounts for the evolution of human altruism:

It seems likely that, during our recent evolutionary history (at least the last 5 million years), there has been strong selection on our ancestors to develop a variety of reciprocally altruistic actions. Humans routinely help each other in times of danger. . . . We routinely share food, we help the sick, the wounded, and the very young, [etc.].

Many behavioral scientists agree that the survival value of reciprocal altruism in human beings caused the genes responsible for it to be selected by evolution during the eons of tribal life, since tribes high in cooperation were likely to fare better than tribes low in it, and to become part of contemporary humankind's inheritance.

But as Trivers himself indicates, reciprocal altruism is based on the expectation that help or favors will be returned, and that "cheaters" (those who do not reciprocate) will not be helped. Thus what he is describing, say critics of his theory, is cooperation—a valuable but selfish form of behavior in which one person benefits another in the expectation of receiving return benefits at some time in the future.

Reciprocal altruism has nothing to do with kindness, unselfishness, and self-sacrifice. It doesn't explain what motivates all those who comfort, help, or rescue others with no thought of reward. It doesn't account in any way for the behavior of the Good Samaritans of the world.

Reward may, in fact, counteract the impulse toward true altruism, according to the evidence of some experiments. In one of them, a team of researchers asked housewives to grant them a five-minute interview; they gave half of those who agreed a small sum, but the other half nothing. A while later, the researchers approached the same women and asked them to submit to a twenty-five-minute interview; this time, the ones who had previously been paid were less willing to do so than the ones who had not. This seemingly paradoxical behavior, says Shalom H. Schwartz, professor of psychology at Hebrew University of Jerusalem, indicates that payment decreases the intrinsic motivation to help altruistically—the very opposite of the way reciprocal altruism works.

Group Selection

Some years ago, many biologists held that altruism evolved through "group selection." In certain species, including humankind, some individuals will act against their own interests for the good of the group in such ways as fighting to defend it or withholding their own reproduction. (Like the slime mold, some seabirds do not reproduce when population density threatens to overfish their feeding grounds.)

This seemed to solve the problem by shifting evolutionary competition from the individual to the group. A group with some altruists in it would have a better chance of survival than a group without any; ergo, altruism is selected by evolution. Witness such cases, already described, as those of the social insect warriors and the birds and monkeys that issue warning calls.

But the theory cannot account for altruism in any species whose members have considerable genetic variation. A group of such a species—most notably, human beings—would contain both altruistic and selfish members, and the survival of the selfish at the expense of the altruistic would not preserve the altruistic genes. Recent mathematical analyses and computer simulations, compressing millennia into minutes, have shown that groups containing altruists would have a survival edge over groups without altruists only in the short run; before they could outsurvive them, they would have lost their altruists by internal competition from the selfish members.

Such analyses have caused the group selection explanation to be more or less discarded in recent years.

Kin Selection

Many years ago the brilliant English biologist J. S. Haldane jested that he was prepared to lay down his life for two of his brothers or eight of his cousins. He thereby anticipated the theory advanced in recent years by sociobiologists that the evolutionary route to altruism is kin selection.

That theory goes as follows: Since human siblings (other than identical twins) have half their genes in common, cousins an eighth, and so on, the altruist, by acting to benefit his blood relatives, tends to preserve his own genes—including his own altruism gene. If he saves the lives of two brothers or eight cousins at the cost of his own, the odds are that no part of him, genetically speaking, has vanished. "Genes, then, can be favored by natural selection," say zoologists Ridley and Dawkins, "if they cause their bearers to increase the survival of their other genetic relatives."

There's one problem: How could any primitive human being—or most contemporary ones—decide whether any given act of self-sacrifice, let alone of everyday helpfulness, makes genetic sense? As Trivers straight-facedly writes, "In kin-directed altruism, the main problem for the altruist is to ensure that the degree of relatedness times the cost-benefit ratio of the act is larger than 1." That conjures up the image of Ichi or Zug or whatever his name is pausing before rushing into the spear-and-club battle to punch the buttons of his hand-held computer in order to determine . . . well, enough of that.

Edward O. Wilson, the Harvard University sociobiologist, suggests a simpler decision-making mechanism: Our altruistic emotions may stem from genes that were selected by evolution over thousands of generations by the tendency of human beings to favor their relatives. J. Philippe Rushton goes further, these days: He espouses the theory that we somehow "detect" genes similar to our own—even in people not known to be relatives—and act altruistically toward those who bear them.

That sounds a touch mystical. But there may be a down-to-earth explanation: If we tend to be altruistic toward those we live with, are close to, and who resemble us, but not to other persons, our behavior will tend to preserve our genes. Without the need for calculations, Trivers's formula may be roughly equated with the ties that bind.

And this has been shown to be the case in small, in-grown human groups. The anthropologist Napoleon Chagnon of the University of California at Santa Barbara has spent many years studying the Yanomamö, a violent and warlike group of Indians who live deep in the Amazonian jungle of Brazil and Venezuela. Recently he and a colleague statistically analyzed the relatedness of the men on both sides of a tribal ax fight. All the warriors taking part in the fight were related, more or less, to all the others. But the researchers' computations showed that the average degree of relatedness *within* each group was considerably higher than the average relatedness *between* the two groups. The primitive Yanomamö didn't need hand-held computers; they just *knew.*

So kin selection theory makes good sense and, many researchers feel, satisfactorily explains how a tendency toward altruism evolved in the human species.

But it accounts only for the kinds of altruism that evolved before the development of larger societies. The very heart of the altruism mystery—at least the one this book is concerned with—is why we behave compassionately and benevolently not only toward our brothers and cousins but toward the neighbor with a heart attack, the stranger in a wrecked car, the unseen and unknown person who will survive an operation because we have given our money or blood to save their lives.

Kin selection theory says nothing of the influence of culture—the absorption, by children, from the society they are immersed in, of all the kinds of behavior attached to concepts like "ought," "should," "good," and "right." These may all have been invented too recently to be part of evolutionary selection. As the paleontologist/polymath Stephen Jay Gould says, "Humans may devise good solutions without waiting for new genetic propensities, and then teach them to their kids and neighbors." Cultural notions of good behavior add to, and may well exceed, all the influences of biological evolution.

That's why the kinship selection theory accounts for only a special and limited kind of altruism—a kind that would have made the Good Samaritan stop to help a relative or fellow townsman but pass by the wounded Jerusalemite without so much as a pitying glance.

Carolyn Zahn-Waxler, despite her feeling that the human organism has a "hard-wired" tendency to respond altruistically, believes that culture and training develop this tendency in far more extensive and varied ways than the kin selection theory can encompass. In a recent critique of that theory she wrote:

> It implies that we will be more altruistic to kin than to nonkin and for biological, not social, reasons. In real life, however, our biological and social worlds are usually totally confounded [i.e., intermingled]. Also, in humans, individual acts of violence and murder as well as altruism are very commonly directed toward family members. . . . [Finally,] the theory does

not readily explain the behavior of individuals who are quite capable of nurturing adopted children, particularly children from other cultures and races.

Carolyn Zahn-Waxler knows whereof she speaks; her own teenage daughter, Rebecca, is adopted and of Korean origin.

THE ROOTS OF HUMAN ALTRUISM

Out of this welter of intriguing but often conflicting data we can draw several conclusions:

- Evolution built into the human species tendencies toward certain kinds of altruism akin to those in some animal species: reciprocal altruism and kinship selection. But these genetically determined tendencies do not produce the uniquely human and civilized forms of altruism: acts of benevolence that cost the giver something but bring no return gift, often in behalf of strangers or unseen and unknown persons.
- Evolution also built into the human species certain neural and emotional reactions to distress in others that are the raw material out of which socialization and experience fashion a wide variety of altruistic behaviors. The capacity for empathy is probably the principal such predisposition.
- While part of our altruism is akin to that of animals, by far the larger part is culturally and experientially determined. The human mind has an immense capacity to learn forms of behavior specified not by biological but by cultural evolution: language, mathematics, music, and art; the uses of tools and money; the forms of governance; writing and reading; religious rituals and scientific research; sexual practices, love, and family life.

    And altruism.

    Biology makes us potentially responsive to need in other people, but the degree to which we respond, the forms our responses take, and the sense of "oughtness" that powers them are the result of our experiences, including the values, emotions, ideas, and behavior patterns that we learn at home, in school, and in the world around us.

CHAPTER THREE

When in Rome—

GROWING CONDITIONS

Depending on the soil and weather, a seed can remain dormant, sprout but do poorly, or flourish. The newborn infant's biological predisposition toward altruism is like a seed; the culture—the way of life—of the society in which the child grows up is like soil and weather.

Other influences on the development of altruism such as parent-child relations, schooling, and social experience are analogous to the gardener's art. In a favorable environment, even an untended plant will grow, though not to its potential; in an unfavorable one, despite diligent cultivation it will struggle for life; and given a benign environment and skillful gardening, it will thrive and develop fully.

To understand, therefore, how an infant can develop into anything from an Adolf Eichmann to an Albert Schweitzer, we first need to see to what extent society itself either promotes or hinders the development of altruism. We start with two extreme specimen cases: a society in which people are unusually kind, generous, and loving, and a society whose people are quite the reverse.

The time is the early 1960s,* the place the remote northwestern corner of Botswana in southern Africa. Near a waterhole hard by

*The anthropological observations I am drawing on were made at that time.

the Kalahari desert is a village of eight thatched huts; here thirty-odd people live part of the year. They are a band of !Kung (the ! indicates a click—a speech sound of the !Kung language that cannot be represented in our orthography). At other times of year, when they must go traveling in search of food and water, they live in temporary camps, without huts; at night they huddle, shivering, around a fire, with nothing between them and the sky.

The !Kung, formerly called Bushmen or Hottentots, are a small, yellow-skinned people with high cheekbones and sharply defined features quite unlike those of the dark, Negroid, much larger Bantus who live all around them; the only physical feature the !Kung and the Bantus have in common is hair that grows in tight spirals. The men wear leather loincloths and, in chilly weather, leather capes; the women wear leather aprons and capes; both sexes go barefoot and, except for the elderly, walk with lithe grace.

The !Kung are a foraging people—classic hunter-gatherers who live off the land, following certain traditional routes with the seasons in search of game, birds, and reptiles, edible roots and nuts, and water, the scarcest and most valued commodity in this area.*

The !Kung village is noisy; there is much raucous conversation, laughter, teasing, storytelling, and gossiping as the women work at preparing food, the men at making poisoned arrows for hunting. Nearby, three men squat in front of one hut talking among themselves; although they are blind (eye diseases are common in this area), they are well fed and adequately clothed. For unlike many primitive peoples living at a subsistence level who abandon or drive away those who can no longer hunt or gather food, the !Kung take care of their blind, sick, and crippled.

Nearby, lying in his hut, is Kasupe, a man in his fifties who has a badly infected leg and cannot work; during the course of the day children and women from all the other households bring him and his wife and four children food. Other men and women drift by from time to time to perform healing procedures and ceremonies for Kasupe; caring for the ill is everyone's task.

On a typical day some of the able-bodied men will drift off in the morning, one by one, to hunt, and women will leave in small groups to go gathering. The other men and women remain in camp with the children, some working, others lazing about; no one dic-

*Since the 1960s, political developments in Botswana and Namibia—whose shared border lies across the !Kung's traditional nomadic route—have forced the !Kung to settle down and become herdsmen and agriculturists.

tates who must gather or work or how much anyone must do. Late in the day the hunters come back bearing snakes, a rat, and a large guinea-fowl, the women carrying nuts, fruit, a few gourds, and an ostrich egg. The food is ceremoniously divided up and passed out to all in the camp—including those who stayed home and did no work—with much gabbling and chattering but no jealousy, sour looks, or quarreling.

Sometimes a few !Kung from a distant band will arrive and ask permission to camp nearby and eat the food of the area. After a good deal of chaffering and teasing—during which everyone offers them food—they are invariably granted the permission. As a !Kung man explained to Richard Borshay Lee, a visiting anthropologist, "If they come to you first, it is all right. It's when they eat alone and you come along later to find them there, that's when fights start." The permission, however, creates an obligation; those who grant the favor can later ask to eat in an area that belongs to the visitors. ("Belong" does not signify legal ownership but a right conferred by custom and presence.)

!Kung life, though marginal in terms of food and artifacts, is for the most part socially idyllic. The men and women talk endlessly, and often sing or dance; they are cheerful and friendly even when performing tedious chores, such as digging up roots during the dry season and painstakingly squeezing moisture out of them to drink. They are loving toward their infants and indulgent with older children, rarely scolding or hitting them. Healers do their best for the sick—without recompense—and adults and children, whenever they stop by a neighbor's hut to chat, are expected to help themselves without asking to some of the nuts piled up at the door.

Not all is peace and love: Fairly often a wife who has discovered her husband's infidelity will rage at him publicly, or a man or woman will fiercely denounce some neighbor or visitor from another band who, they feel, has been stingy to them (stinginess is the worst sin among the !Kung). Yet by and large they almost never do anything worse to each other than scream and scold; they are, in the words of anthropologist Elizabeth Marshall Thomas, "the harmless people."

The !Kung are remarkably protective of each other's feelings. If a hunter has made a big kill some distance away—an antelope that he needs help bringing back—he will return to camp and sit down in silence. Someone will say, "What did you see today?" and he will reply, "Ah, I'm no good for hunting, I saw nothing at all . . . maybe just a tiny one." Then everyone knows he has made a big kill but doesn't want other hunters to feel he is superior to them. When other men go with him the next day to butcher the antelope and bring the meat home, they joke about how small and worthless the kill is and he agrees with them. As ≠Tomazho, a healer, explained to Lee when he was living with them:

> When a young man kills much meat, he comes to think of himself as a chief or big man, and he thinks of the rest of us as his servants or inferiors. We can't accept this. We refuse one who boasts, for someday his pride will make him kill somebody. So we always speak of his meat as worthless. In this way we cool his heart and make him gentle.

The open-handed sharing of food is not unique with the !Kung; most hunter-gatherer societies parcel out available food as if they were one large family, and the sharing and gift-giving in such societies are motivated by custom and obligation as much as by compassion and generosity. Still, the !Kung are unusual. Their culture, far more than that of most of the world's peoples, is largely one of kindly and generous customs and makes most of them into altruists of a kind.

How the !Kung culture came to be that way is anyone's guess; certainly not because of economic plenty (!Kung life is one of mere subsistence), good leadership (they have no leadership), or any other easily identified social or economic determinant. Since their history is unwritten and not even passed down in the form of a folk epic memorized by bards, we cannot know. The only conclusion we need to draw at this point is that the culture of a society can, indeed, promote altruism.

The time, 1965; the place, a mountainside village of six thatch-roofed huts in the northeastern corner of Uganda, 1,700 miles to the northeast of the !Kung territory. Here lives a band of the Ik (pronounced "eek"), a people as different from the !Kung as if they came from another planet.

Unlike the !Kung village's scattering of huts in the open, the Ik village is surrounded by a stockade fence in which there is only one tiny entrance. That may not seem strange, but what is very strange indeed is the interior design: Six smaller stockade barriers subdivide the enclosed area, each surrounding a hut and isolating its owners from their fellow-villagers. This unconvivial and antisocial arrangement grows out of the Ik's mistrust and fear not only of outsiders but of their relatives and neighbors; it is no idiosyncracy of this particular band, for the half dozen other nearby Ik villages are all laid out much the same way.

The Ik have much to be fearful of besides each other. A small people (five feet tall on the average), dark-skinned and Negroid of feature, they are currently living below the level of subsistence. Most of the adults and children have no clothing (they are totally naked or wear at most a strip or two of fur dangling from a cord about the waist), and they are all scrawny and bony. The few elderly adults in the village are seriously emaciated. The Ik are in deep trouble.

They used to be successful hunter-gatherers, but in recent years the government of Uganda has forced them to give up their hunting-gathering treks through the mountains of that country and neighboring Kenya and become agriculturists. But the Ik know only the most primitive methods of farming, their fields are open to the ravages of animals, and this year the rains have failed. There is almost nothing to eat; they are barely hanging on with what little they can grow and whatever they can gather in the stony mountains and parched valleys. The men occasionally have some success hunting, but most areas in which there is game are now out of bounds to them, and poaching on the goat herds of neighboring peoples can bring bloody retaliation or imprisonment.

In so grave a situation, social groups ranging from families to large societies usually cling to each other; crisis strengthens those doctrines or customs that make for mutual helpfulness. But if the Ik ever had any such, they must have been shallow-rooted; today their world is a travesty of a human society, a reality grimmer than such bleak fantasies as *1984* or *A Clockwork Orange.* Instead of sharing food, when the Ik find any they eat it in secret, wolfing it down as fast as possible so as not to have to give any of it to their mates, children, or fellow villagers.

Colin Turnbull, an American anthropologist who lived among the Ik, tells an illustrative story:

Lomeja, a man in his twenties, hides his bow and arrow outside the camp one night so no one will realize he is going hunting the next day. But his half-sister, Niangar, sees him leave in the morning and tells her husband, Lotibok, who silently tracks Lomeja. When he kills an antelope, Lotibok waits in hiding until Lomeja has cleaned it, then appears, claiming to have come this way by accident, and offers to help cook it. Lomeja can only sourly accede. Although they carry the meat to a wooded glen and use as little fire as possible, two other men of their village spot a wisp of smoke and come running. They find Lomeja and Lotibok cramming meat into their mouths as fast as they can in an effort to get it all down before anyone comes along, but now they have to let the newcomers join in. The four men succeed in finishing off all the meat without being discovered by anyone else and without saving any to take back to their families and fellow villagers.

The old people tottering around are dying; they cannot procure food for themselves, and most people, including their own children, will not give them any. The Ik feel it is a waste of good food to give it to old people. One day, Turnbull, who has been living among the Ik for many months, brings a dish of food to two old men, one of whom has been particularly friendly to him. The old men tremble at the sight of the food and ask Turnbull to close the gate to their compound so no one will come in and share. He does so, waits until they have finished, and then leaves with the empty plate—and finds a disapproving crowd clustered outside, muttering angrily about his having given food to those who will soon be dead.

Later, one of the old men, Lolim, becomes ill and weak; Turnbull brings him food in a tin mug, but the moment he leaves, Lomongin, a younger man, begins snatching bits of food out of Lolim's mug while the old man, crying, tries to stop him and keeps stuffing food into his own mouth. Some time later, Lomeja, the hunter, is shot by a raiding group of non-Ik and lies dying; Turnbull prepares a cup of sweet tea for him, but when he turns to look at Lomeja's bandages, he hears a woman's laugh behind him and sees Lomeja's sister running off with the cup of tea, which she has torn from her dying brother's hand.

Bands of children head off into the mountains and valleys in the morning, chattering gaily to each other. But they're not going out to have fun, they're going out to forage; they have to, for unless they find food for themselves, they will not eat. Ik parents care for their children until about age three or four and then "put them out"; from that point on the children may not sleep in the house but only in the compound outside it, and must find their own food. So they team up with other children in self-defense and forage together until they are old enough to live as adults.

Not all make it. An emaciated young girl, Adupa—who has

been put out—trails around after her parents begging for food until, infuriated, they shut her into the compound; too weak to break out, she dies a few days later. Two brothers squat by a fire; Murai, the older, has found some food and is eating, while Liza, the younger, who is starving, watches but knows better than to ask for any. Some time later, when Liza dies of starvation, Murai waxes philosophic: "Surely it is better that one lives than that both should die."

At times, however, the Ik can be gay. Although they are not talkative, they do sometimes chat and joke, but they have a morbid sense of humor: They shriek with laughter when Turnbull stumbles on a steep path; they eagerly watch a tiny child crawling toward a fire and laugh gaily when it touches the coals and screams; and when Lo'ono, an old blind widow, falls on a hilly pathway, rolls into a gully, and lies on her back with her arms and legs feebly flailing, they stand on the ledge above, looking down with amusement at the spectacle.

Anthropologists almost always come to like the people they live among, but Turnbull, after living with the Ik, pronounced them "as unfriendly, uncharitable, inhospitable and generally mean as any people can be." He did, however, make excuses for them: He thought it likely that the Ik once lived more like a normal people but that hard times forced them to abandon all kindly and generous feelings—which, in his opinion, "far from being basic human qualities, are superficial luxuries" that people cannot afford except in times of plenty.

Yet other anthropologists have lived among people who, though not in dire circumstances, were just as uncharitable and generally mean (see Margaret Mead on the Mundugumor of New Guinea or Napoleon Chagnon on the Yanomamö of the Amazonian jungle); their meanness was the expression of their own cultural values interacting with the innate human potential for aggression. But different cultural values, those of the !Kung, for instance, develop and promote the innate human potential for altruism even in, and sometimes especially in, hard times.

MORE (OR LESS) ALTRUISTIC CULTURES

The !Kung and the Ik are extreme examples of the extent to which culture can either foster or choke off the development of altruism.

Both of these, however, are preliterate cultures and minuscule communities, without variations in class, community size, or other social factors. Highly developed societies with both large and small communities, a class structure, and ethnic subgroups are far more complex, and it is much harder to make valid generalizations about their typical level of altruism.

Still, many travelers have had the distinct impression that the people of some countries are relatively helpful and kind, and of others unhelpful and unkind, at least to strangers and foreigners. These perceptions lack the rigor of scientific findings but they do have value: As observations made in natural settings, they are a kind of informal anthropology. A couple of testimonials:

Daniel Bar-Tal, no mere traveler but a social psychologist—and an expert on altruism to boot—told me, "As a child, I lived in Poland, then went with my family to Israel, and later studied for some years in the United States. Very different, one from the other, as to altruism. Of the three, the people in Israel have by far the most altruistic outlook. In particular, in a kibbutz [an agricultural commune], from the moment you first open your eyes you're aware of responsibility for and to other people."

Ervin Staub: "In my student days, I hitchhiked in Sweden and other Western countries, and to my surprise, it was very hard going in Sweden. Their social system makes them a caring society, but there's a difference between that kind of rule-directed caring and self-motivated caring or personal altruism. But the English also surprised me: They're aloof and seemingly uncaring, but if you stop on a street with a map in your hand and look puzzled, you practically have to beat them off, they're so eager to help."

A handful of laboratory experiments and field studies confirm the import of these observations, namely, as Staub puts it, "The cultures of certain societies make it difficult or impossible for individuals to evolve toward altruistic behavior. The cultures of others guide them and shape them toward it." Some of the research findings:

- A series of studies by Bar-Tal and others validate his comments about altruism in Israel. In most of them children were told stories in which a person needed help of some kind—in some cases at little cost to the potential helper, in other cases at very great cost—and were asked what they themselves would do in each situation. The kibbutz children gave by far the most altruistic answers, the American children the least, and Israeli city children intermediate ones.

- Chinese psychologist Hing-Keung Ma asked a number of high school students and adults in London and in Hong Kong what they would do if someone—the questionnaire named persons ranging from a close relative to a total stranger—was in serious need of help. Overall, the Hong Kong respondents felt more altruistic, and toward a wider spectrum of persons, than the Londoners. This does not contradict Staub's impression of the helpfulness of the English; helping a foreigner with directions and helping persons in a serious crisis are different measures of altruism. In any case, Ma's study shows a difference in altruism between people of comparable age and background in two countries.

- Researchers from the University of Pennsylvania had undergraduate volunteers in Philadelphia and in Madras, India, play several versions of a game of chance. The player could choose either to gamble and keep whatever he won, or take a flat fee for being in the experiment, play to win, and give his winnings to a volunteer whom he did not know but who, he knew, was unpaid. The Americans more often made choices and wagers that benefited the unknown, unpaid volunteer than did the Indians, whose strategies were aimed chiefly at benefiting themselves.

Such data should be interpreted with caution: They tell us something about the kind of people sampled in each country, but the findings may not apply to other kinds of people in those countries. Any generalization about the altruism of a large heterogeneous society with a variety of religions, subcultures, and lifestyles, is bound to have many exceptions. The level of altruism typical of middle-class Parisians may be different from that of workers in Marseilles or farmers in a village in Normandy; a generalization about altruism in an upscale Boston suburb may not be valid for a town in rural Mississippi.

One study found the difference in levels of altruism between middle-class and working-class men in England greater than that between men of the same class in the two countries. Similarly, in an experiment mentioned in Chapter One, researchers noted the clothing of people who picked up wallets dropped in front of a paperback bookstore and an "adult" bookstore; two thirds of the well-dressed people but only one fifth of those in work clothes returned the wallets.* But these findings do not contradict the idea that different societies have different levels of altruism. The *culture* of a society—all its shared customs, beliefs, laws, and knowledge—is the environment in which altruism flourishes or withers, but different classes, regions, or communities within a society may have somewhat dissimilar subcultures.

The difference in the altruism levels of different kinds of communities in the same country was documented by the study referred to earlier in which researchers tested the helpfulness of passersby in squatter communities and better residential areas in Ankara and Istanbul. Working separately, the researchers, a young Turkish man and Turkish woman, asked some passersby to make change, others to answer a short questionnaire, and in front of still others dropped the top box of an awkward load and made ineffective efforts to retrieve it.

In every case the residents of the squatter communities were more helpful than people living in better communities (94 percent of squatter residents, but only 54 percent of other urbanities, helped with the dropped box). The study's principal investigator, Charles Korte of North Carolina State University, hypothesized that the more active street life of the squatter neighborhoods and the lower socioeconomic status of their residents make helping a stranger in a public place feel more natural to them than it does to the more formal residents of better neighborhoods.

HOW CULTURE MAKES ALTRUISTS

How does culture do this? It does so by means of its *values* and *norms,* the accepted guidelines and prescriptions for behavior that children absorb from everyone around them beginning in infancy and continuing into adulthood.

Values are the broad, abstract ideas shared by a group of people about what is right and wrong, good and bad, beautiful and ugly, and so on; norms are the specific rules of behavior—customs, religious injunctions, and laws—that express or carry out those values.

Honesty, for instance, is one of our society's values; among the

*Also, curiously, wallets were returned by 75 percent of patrons of the paperback bookstore but by only 44 percent of patrons of the "adult" bookstore.

many norms that derive from it are our expectations that we and others will not cheat in games and transactions, and that people will tell each other the truth.

Such values as kindness, generosity, helpfulness, and concern for others are involved in altruism. Since nearly every other society and nearly every religion holds these values in esteem, why are there such great variations in the average altruism level of different peoples? The answer is twofold.

First, there is no one-to-one relation between values and norms. Two peoples may both believe in kindness but spell it out very differently in their specific rules of conduct; one may have a norm enjoining them to be kind to everyone; another may have a norm extending kindness only to peers and another permitting the brutal treatment of inferiors or slaves.

Second, certain other values and norms may conflict with, and take precedence over, those of altruism; in the cutthroat business world, success ranks higher and has more sway over behavior than concern for one's competitor.

Consider the Italians, who are so warm and helpful toward foreigners—but not, according to Luigi Barzini, toward other Italians who are their equals, and definitely not toward their inferiors. In *The Italians,* a work of amateur anthropology on a par with de Tocqueville's *Democracy in America,* Barzini says that the Italian character was molded by many centuries of oppression, and that people adapted to it by learning to be outwardly gay and charming (though desolate and desperate inside), and *simpatico* and helpful to their superiors (but domineering and cold toward their inferiors). The traveler may never be aware of this:

> It is not surprising that few foreigners see these things when only a tiny minority of the natives are aware of them. . . . The Italian social structure can be compared to the olive tree, that most Italian of all trees, which looks entirely different when seen from above from what it looks [like] when seen from below. The leaves are glossy dark-green on top and powdery grey underneath. The faces of the Italians look flattering, smiling, and kindly from above but overbearing, insolent, pitiless from below. Foreigners are automatically promoted to be honorary members of the ruling class. They occupy a position of vantage. Theirs is the bird's-eye view of the olive tree.

There are far more extreme cases: subcultures in which, although altruism is taught by religion, other values and norms poison the social soil and blight the development of concern for anyone other than the members of one's immediate family.

Such a milieu is the typical Greek mountain village, whose culture embodies traditional Judeo-Christian values but also others totally antagonistic to these. Juliet du Boulay, an Oxford anthropologist who lived in the village of Ambéli, in Euboea, for some time, says that one of the important local norms is that of hospitality: Every family regards it as a matter of honor and pride to give a lavish welcome, with abundant food and wine, to any visitor or stranger from outside the village. But this generosity appears to stem from a motive rather different from compassion or benevolence:

> The house . . . is a sanctuary from the hostility of both nature and society. . . . The villager's attitude to hospitality illustrates particularly clearly the living reality of this image of the house. . . . It is the index of a house's security and an element in the honor of its owners to be able to provide for the unexpected, and to give hospitality where it falls due.

For the older villagers, hospitality is sacred, with supernatural sanctions; not to extend it could bring ill fortune:

> In the giving of hospitality, the part played by the fear of misfortune attending the house that turned away the stranger was, in the old days, clear; and certainly in the thinking of the older generation in Ambéli the necessity to placate or win over the equivocal presence that the stranger represented seems to have been strong.
> . . . Nevertheless, whatever negative motives may be attributed to rural Greek hospitality, its effect is to cause not only a remission of fear and caution on the part of the house but a positive release of generosity and affection . . . [enabling its members to] relate positively to the society from which in the normal course of events it is separated by mistrust and hostility.

Despite their good treatment of the stranger, the people of Ambéli are often anything but generous and kindly toward their fellow villagers. Although they do expect to give help to a wide range of others, their utter devotion to the welfare of the family is so dominant a norm as to generate behavior to others that is the antithesis of altruistic. When obligations to the family and others conflict, says du Boulay, it is often a man's "moral duty to quarrel with, cheat, or deceive the [other villagers] in support of the house." Another paramount norm (probably of ancient origin), *egoismós* or self-assertion, has a similar effect:

> To "make a fool of" someone else is an effective way of enhancing one's own ego and of damaging that of another. . . . [Hence] the slightest unintentional insult may be interpreted as gratuitous offence and give rise to a quarrel. . . . It is as an expression of egoismós that the community as a whole indulges in socially regulated forms of stealing, such as tapping a pine-tree belonging to someone else, or cutting firewood from a neighboring property.

The other members of the family are no kinder to their fellow villagers than the men:

> The pious mother of a family, for instance, involves herself in quarrels, abuse, and unrelenting hatreds in defense of her house; a child is conditioned to deceit from a tender age, because deceit is necessary to safeguard the family from the curiosity and malice of the community.

Thus the culture of the Greek mountain village is a stony ground on which the seed of altruism can barely exist; yet in many villages in other countries, people act much like members of an extended family. It is not the site or size of the community but the local culture that is either favorable or hostile to the development of altruism.

Similarly, one cannot generalize about large cities: The altruism of their residents varies considerably and in many ways. Some years ago, Roy E. Feldman, a social scientist at the Massachusetts Institute of Technology, conducted five experiments in Boston, Paris, and Athens, two of which bear directly on altruism. In one, Feldman had his assistants—some of them natives of the country, others foreigners—stop people on a main shopping street and ask directions; in the other, the assistants asked people in subway stations to please mail a letter for them to a friend who was expecting them.

In all three cities, many of the people who were asked for help gave it, but Parisians and Athenians were considerably more willing to give proper directions to fellow citizens than to foreigners (to whom 45 percent of Parisians either gave no directions or wrong ones). Bostonians were relatively even-handed; six out of seven gave correct information, whether the asker was American or foreign. In response to the request to mail a letter, a somewhat larger favor, the Athenian men—only men were accosted in the experiments—were startlingly unhelpful to the Greek experimenters (93 percent refused) but relatively helpful to the foreign ones (only half refused). In both Boston and Paris, a large majority helped both kinds of askers, though Parisians, inconsistently, were more helpful to foreigners than they had been with directions. In all three cities, people of the middle or upper class were more helpful to foreigners than were lower-class people.

Feldman summed up the results of his five experiments as follows:

> In general, when a difference was observed, the Athenians treated the foreigner better than the compatriot, but Parisians and Bostonians treated compatriots better than foreigners. We could, however, also differentiate between socio-economic correlates within the cities studied. This means that we can do considerably better than speak of Parisians, Athenians, and Bostonians in sweeping terms. We can make meaningful statements about subgroups of these populations.

Clearly, the norms governing responses to the needs of others are complex and highly variable. The curious hostility of Greek men toward their compatriots, for instance, the oddest of Feldman's findings, is the result of a particular norm Greek men live by: They cooperate with and help only those other Greeks to whom they are bound by personal loyalty; foreigners, however, not being Greek at all, are treated according to other rules—those of good manners and hospitality.

In Paris, apparently, people are governed by more familiar norms: loyalty to the compatriot, indifference to the foreigner.

As for Bostonians, the data suggest that they are not very class-driven, certainly not motivated by tribal loyalties, and not particularly xenophobic. It would seem that the culture around them is a milieu fairly favorable to the development of altruism.

* * *

Thus, in every culture a wide variety of norms prescribe the kinds and bounds of altruistic behavior, and so determine the limits to which altruism will develop in the average individual.

Some norms are very specific, spelling out exactly who may be offered help, and how much of it. In this country we are expected to offer help without regard to class or race; to rescue (if possible) or summon help for someone in grave danger (drowning, pinned in an auto wreck, and so on); but *not* to sacrifice our lives for strangers or even people dear to us. Some norms are very specific, and merely prescribe customs; others are broader, and are statements of moral principle. The most important norms of altruism, according to the experts, are three of the latter kind. They are:

- The "reciprocity norm": Give, and unto you will be given; do good to those who have done good to you. This norm, of course, accounts for all kinds of cooperation and mutual help but does not call for benevolence or helping with no thought of return, nor is it extended to unknown or unseen strangers. That kind of altruism is based on the other two major norms.
- The "norm of aiding" or "norm of social responsibility": Help those who are dependent upon you—your children and spouse, friends or colleagues who need your assistance, acquaintances and strangers in your society, or even outside it, who would suffer greatly or perish without your help.
- The "norm of fairness": This is actually a set of norms promoting equality, humanitarianism, and "equity" (dividing or sharing). When we try to right what we consider a wrong— the abominable housing conditions of many migrant workers, for instance—we are acting according to this norm.

The norms of many kinds of behavior—marriage and divorce, criminal conduct, professional education, and so on—are embodied in law and enforced by society. That is not the case with the norms of altruism; they are merely social expectations of how people should behave.* But if altruistic behavior seeks no reward and often involves some cost, and is not enforced by law, why do most of us behave, at least some of the time, as the norms say we should? Why

---

*But in a few jurisdictions "Good Samaritan Laws" oblige spectators to help someone in distress; this will be discussed in Chapter Five.

are they stronger than the drive of self-interest?

One reason, says social psychologist Janusz Reykowski of the Polish Academy of Science, is the pressure to conform. If our actions are visible to people around us, we tend to do what they expect of us and avoid doing what would make them disapprove of us, even if this conflicts with our own preferences. It is easy to throw away a mailed request for a contribution to a worthy cause, but when there is a fund drive in one's office and everyone else is wearing pins reading "I GAVE," it is hard not to follow suit. Similarly, physicians or other professionals working in a group setting will often do more for needy clients than is legally required of them, but those in strictly private practice are less likely to.

Laboratory experiments have demonstrated the conformity motive in altruism. In one, a Bulgarian graduate student had a group of college students in Sofia rate each other as either prosocial or egocentric, and answer a brief questionnaire on the desirability of helping fellow students. The researcher then told half of them, truthfully, that 90 percent of the group approved of helping fellow students, but told the other half falsely that a majority did not. Later, a confederate, posing as a researcher from a scientific institute, asked the students if they would help him out of a difficulty by scoring some questionnaires for him. Many of those who thought their group favored helping volunteered; few of those who thought their group did not did likewise. Moreover, prosocial students were more influenced by the false information than egoistic ones. What looked like helpfulness in the former was largely conformity; if helping were "in," they'd help, if not, they wouldn't.

But conformity is obviously not what motivates us in all those cases where we obey the norms of altruism even though no one else knows of our behavior. Why do we? It is a crucial question; it goes to the heart of the mystery, the good deed performed without reward. The answer, psychologists say, is that we have "internalized" the norms; we have made them part of our own personal sense of right and wrong, so that acting according to them feels like what we *should* do, *the right thing to do, the only way, the natural way, to act* in the circumstances.*

Natural it is not; the norms of altruism are as arbitrary and man-made as language or clothing (although religious people regard some norms as God's handiwork). But they don't *feel* man-made;

---

*How we internalize the norms is discussed in Chapter Six.

they feel like part of the "real me" because we have breathed them in with every breath from the day we were born. (And of course that is just as true of other people with quite different norms.)

For example:

- Practically all of us will help a small child who is lost and crying, even if no one sees us doing so; we would be ashamed of ourselves if we did not. Practically all of us will offer to walk a blind stranger across an intersection, again without the reward of social approval.
- Many of us give to certain causes whether or not anyone else knows we do so, even when our giving is impossible to justify logically. "Take the case of National Public Radio," says social psychologist Bibb Latané of the University of North Carolina. "If everybody sends in a few bucks, everybody's better off because NPR survives and they get to listen to its programs. But why do *I* send in my few bucks? There's no effect whatever from my doing so or not—no one person's contribution can possibly make any difference. Yet I *do* it, and so do a great many other people."
- Nearly half of adult Americans perform at least some volunteer work, many of them without public acclaim but out of a sense of duty; in particular, retired people, with time on their hands, feel it is incumbent on them to do something useful for others. Recall, too, the volunteers who handle the suicide hot line of Samaritans; they work unseen and unknown, without even the payoff of the appreciation of those they help.
- Nearly three quarters of American families give to charities, many or perhaps most of them without recognition or social reward of any kind. A flood of contributions from a great many donors of all sorts poured in to various agencies when, in December 1988, a major earthquake in Armenia killed an estimated twenty-five thousand people and made four hundred thousand homeless.
- Some millions of people respond to every blood drive or regularly give blood on their own, without reward other than a label to stick on their lapel if they wish. One such regular is social psychologist Jane Piliavin of the University of Wisconsin. Although she had been doing altruism research for years, she never asked herself why she was a chronic giver

of blood until one morning, while brushing her teeth, she looked at herself in the mirror and said, "You've given about two gallons of blood so far. *Why?* Why *do* you? Why does *anybody,* do such a thing?" After several years of field research she concluded that while first-time donors give in response to external appeals and pressures, regular donors "have no external reason. Their reasons are internal—just the knowledge that someone else, unknown to them, has the need."

HOW CULTURE MAKES EGOISTS AND SADISTS

Assuming we internalize our society's norms (and the values they derive from), as nearly all of us do while growing up, why aren't we more altruistic than we are? Why does our behavior often fall far short of society's ideals?

Part of the answer is in those individual biological differences that we have already seen, and in psychological ones that we will look at later.

But another part is that in our culture, as in that of Ambéli and many other places, other norms conflict with the altruistic ones. We are taught: "Help those who are in trouble," but also: "Don't stick your nose into other people's business." We learn that all people are entitled to equal treatment, but also that those who are smarter and work harder than others are entitled to a larger slice of the pie. We are told that we should accept responsibility for others but also that people should stand on their own feet and shoulder their own burdens.

In any given situation, therefore, we may have to choose between contradictory inner injunctions. Which of them we heed is determined by a variety of factors, one of the most important being where our attention is currently focused by circumstances. If for some reason we are preoccupied by a nonaltruistic norm, we may never consider the altruistic one, even if it is part of what we regard as our real self.

This was illustrated by an amusing—but disturbing—experiment conducted at Princeton University some years ago. Psychologist John Darley, a faculty member, suggested to Daniel Batson, then a graduate student, that they explore to what extent being in a hurry would interfere with the helping impulse. Batson, having been a divinity student before turning to social psychology, came up with the idea of getting volunteers from the Princeton Theological Seminary in whom the aiding norm—the Good Samaritan norm, one might say—should rank high.

He and Darley then worked out the plot of the experimental situation: The volunteers would be in a hurry to carry out some assigned chore when they would unexpectedly come across someone seemingly ill and in need of help. Batson and Darley then wickedly added a special twist: The seminarians would come across the ill person while on their way, somewhat late, to deliver a brief talk—some of them on the Good Samaritan, others on another and self-oriented topic. Could a seminarian on his way to talk about the Good Samaritan possibly fail to act like one even if he were late for an appointment? Or, since he was hurrying on faculty business and faculty assistants were waiting for him, would norms of obedience and promptness overpower the helping impulse?

In a room in Green Hall, Princeton's collegiate-Gothic psychology building, one of Batson's assistants gave each volunteer printed instructions to spend the next few minutes preparing a three-to-five-minute talk that would then be tape-recorded. The instructions directed half the volunteers to speak about the Good Samaritan parable, and the other half to speak about what kinds of jobs or professions seminary students would find most rewarding. The assistant told each volunteer when to leave for his speaking appointment, directing him to take a shortcut through the alley on the west side of Green Hall to another building where a second assistant would meet him and record his talk. (Later, Batson told each volunteer what the real purpose of the experiment had been.)

To some of the volunteers (who came in one at a time and did not hear what the assistant had said to others), he said, "It'll be a few minutes before they're ready for you, but you might as well head on over." To others he said, looking at his watch, "Oh, you're late. They were expecting you a few minutes ago. The assistant will be waiting for you so you'd better hurry." As he sent them off at fifteen-minute intervals, he alerted a confederate on a walkie-talkie. The confederate, another college student, was stationed inside a door opening onto the alley—it was December, and too cold to stay outdoors—and at the alert he would come out, slump down in the doorway, head down and eyes closed, and, as the seminarian approached, cough twice and groan.

A total of forty volunteers walked down the alley on their way to their appointment and came upon the coughing and groaning student. Some went right by, some hesitated and then continued on, and some stopped and said things like, "You all right?" or "Can I help you?" The confederate told those who spoke to him that he'd just taken pills for a respiratory condition and would be fine if he just rested a few minutes; he needed no help. Several seminarians insisted on getting him in out of the cold, and he let them do so in order to get rid of them before the next call came on the walkie-talkie.

The results, as Batson recalls with mingled ruefulness and amusement, were disconcerting:

"Only sixteen of the forty seminarians offered any kind of help," he said. "That surprised me, but what surprised me far more was that those who were on their way to talk about the Good Samaritan parable weren't any more likely to stop and help than those who were on their way to talk about jobs. The hurry variable was extremely strong—it overcame any difference there might have been in what the students were supposed to be thinking about. In fact, when we debriefed them, we learned that some of those who had been in a hurry hadn't even *noticed* anyone in distress en route, although they had practically stepped over the victim."

In a report of their study published in the *Journal of Personality and Social Psychology*, Darley and Batson concluded:

> According to the reflections of some of the subjects, it would be inaccurate to say that they realized the victim's possible distress, then chose to ignore it; instead, because of the time pressures, they did not perceive the scene in the alley as an occasion for an ethical decision.
>
> For other subjects it seems more accurate to conclude that they decided not to stop. They appeared aroused and anxious after the encounter in the alley. For these subjects, what were the elements of the choice they were making? Why were the seminarians hurrying? Because the experimenter . . . was depending on [them] to get to a particular place quickly. . . . A person not in a hurry may stop and offer help to a person in distress. A person in a hurry is likely to keep going, even if he is hurrying to speak on the parable of the Good Samaritan.

Another constraint on the altruistic impulse is that certain social settings have selfish or cruel norms of their own; in such a milieu, a reasonably decent person can become an avaricious egoist or even a sadist.

milieu, a reasonably decent person can become an avaricious egoist or even a sadist.

What was most shocking about the Watergate and Iran-Contra scandals was that many respectable and seemingly moral people committed criminal acts; we keep forgetting how often power corrupts. What was most horrifying about the My Lai massacre of nearly five hundred Vietnamese villagers was that it had been committed by normal young American men; we keep forgetting that war and military discipline can make monsters of ordinary people.

The world of political power and the world of war are only two of many social scripts that cast people in roles calling for behavior contrary to the norms of their culture; almost involuntarily—even unwittingly—they tend to play the part they have been assigned.

Professor Philip G. Zimbardo, a social psychologist at Stanford University, dramatically demonstrated this in a study of the psychology of imprisonment. He and three assistants signed up a group of college men to serve as either prisoners or guards in a simulation of the imprisonment phenomenon. One quiet Sunday morning the "prisoners" were "arrested" by police in squad cars, handcuffed, booked at the police station, and then taken to the "prison" (a special set of cells built in the basement of the Stanford psychology building), where they were stripped, searched, deloused, and issued uniforms.

Zimbardo and his team had selected the ten prisoners and eleven prison guards from a larger pool of would-be volunteers, all of whom had been interviewed and given personality tests. The researchers chose only those they evaluated as emotionally stable, mature, and law-abiding. These average middle-class white college men all agreed in advance to be either guards or prisoners during the two-week experiment; each was assigned to one part or the other by a flip of a coin.

The warden (one of Zimbardo's colleagues) and the guards compiled a list of sixteen rules the prisoners would be required to obey: They had to be silent during meals, rest periods, and after lights out; they had to eat at mealtimes but not at any other time; they had to address each other only by their ID number and any guard as "Mister Correctional Officer"; and so on. Breaking any rule could result in punishment.

The guards, for their part, had billy clubs, whistles, handcuffs, and the keys to the cells; their instructions were to maintain "law and order" in the prison and they were given considerable freedom to improvise their own tactics and strategies for prisoner control.

Quite soon, the interaction between the guards and the prisoners assumed a familiar pattern: The guards began to regard the prisoners as inferior and dangerous, the prisoners to see the guards as bullies and sadists. A typical guard experience:

> I was surprised at myself. . . . I made them call each other names and clean out the toilets with their bare hands. I practically considered the prisoners cattle, and I kept thinking I have to watch out for them in case they try something.

Shortly the prisoners staged a rebellion, ripping off their numbers and barricading themselves inside their cells by pushing the beds against the doors. The guards sprayed a fire extinguisher at the prisoners to force them away from the doors, broke into the cells, stripped the prisoners and took away their beds, and generally harassed and intimidated them.

From then on the guards began making the prisoners obey additional rules and perform tedious and useless work, punishing them for "infractions," and waking them repeatedly at night for head counts. The prisoners, for their part, became increasingly humiliated and obsessed with the unfairness of their treatment, yet felt so collectively demeaned and had so little respect for each other that after days of living together many of them still knew nothing about the others. Some grew rather disturbed, one so much so that by the fifth day the experimenters were planning to release him early. As Zimbardo and his assistants later wrote:

> What was most surprising about the outcome of this simulated prison experience was the ease with which sadistic behavior could be elicited from quite normal young men, and the contagious spread of emotional pathology among those carefully selected precisely for their emotional stability.

The researchers illustrated the development of sadistic behavior by quoting excerpts from the diary of Guard A, who, prior to the experiment, had written of himself:

> As I am a pacifist and [a] nonaggressive individual, I cannot see a time when I might guard and/or maltreat other living things.

But by the fifth day he noted in his diary:

> I have singled him [one prisoner] out for special abuse both because he begs for it and because I simply don't like him. . . . The new prisoner (416) refuses to eat his sausage. . . . I decided to force feed him, but he wouldn't eat. I let the food slide down his face. I didn't believe it was me doing it. I hated myself for making him eat but I hated him more for not eating.

On the sixth day. Zimbardo and his team abruptly terminated the experiment at midpoint for the good of all concerned. The value of their study, they later wrote, "derives precisely from the fact that normal, healthy, educated young men could be so radically transformed under the institutional pressures of a 'prison environment.'" But the volunteers' abnormal behavior, they said, was actually an "appropriate" adaptation to the prison setting.

What the Stanford researchers had seen has often been reported as occurring in real prisons and prison camps. The most hideous and infamous instances on record are to be found in accounts of the behavior of the guards and officers in charge of the Nazi concentration camps and death camps. It is less well known that the social setting the Nazis created corrupted many of their prisoners and turned them, too, into beasts. In *Survival in Auschwitz*, the Italian writer Primo Levi described the death-camp system in which certain prisoners were given particular privileges and power over the rest and, as a result, became "monsters of asociality and insensitivity" who took out their hatred of their oppressors on those they had some control over. Nearly all the other prisoners were dehumanized too; struggling to survive by wangling an extra ounce of bread or escaping a hard work assignment, they lost all impulse to aid their fellows, and those who faltered or weakened found no one extending a helping hand.

Yet Levi did not conclude from his experiences that human beings are fundamentally brutal and egoistic but rather that the world of the camp made many of them that way. And he pointed out that when that unnatural world dissolved, the dehumanized prisoners almost at once reverted to more humane ways. His diary entry for January 19th, 1945—the day after the Germans fled the camp but before rescuers arrived—records this tiny but memorable event:

When the broken window was repaired and the stove began to spread its heat, something seemed to relax in everyone, and at that moment Towarowski (a Franco-Pole of twenty-three [with] typhus) proposed to the others that each of them offer a slice of bread to us three who had been working. And so it was agreed.

Only a day before a similar event would have been inconceivable. The law of the Lager [camp] said: "Eat your own bread, and if you can, that of your neighbor.". . . . It was the first human gesture that occurred among us. I believe that that moment can be dated as the beginning of the change by which we who had not died slowly changed from Häftlinge [prisoners] to men again.

An optimistic concluding note: As some social scripts turn ordinary people into egoists and even sadists, others lead them to outdo themselves in kindness and helpfulness. What is most notable about heroic rescues is that so often the rescuers are average men and women who lived up to the part thrust upon them; what is most inspiring about those who, after floods and earthquakes, labor incessantly at comforting and caring for its victims is that generally they are ordinary people who rose to the occasion.

Finally, when a group of people has only a limited amount of some needed resource, as in a water-shortage crisis, they must resolve a difficult dilemma: If each does what is best for himself, all will suffer—but for anyone to altruistically take less than he can get would be self-destructive unless the others did likewise. Such situations, which have been studied by social scientists both in real life and in the laboratory, often produce selfish and harmful behavior: In 1987, when San Franciscans were asked to voluntarily cut down their water consumption by 10 percent because of a shortage, use rose by 6 percent.

But when it becomes plain that individual self-control is not working and that the problem is growing worse, groups often resolve the dilemma by voting or agreeing to create an authority to supervise rationing of the resource. Such a solution is in everyone's best interest in the long run; it transforms selfishness into mutually enforced altruism.

This happens most often in small face-to-face groups; in large impersonal ones, the population may rely on already existing authorities to exert the necessary control. Such was the case in San

Francisco, where the Public Utilities Commission announced a program of mandatory rationing in May 1988, granting each user a reduced allotment based on 1987 water bills, with penalties to be imposed on those who used more than their allotted quantity.

WE AND THEY

The most obvious fact about altruism is that people tend to practice it toward those in their own group but not those outside it, for whom they feel anything from indifference to hatred. To some people, their own group can be as large as their society, or even much of humankind; to others it can be as small as their own immediate family. Wherever they draw the line, those within it are We (the "ingroup," as social scientists say), one's fellow human beings, who merit help when in need; those outside it are They (the "outgroup"), aliens, who do not.

History provides ample proof of this generalization: Those who have made war or been warred upon, and those who have persecuted, enslaved, or sought to exterminate another people, have unfailingly seen their enemies and victims as either evil or subhuman, and in either case deserving of what is done to them, but seen their compatriots as brothers and sisters who deserve their loyalty and support. These are abstractions; to better comprehend their meaning, look at a single minuscule incident, a real-life parable offered by sociologist Ronald Cohen:

> Some years ago I roomed with a German who had been assigned on his first tour of duty during World War II to a concentration camp—a phenomenon he did not fully believe existed until he got there. One night he told of a strange event at the camp that nearly drove him mad. Another, older, more seasoned guard was assigning every tenth person to die. When he got to a particular tenth one, instead of telling him to step forward for execution, the guard raised his eyebrows almost imperceptibly and chose the eleventh. The tenth, he explained later, was a *Landsmann* [compatriot] from the same town and they had known each other before the Hitler period.

The guard had effortlessly sent Them to die, but could not do so to one of Them who was also, in his eyes, one of Us.

The tendency of human beings to make such distinctions and to treat members of Us with humanity, Them with barbarity, is both strong and all but universal; two thousand years of preachments about the Good Samaritan have done little, if anything, to change that. It has not only been Goths, Huns, and other barbarians who have relished slaughtering their enemies; civilized people, whose religions exalt altruism and the love of humankind, have done likewise.

Such as, for instance, the Crusaders. In June 1099, when the armies of the First Crusade laid siege to Jerusalem, held by the Fatimid Moslems, the caliph offered peace and guaranteed the safety of Christian pilgrims and worshipers. But Bohemund and Godfrey, the leaders of the Crusaders, demanded unconditional surrender, and the defenders, after resisting for forty days, surrendered. The Crusaders entered the holy city; here is the joyous eye witness report of one Raymond of Agiles, a Christian—and a priest:

> Wonderful things were to be seen! Numbers of the Saracens were beheaded . . . others were shot with arrows, or forced to jump from the towers; others were tortured for several days and then burned in the flames. In the streets were seen piles of heads and hands and feet. One rode about everywhere amid the corpses of men and horses.

That was in the semicivilized Middle Ages. But it was in our own time that some American hawks were all for dropping the bomb on Moscow before the Russians had perfected their own bomb, and it was only a year or so ago that some Administration strategists were arguing the feasibility of nuclear war, particularly if we struck first and hardest.

Is We-They thinking inevitable? Is it so deeply rooted in us than nothing can alter it? If so, altruism research is a useless academic exercise—but if not, then scientific understanding of its causes may enable us to find ways to combat We-They feelings.

One cannot deny that a good deal of the scientific evidence about the We-They tendency is disheartening. Specifically:

• Sociobiologists argue that We-They thinking has been built into us by evolution. Edward O. Wilson writes, "Our brains do appear to be programmed to the following extent: We are

inclined to partition other people into friends and aliens.
. . . We tend to fear deeply the actions of strangers and to
solve conflict by aggression." He argues that those early humans who thought in this fashion had the advantage over
those who did not, and that the trait was therefore selected
by evolution and is now inherent in human nature.

- Psychologists see the We-They tendency as part of a key
process of human thinking, namely, categorizing—grouping
things according to their similarities and differences. Although categorizing is essential to thinking, it can be the
basis of prejudice; we are likely to exclude from the category
of humans worthy of our concern and caring those who
merely speak, dress, and/or worship differently from us.

- Social psychologists and sociologists point out that the We-
They tendency can be socially useful: Hatred of Them unifies
and solidifies the feeling of being Us, thereby strengthening
the ingroup. It can also be personally useful: The sense of
We-ness created by having a common enemy is reassuring,
exhilarating, and *feels* good. Thus, for both societal and personal reasons We-They thinking is hard to combat.

- Social psychologists and sociologists have also gathered
many data showing that human beings, even if they believe
in equality, prefer others who are mentally and physically
similar to themselves. Most people choose friends and mates
who are like them in intelligence and social background;
more broadly, they feel more comfortable with and closer to
others who are like them in skin coloring, shape of nose, type
of hair, style of dress, accent and speech patterns, than those
who differ markedly.

Such feelings, when exacerbated by fear or competition, can
generate savagery in ordinarily civilized persons, even in presumably pleasant and peaceful settings. In 1985, English soccer fans
rioted and attacked Italian fans at a game in Brussels; thirty-nine
people were killed and 450 injured. If nationalistic and ethnic hatred
can justify such behavior in the minds of spectators of a sport, it is
not surprising that such feelings have provided the rationalization
for many a war over territory and nationhood.

Almost always, the hatred of Them is masked, assuming the
visage of a fight for territorial rights, political power, morality, or
liberty. Just such motives have been trumpeted by both sides in the

endless bloody struggles of Christians and Moslems in Lebanon, the recent eruption of ancient ethnic antagonisms between Serbs and Albanians and between Serbs and Slovenians in Yugoslavia, and the astonishing outbreak of savage rioting in the Soviet republic of Azerbaijan between Azerbaijanis and Armenians.

But occasionally someone will take off the mask and reveal the truth—the ugly features of We-They hatred. During the savage conflict between Moslems and Hindus that followed the end of British rule over India and led to the separate existence of Pakistan, the leader of the Moslem League, Mohammed Ali Jinnah, grew indignant when asked if the Hindus and Moslems could not be reconciled and reunited as one country:

> How can you even dream of Hindu-Moslem unity? Everything pulls us apart. We have no intermarriages. We have not the same calendar. The Moslems believe in a single God, and the Hindus are idolatrous. Like the Christians, the Moslems believe in an equalitarian society, whereas the Hindus maintain their iniquitous system of castes.

Recently, Meron Benvenisti, an Israeli historian and former deputy mayor of Jerusalem, eloquently lamented the powerful, senseless chauvinisms that were defeating the efforts of liberals like himself to bring the Jews and Arabs of Jerusalem into one community.

> Jerusalem is held together by force; take away Israel's coercive power, and the city splits on the ethnic fault line. ... Violence courts violence in a magic circle. Exotic growths— chauvinistic, fundamentalist—blossom on the rotting soil of atavistic urges. ... So basic is the cleavage that a decisive component of the self-identity of Jews and Arabs alike is not who they are, but rather, who they are not.

Benvenisti himself has lived for some years on Ein Rogel Street, a hilltop alley where Jews and Arabs live side by side in what they hoped would become neighborliness but has not:

> We had devised a complex and delicate system of social interaction, to avoid offending the sensibilities of one another. We sensed that we were destined to live in the twilight

world—so strange to luckier people but so real to us, for whom violent conflicts and neighborly relations are part of one human world. And we hoped that each day would bring us closer to a peaceful solution, that personal coexistence would somehow mitigate communal strife. . . . Yet during [my children's] lives on Ein Rogel Street they have not acquired a single Arab friend, nor even exchanged more than a few sentences with their Arab peers, and those not always friendly.

Between my children and my neighbor's children is a wall of glass. Through it they glimpse familiar human forms, but they don't relate to them; the forms have three dimensions but remain meaningless. They do not exist as people in the same psychological world.

Which is why Benvenisti sees almost any focused issue, such as the Israeli-Arab conflict over control of the Temple Mount, as "a time-bomb with a destructive force of apocalyptic dimensions" ticking at the heart of the city.

The differences between Hindu and Moslem, Moslem and Christian, Jew and Arab, are substantial, but even differences of the most trivial kind can generate feelings strong enough to cause favoritism to Us and unfairness to Them. To demonstrate how astonishingly little it takes to induce such behavior, the English psychologist Henri Tajfel and his colleagues had teenage English schoolboys sit together, four at a time, watching dots flash on a screen; each wrote down his estimate of how many dots he saw at each flash. Afterward, some of the boys were told that they belonged to a group that tends to overestimate in such guessing, while others were told that they belonged to a group that tends to underestimate. (There were, in fact, no such groups.) Each boy was then asked to say how a sum of money should be divided between two other boys about whom he knew nothing except that one was said to be an overestimator and the other an underestimator. Little as that was to go on, it was enough: Over 80 percent of the boys allotted more money to those who shared their supposed estimating tendency than to those who did not.

Adults exhibit the same propensity in everyday situations of all sorts, as shown by a variety of experiments: "lost" wallets whose owners could be identified as to race or ethnic background; stamped letters, ready to mail but apparently dropped, with senders' and addressees' names of a recognizable ethnic group; and, most often, the accidental spilling of some large batch of objects that have to be picked up (a carton of data cards, a box of pencils, a container of paper clips). In each case, the aim was to see whether passersby or spectators more readily help someone of their own ethnic or racial group than someone of a different group. For the most part, they do.

What experiments reveal in minuscule form—sympathy for people like ourselves, indifference or antipathy toward those who differ from us in looks, manners, or beliefs—explains some of the most monstrous behavior of humans toward fellow humans in the real world. Torture of political enemies is a case in point. American psychologist Janice Gibson and Greek psychologist Mika Haritos-Fatouros studied men who had been torturers in the Greek Army Police Corps during that country's military regime (1967 through 1974). They concluded that the torturers were not freaks but more or less ordinary people who had been taught, by means of brutal training and indoctrination, to see themselves as a close-knit elite, and their prisoners as belonging to the "outside world," as "worms" who had to be "crushed," and, of course, as Communists, a virtually nonhuman category.

Hans Frank, Nazi governor of Poland, and an expediter of the extermination of Polish Jews, wrote in his diary that he considered Jews a lower species of life, a kind of vermin which upon contact infected the German people with deadly diseases; when the Jews were all slaughtered, he wrote, "a sick Europe [will] become healthy again."

The eighteenth-century Boers who, in South Africa, butchered the peaceful !Kung; the American settlers and soldiers who sought not to conquer but to kill off the Indians; the contemporary Brazilian developers who have been trying to rid great areas of the Amazonian forest of Indians—all these, and many others like them, have seen their prey as pestiferous and dangerous animals toward whom one need feel no humane sentiment.

But not only murder kills; as Elie Wiesel has said, indifference does, too—the kind of indifference to others' suffering that allowed so many Poles to look away as their Jewish compatriots were arrested and shipped off to the death camps. For to most Poles, the Jews in their country were Others, aliens who spoke an ugly language, rejected Christ, and whom they forced to live apart, in their own neighborhoods and villages. The end result: Only 10 percent of Poland's 3.5 million Jews escaped death.

In contrast, the Danes, with a democratic tradition and a relatively tolerant religion, had long allowed Jews to merge into Danish life, living among them, dressing and speaking and behaving like them. The Danes, accordingly, saw their Jews as fellow Danes, even though not fellow Christians; they could not feel indifferent to their fate during the Nazi occupation. When the German effort to round up Danish Jews for deportation to the death camps was about to get under way, a rescue movement sprang up overnight; large numbers of Danes conspired to hide Jews and to ferry them in small boats of every kind to safety in Sweden. The end result: 95 percent of Denmark's 7,800 Jews were rescued.

Can we get people to draw larger boundaries to what they consider Us?

In part, the categories we think in as adults are based on formative experiences in the home. Parents are role models for their children; if our words and actions express a broad and catholic view of humankind, our children are likely to adopt such a view, while if our words and actions suggest the existence of a small, preferred, elite Us and a vast, undesirable, unwanted Them, our children are likely to grow up bigoted.

Outside the home, can we do anything in our schools, our communities, and the larger world to induce people to see people unlike themselves as fellow human beings, as neighbors to be loved as themselves?

Many well-meant efforts to do so—everything from interracial block parties to the international One World movement—have either not caught on or had only limited and temporary success. Most of them were based on the "contact hypothesis"—the belief that merely having people of different backgrounds or races work, study, or play alongside each other would break down their mutual antipathies. But the hypothesis was wrong. School desegregation, the most notable such effort, has not had the desired effect; according to a number of studies, in desegregated public schools and colleges the members of the different races usually create their own encapsulated groups, and antagonisms remain unchanged.

But a small number of sophisticated experiments based on social-science findings have been successful. For economic reasons, such trials have thus far been conducted only with small groups, but the principles should be applicable to larger ones.

- A classic study of boys in summer camp, conducted by psychologist Muzafer Sherif, showed, first, that it was alarmingly easy to create ingroup loyalty and intergroup hostility. Boys were assigned to two separate lodgings and allowed to give their groups names; that was enough to cause them to quickly develop partisan feelings and, when they played competitive athletic games against each other, they were openly hostile, even to the point of stealing and burning each other's banners, calling each other names, and scuffling later in the mess hall lines.

  In the next phase of the experiment Sherif sought to dissolve the hostility by putting the two groups together in noncompetitive enjoyable activities such as a morning swim. Mere togetherness, however, not only did no good but actually exacerbated hostility.

  Sherif then arranged to have the boys go on a day-long outing during which the one truck available to get food was immobilized by a supposedly dead battery. The only solution was for the boys, all together, to push and haul it to a place from which it could coast downhill and be started. After that experience and several others that also required the boys to cooperate for their mutual good, they began to see themselves as one group rather than two. Name-calling and jostling in the food lines died away, friendships between members of the two groups sprang up, and when a bus taking the boys back from a campfire stopped at a refreshment stand, those in one group, with five dollars left in their kitty, treated their former enemies to milkshakes.

- Many experiments and programs in which a school sports team is made up of members of different races have had results similar to that of the Sherif experiment. Working together toward the common goal of team victory leads those on the team to see others on the team who are of a different race as Us, not Them. This is very different from what occurs in token or proportional allotment of places on a panel or board to members of different racial or ethnic groups; when individuals "represent" a subgroup, their subgroup identity is not minimized but emphasized, and intergroup animosity is not diminished but maintained.

- Social psychologist David W. Johnson of the University of Minnesota and various colleagues have conducted experiments in cooperative learning in which students are assigned to interracial groups that use team-study methods to learn the course material. When students drill each other, quiz each other, and correct each other, they learn not only the material but something else: They develop wider friendship circles and more positive interracial attitudes than comparable students not in such groups.

• Even seating arrangements or other spatial relationships can accentuate or weaken ingroup partisanship. Samuel L. Gaertner and John F. Dovidio had groups of four students (two men, two women) meet separately and discuss, until they reached agreement, what would be the most important steps to take if they were in a plane that crashed in northern Minnesota in the winter. When each group had reached a consensus, the groups were combined, two at a time, into eight-member groups whose members were asked to agree again about the steps in the survival plan and to choose a leader in their imaginary winter crisis.

Some of the eight-member groups were seated around a circular table with the members of each original four-person group side by side facing the members of the other one. Other eight-member groups were seated so that members of the two original groups were alternated all the way around. This superficial manipulation was surprisingly effective: 62 percent of the people in the segregated seating, but only 48 percent of those in the integrated seating arrangement, voted for one of their own group as leader. Moreover, those in the integrated seating plan were much more likely to feel that their eight-person group had acted as a single unit (not as two units) than those in the segregated seating plan. Finally, those who saw their merged group as two units continued to like their former subgroup members more than people from the other subgroup; those who saw the merged group as one unit lost this bias.

This is only a sampling of the experiments showing that it is possible to use behavioral science knowledge to enlarge the boundaries of the We feeling; applied science, rather than moral exhortation, may some day bring us closer to the ideal of the Brotherhood of Man. That, at any rate, is the belief and hope of many of the altruism researchers I have talked to.

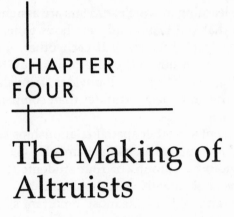

CHAPTER
FOUR

The Making of
Altruists

HOW ALTRUISTS GET TO BE THAT WAY

Journalists and biographers often ask those who have done something notably altruistic what made them the way they are. The answers, though interesting, are rarely enlightening; altruists themselves know very little about why they behave as they do.

Most of them, like nearly all of us, explain themselves largely in terms of a few crucial experiences that they believe shaped them. But similar experiences can have quite different effects on different people, since, as we have seen, both biology and the cultural milieu play a considerable part in what we become.

More important, developmental psychologists now believe that the adult personality cannot be accounted for largely by a few critical experiences but is the product of a continuing interaction, from birth to adulthood, between each new experience and the personality as it has developed up to that point; the impact of any experience depends on all that the infant began with and everything that has occurred to it.

But that isn't how it feels to us or how we perceive it. Unwittingly, for reasons of psychological economy, we construct simple, rational explanations of why and how we became the kinds of persons we are; we simplify, forget, or repress much of what was important in our past. And as longitudinal studies of individuals made by psychologists have shown, over the years we unconsciously and continually revise our autobiographies to harmonize with our current mood and condition.

For such reasons, altruists, when asked what made them that way, usually offer only little odds and ends of biography or family life by way of explanation. For instance:

- Joyce M. Black, a handsome, well-to-do New York matron, has served on seventy-five boards, commissions, and advisory panels dealing with health or welfare matters in the past thirty years; she has sometimes been called "the ultimate volunteer." When a *New York Times* reporter asked her why she has devoted so much of her time and energy to good works, Mrs. Black said, "I was born into a good life and encouraged to give back what I could." The reporter persisted, and Mrs. Black added a second explanation: As a young adult, she had contracted poliomyelitis and vowed that if she recovered, she would work at helping others. Both are good answers, as far as they go—which isn't very far, since most other people with similar experiences do not become super-volunteers.
- Reginald Andrews, the young black man who jumped under a subway train to rescue a blind man, when asked by a reporter why he did it, said only, "I knew what I had to do." But pressed further, he thought a bit, then added that he had a blind sister and "if it had been my sister there, I wouldn't want anyone to just stand around." Yet in many an emergency situation, some or most bystanders, who also know what they should do and have close ties to someone who might some day be in a similar crisis, do nothing but stare, or hurry away. There must be much more behind Reginald Andrews's act than he said, or could say.
- Mrs. Marjorie Judge of Southampton, New York, a sweet-faced, middle-aged, retired teacher, currently spends half a day each week as a hospice volunteer in the home of some dying person. Throughout the nation, eighty thousand hospice volunteers, many of them retired, spend at least several hours a week reading and talking to terminally ill people, holding their hands, feeding them, performing household tasks, in many cases providing actual nursing care, and knowing all the while that those they are befriending and helping will soon die. Why do they do it? Surely not because

it gives them something to do; there are pleasanter ways to fill one's time. And surely not for the rewards of company; it is they who are the givers, the dying who are the rewarded. I asked Mrs. Judge, among others, why she does it; like the rest, she seemed hard put to explain it. Here are the highlights of our talk:

Q: What made you want to spend time ministering to dying people?

A: Oh . . . I had always done things like this. At nineteen I was a counselor at a camp for handicapped children—kids in wheelchairs, kids in braces, spastic kids, all that. Later I was a recreation volunteer on a psychiatric ward at a large hospital. And as a teacher, I always worked with problem kids in school.

Q: But what made you like that? Why were you drawn again and again to such activities?

A: I don't know. . . . I've always been very people-oriented, I need people around me.

Q: Why in so giving a relationship to them?

A: Oh, I think it's a two-way street, I feel I come away having received more than I have given. If it weren't satisfying, I think I couldn't do it.

Q: That still doesn't tell me what made you an altruistic kind of person. What do you think did?

A: *(Long pause.)* I don't know. *(Long pause.)* My mother was a very loving, giving personality. *(Long pause.)* Also, my generation was an idealistic one. When I went to college, we all wanted to make the world a better place. But I don't call what I do altruism. I never use that word. To me it sounds—I don't know—impractical, or pretentious. I do what I do because I feel good doing it.

Can diligent research by a biographer find more enlightening answers? Sometimes it can, although since biography involves no controlled experiments, it can yield only untestable hypotheses. Still, sometimes such hypotheses can be rather persuasive, especially when the biographee's life is well documented, as, for instance, in the case of Florence Nightingale, one of the great altruists of history. For not only were the details of her life a matter of public record but she left a mass of revealing correspondence and private diary notes; we have ample grounds for a number of conjectures, which, taken together, add up to a reasonably convincing interactional explanation of her behavior.

Florence Nightingale was the strikingly good-looking daughter of wealthy upper-class English parents; her father, a country gentleman, was a propertied man of leisure. Born in 1820, she was reared to live the fashionable and pampered life of a gentlewoman, but from her teens on she found that prospect repugnant. Though she was at times half in love with one or another of several eminently desirable suitors, sooner or later she rejected each of them, choosing instead the bitterly hard, lonely life of the reformer of the hospital system and of nursing practice, often working in malodorous and disgusting conditions, and for many years fighting a seemingly hopeless battle against bureaucratic conservatism. Why did she? The biographical record suggests a number of possible hypotheses, none of which, by itself, seems sufficient:

- Though surrounded by every advantage, reared by a devoted nanny, and cherished by her father (she got along poorly with her mother), Florence Nightingale was a "strange, passionate, wrong-headed, obstinate and miserable" child, says her biographer, Cecil Woodham-Smith. Nightingale herself wrote in a private autobiographical note that as a very young child she felt sure she was not like other people but was a monster, and feared she would do something strange in company that would give her away.

   Might it be that because of her natural moodiness and wilfulness, she was treated like a misfit and outsider, and these experiences made her particularly responsive later to others who suffered and were outsiders to the good life?
- Her mother's father, a wealthy merchant, was a distinguished humanitarian who, in Commons for forty-six years, fought for the oppressed, first as an abolitionist, then as a champion of factory workers, and later as a defender of the rights of Dissenters and Jews. Her father was an outspoken supporter of the Reform Bill of 1832, which gave the vote to many who had not had it, and a reader and thinker with a lifelong interest in ethical questions; in tutoring Florence he must have conveyed his values to her.

   Could her life have been an effort to follow the example set for her by her admired grandfather and father?

- Long before she ever thought of nursing as a career, Florence displayed a fondness for nursing sick pets and taking care of babies. As a young woman, she volunteered to spend what turned out to be many weeks nursing her ailing grandmother and her grandmother's dying nurse.

  Might the satisfactions of doing good have been so rewarding as to make her seek more of them on a vastly larger scale?

- At seventeen, when her family was preparing for an extended tour of Europe and a round of glamorous events and entertainments, she wrote, "On February 7th, 1837, God spoke to me and called me to His service." Exactly what kind of service, the voice did not specify. Only after years of agonized searching did Nightingale decide that she was supposed to help the poor and wretched in some way, and only years after that did she identify her particular mission as the reform of hospitals and nursing.

  Could the voice she heard have been that of her unconscious, showing her a feasible way to reject marriage and a life of privilege?

- For many years before she entered nursing (over the strenuous objections of her family), she alternated between taking part in the social whirl and enjoying the attentions of suitors, and detesting and shunning that life. She suffered frequent attacks of the vapors, near-breakdowns, and spells of compulsive fantasying; these mysterious ills largely disappeared once she had found her vocation.

  Could guilt over her rejection of marriage and her mother's way of life have made her seek expiation in the form of hard, revolting work in a good cause? Or did the guilt arise from her several intense attachments, never physically consummated (as far as anyone knows), to women? (Of a cousin, she wrote, "I never loved but one person with passion in my life and that was her.")

- After years of studying hospital management and nursing, and gaining experience in a German orphanage and a hospital in Paris, she became superintendent of a London sanitorium for indigent governesses. The next year, during the Crimean War, she was sent to Crimea by the government to oversee the nursing of sick and wounded British soldiers. There she carried out bedside and supervisory duties amid ghastly sights and sickening stenches, performed labors that would have shattered the nerves of any other gentlewoman of her era, and battled against War Office indifference and red tape until she had succeeded in bettering conditions.

During the next four decades, she fought to reform the military hospital system (she became general superintendent of the Female Nursing Establishment of the army's military hospitals); wrote reports, tracts, and a primer on nursing; founded a model nursing school that soon was widely emulated; and transformed nursing from unskilled part-time work, performed largely by prostitutes, into a skilled, respectable, helping profession. She became a national heroine, loved by the people, feared by her adversaries (and sometimes her friends and colleagues), and honored by King Edward VII, toward the end of her life, with the Order of Merit—the first time it had ever been given to a woman.

Was the sight of dreadful suffering and of the relief she could bring the crucial experience that drove her ever on?

Or could the rewards of power and status, first experienced at the sanitorium in London and then on a much greater scale in the Crimea, have been the prime mover?

There you have eight conjectural explanations of Florence Nightingale's extraordinary altruism. How can we make sense of all this? Which hypothesis seems most plausible?—or could it be that all of them, taken together, offer a plausible explanation? Start with a child who had innate tendencies toward moodiness, sensitivity, and withdrawal; proceed to the early experiences of differentness and of maternal rejection that these predilections created; continue on to all her other experiences, each acting, in that social setting, upon the personality and values built up in her to that point; and we have something like an interactional explanation of Florence Nightingale's altruism.

Yet all this is only suggestive, not conclusive; it is strictly *post hoc* hypothesizing that cannot be put to the test. For evidence of a stronger sort, let us turn to data of a different kind: that gathered by developmental psychologists through painstaking observation of, and experimentation with, infants, toddlers, schoolchildren, and young adults. These data reveal that, like the growth of the mind and its abilities, altruism gradually develops to a greater or lesser degree in nearly all human beings in the course of normal development; it is not rare or idiosyncratic, as Florence Nightingale's biography might lead us to suppose, but typical of us. If crime, war, and genocide are evidence that we are beasts, the developmental study of altruism provides evidence that we are, paradoxically, compassionate beasts.

THE NATURAL HISTORY OF ALTRUISM

It was the Swiss child psychologist Jean Piaget who first portrayed the mind as developing via an inevitable and ever more complex interaction between the organism and experience. Piaget conceived of the infant's mind as a structure, embodied in the growing brain, that interacts with simple experiences; these events modify and add to that structure, making it more complex and capable of having other, more intricate interactions with the world, which modify and build upon it still further, and so on.

Piaget, a gentle bird-boned little man, spent decades tirelessly crawling around on the floor with toddlers, playing games with older children, and plying still older ones with brain-twisters and puzzles, all in an effort to observe the nature of thinking at each age. Although he did not study the development of altruism, his work casts light on it, and we need to spend a moment looking at his results.

Piaget found that human intelligence develops through an unvarying sequence of four stages. During the first, from birth to about a year or year and a half, infants perceive things outside themselves but have no mental symbols or images of them. If you show a baby a toy, then hide it or drop it out of sight, the baby does not look for it but is as unaware of it as if it had ceased to exist.

By the end of that period, however, the baby's repeated experiences of external objects, plus the development of the brain and its ability to store and retrieve memories, enable the child to use mental images in place of perceptions. If you hide a toy under a pillow, the child, seeing the toy in its mind, will seek it there; the child can now remember absent objects and people, talk about them, and think about them in a simple way.

But not in terms of organizing concepts. No matter how you try to tell a three-year-old that his parents, away on a vacation, will be home in a week, he cannot grasp it; time, in his mind, consists only of "now," "before now," and "not yet." By seven or so, however, the structure of his mind has become developed enough for him to think about the physical world in terms of time, causality, and quantity.

Finally, somewhere between eleven and fifteen the intellect becomes capable of dealing with abstract concepts such as ratio, probability, justice, and virtue, and of hypothesizing, classifying, and logical reasoning.

Although Piaget did not investigate the development of altruism, some of his findings imply that it develops in stages that are related to those of mental development. For instance, not until somewhere in the third stage of mental development, at age seven or later, can a child correctly imagine how objects in a room look to another person standing elsewhere in the room (that is, which object is in front of which). This strongly suggests that as the child gains that ability, he or she should also be able to see things from another's emotional perspective and hence become more responsive to that person's distress.

Piaget's developmental theory offered an explanation of mental abilities so much better than any that then existed in psychology that it rapidly became dominant and spawned a virtual industry of Piagetian studies. Most of them dealt with mental abilities, but some branched off into other areas more closely related to altruism.

Especially notable was the work of the Harvard University psychologist Lawrence Kohlberg, who studied the development of moral ideas—the sense of what is right and wrong—between late childhood and adulthood. Over a twenty-five-year period beginning in 1958, he asked numbers of adolescents and adults for the right answer to various moral puzzles or dilemmas that he created. An example: A woman is near death from a special kind of cancer; only one drug can save her, but it is available only from the druggist who discovered it and who charges ten times what it costs him to make. The sick woman's husband can scrape up only half that amount, but the druggist refuses either to cut the price or to let him pay later. The husband thinks about breaking in and stealing the drug. Should he? Why or why not?

From the answers given by people of different ages, Kohlberg concluded that, like thinking, the moral sense develops through a series of predictable stages. In stage one, children base their moral decisions on avoidance of punishment and obedience to authorities; in stage two, on serving their own needs and trying to strike fair bargains; in stage three, on being a good person in their own eyes and those of others; and so on, ending up at stage six, on universal ethical principles.

Since altruism is partly motivated by moral values, one might suppose it likely that it develops in those same stages. But Kohlberg's evidence for this is rather thin: Most of his dilemmas don't concern altruism, and those that do don't deal with the conflict, typical of real life, between altruism and self-interest.

In his Dilemma V, for instance, the captain of a company of Marines in Korea asks for a volunteer to go back and blow up a bridge so the company can escape its pursuers. Because the volunteer would not be able to get back alive, no one speaks up. The captain must then decide whether to do it himself, or, since he is the only one who knows how to lead the retreat, order someone else to do so. But, as developmental psychologist Nancy Eisenberg points out, this dilemma involves a choice between two moral goals, one altruistic and one not, while in real life we far more often must choose between an altruistic goal and an amoral, selfish one.

But more recently there has been a great deal of developmental research focused directly on the question of how altruism develops. A number of psychologists have borrowed and adapted both Piagetian and Kohlbergian concepts and methods and used them to investigate how altruism develops in the human personality. They use a variety of techniques, all of which require immense patience and attention to detail.

Some altruism researchers spend long hours glued to peepholes, watching toddlers and young children in play groups and classrooms, and clocking and recording the frequency of their empathetic reactions and altruistic acts—and, often, their nonempathetic reactions and hostile acts. (The researchers usually remain hidden in order not to influence the children by their presence.)

Others conduct experiments in which they make children aware of someone's need or distress by telling them about it, showing them a videotape, playing a tape recording in the next room that sounds like crying, and so on. They note whether each child reacts selfishly or altruistically, then ask them why they acted as they did.

Still others tell children little story-dilemmas which, unlike Kohlberg's, involve a choice between self-interest and altruism; they ask the children what the person in each dilemma should do, and why.

The data derived from such studies show that altruistic feelings and behavior do develop in stages related to, but not identical with, those of intellectual or moral development. Some children progress through them faster, others more slowly; some are more responsive and giving at every stage than average, others less so. These differences may be due to the home milieu or the child's social environment. Or they may be due to heredity: Some children are more sensitive and perceptive than others; moreover, a child's innate temperament has a lot to do with how people respond to him or her, and thus to the kinds of experiences the child has.

But sooner or later, and to a greater or lesser extent, nearly all children follow the same course of development: As their experiences interact with their maturing mind and personality, they become more capable of empathizing, better informed about the consequences of selfish and altruistic behavior, and more keenly aware of what is expected of them in our society. A few highlights of the evidence:

- Newborns, as described above, cry when they hear another infant crying; they have no idea who is distressed or why but respond simply to their own discomfort.
- By ten to fourteen months, also as described above, toddlers react in a far more externally directed way to someone else's distress: They stare tensely at the person, or whimper, burst into tears, or run away. They rarely try to do anything directly for the sufferer, although some of them look at or reach out to their mothers as if to summon help.
- From fourteen months on, say Carolyn Zahn-Waxler and her colleagues at the National Institute of Mental Health, children react less and less with tears and distress, more and more with little efforts to do something for the other child or adult such as patting or stroking and, to a lesser extent, hugging and kissing.
- Beyond eighteen months, according to the NIMH researchers, children make more specific and complicated efforts to help: They enlist the help of an adult, embrace the victim, or bring him or her objects that in their own experience are comforting—a toy, a cookie, a bottle, a blanket. An excerpt from a research report:

> A neighbor's baby cries. Jennie [eighteen months old] looked startled, her body stiffened. She approached and tried to give the baby cookies. She followed him

round and began to whimper herself. She then tried to stroke his hair, but he pulled away. Later, she approached her mother, led her to the baby, and tried to put mother's hand on the baby's head. He calmed down a little . . . [but Jennie] continued to bring him toys and to pat his head and shoulders.

- By two to two and a half years, according to several research teams, most children have a repertoire of primitive caring responses: physical contact, inspecting the hurt, gift-giving, protection or defense (for instance, from another child), concerned questioning, advice, reassurance, and so on. By four, most children show a good deal of genuine concern about the well-being of other children, and some perform rather sophisticated acts of altruism. The psychologist Joan Grusec of the University of Toronto quotes a mother's report as an illustration:

> David [age four] has been playing at a neighbor's house for the afternoon. Michael [age six], his next-door neighbor and best friend, has been playing at the neighbor's too. . . . Michael is riding his bike. David spots a car rounding a corner and shouts to Michael, "You should make a signal!" David continues to lecture Michael on "safety" and then I realize that David is being overly concerned because Michael ran in front of a car this winter and was knocked down and since then David has shown a lot of concern about Michael's safety.

- Between kindergarten and second grade, children make a noteworthy leap in altruistic behavior, according to experiments conducted by Ervin Staub. He had a female assistant ask a child to make a drawing and then say, with seeming surprise, that there were no crayons on hand and that she would have to go get some. As she was leaving the room, the assistant would offhandedly remark, about a little girl supposed to be in the next room, "I hope she doesn't climb on that chair again." She would then leave; in her absence there would be a crash in the next room, followed by a child's sobbing. (The sounds, as usual in such experiments, were produced by a tape recording.) Most kindergarten children ignored the sounds or held their hands over their ears; only one out of five ran into the next room to help or went looking for an adult. By second grade, however, half of the children who were alone when they heard the sounds tried to help, and nine out of ten did so if they were with another child at the time.

When Staub queried the children afterward, the kindergartners indicated that they didn't help because they felt they weren't expected to; they weren't old enough or competent enough. Second graders, however, having had two years of the socializing influence of school, felt not only more competent but also responsible for other children.

• From kindergarten through tenth grade, children become ever more altruistic, according to Daniel Bar-Tal. In a series of experiments, he had Israeli children, one at a time, play a game with a research assistant; the children always won a cash prize. In the room was a contribution box and a poster asking for donations for needy children; in some cases there would be no other stimulus to giving, in other cases the assistant would make some comment about the poster, and in still others the assistant would urge the child to give. The results: The older the child, the more likely he or she was to give, and more generously, without suggestion or urging, even if the assistant had left the room and it seemed that no one would know whether the child gave or not.

(But the growth of altruism may not be uninterrupted; like a stock market graph, it may have minor dips, even though long-term movement is upward. Ervin Staub, for one, found a drop in helping from fourth to sixth grade. He thinks one reason is that, toward puberty, children become increasingly concerned with how their peers see them; this tends to inhibit helping, since they are not always sure that help is needed and fearful that offering help may look silly.)

• Between second and twelfth grade, children's motivations for altruistic behavior change significantly. Nancy Eisenberg and a series of colleagues concocted little stories in each of which the protagonist, a child, has to decide between helping someone in need and doing something in his or her own interest; the stories were told to or read by children, who were then asked what the protagonist should do. Here is one such dilemma presented to preschool and elementary school children (it comes in two versions, one with a female, the other a male, protagonist):

> One day a girl named Mary was going to a friend's birthday party. On her way she saw a girl who had fallen down and hurt her leg. The girl asked Mary to go to her house and get her parents so the parents could come and take her to the hospital. But if Mary did run and get the child's parents, she would be late for the birthday party and miss the ice cream, cake, and all the games. What should Mary do? Why?

Eisenberg's major findings: Preschool and young children, whatever alternatives they choose, make their decisions largely on the basis of what will be best for themselves. But as they mature, they become more capable of "role-taking" (putting themselves in the other person's place) and base their decisions more on the nature and urgency of the other person's needs. Furthermore, younger children reason partly in terms of stereotypes of what "good" and "bad" people would do (plus others' needs), while older children draw on their own personal values and their own sense of right and wrong.

Over the total span of the school years, say Eisenberg and her coworkers, children's decisions about how to behave toward others in need evolve through five stages, based respectively on (1) their own needs, (2) direct recognition of the needs of others without role-taking or guilt, (3) social approval plus conventional ideas about good and bad people and behavior, (4) empathetic and sympathetic reactions arising from role-taking, and (5) ethical responsibility, social responsibility, and internalized moral values.

Such is the evidence that altruism is the end product of an interaction between our normal biological equipment and a host of experiences common to growing up. What, exactly, are those experiences?

THE CONSTRUCTION OF ALTRUISM

The Parent-Child Relationship

The child's first experiences are of its parents' responses to its needs and actions. Parents who freely express love and warmth and are generously nurturant give the infant a sense of security, the toddler and preschooler a sense of his or her own worth; these are essential to normal emotional development. More specifically, parental warmth and nurturance are prerequisites for the development of empathy: Without a sense of oneness with other human beings created by a warm and close relationship with one's parents, says Staub, "The similarity of others' distress to one's own may not be noticed or acknowledged."

And, indeed, researchers have found correlations between parental warmth and altruism in children. One study of four-year-old boys found that those who were most generous in experimental situations had particularly warm and affectionate fathers. Another reported similarly that altruistic ten-year-old boys had affectionate mothers. The psychologist David Rosenhan, in a famous study of civil rights workers, found that those who were most deeply committed (most altruistic) had unusually warm ties with their parents.

The opposite is equally true. A recent study found that maltreated or abused preschoolers, when their playmates cry or are unhappy, react not with concern and empathy but by hitting or biting them, or trying to take their toys away. Another reported that children from abusive homes more frequently hit or threatened other children than those from normal homes. Many studies of delinquents, chronic criminals, and viciously antisocial adults have found that many of them had mothers who showed them no affection or love, particularly in the first five years of life. A study of a group of Nazi SS men who functioned as mass murderers in concentration camps and similar units reported that they had had highly authoritarian, punitive fathers.

Modeling

The experience of parental warmth promotes the development of altruism in a second way: Parents are children's first and most important role models, and their responses to the children's needs show the children how to respond to other people's needs. Parents who are cold or aggressive toward their children teach them, in effect, to be cold or aggressive toward others; parents who are caring and giving teach their children to be that way.

Children also model their behavior on their parents' behavior toward people outside the immediate family. A child whose father or mother refuses to get involved in other people's problems is likely to react the same way; a child whose parents are concerned about and helpful to others is likely to behave similarly.

Other people in the children's world—older siblings, admired teachers, and so on—also serve as models. When children see someone act altruistically, especially a sibling or an adult they respect or love, many of them do likewise. In a number of experiments using the same technique as Bar-Tal's, children have played games with an adult in which they won marbles, pennies, or tokens exchangeable for prizes; in some cases the adult player, without saying anything, put some of his own winnings in a bowl under a sign asking for donations for poor children; in other cases the children were asked by another adult to give part of their winnings to poor children and told that it would make those children happy. Both techniques increased children's giving, but "modeling," as the good example is called, worked better than exhortation, particularly with young children.

Models or good examples continue to have an effect even beyond childhood and adolescence. In an experiment mentioned in Chapter One, researchers stationed a young woman next to a car with a flat tire on the shoulder of the road and observed what fraction of passing motorists stopped to help her. Then they repeated the experiment with another young woman some distance farther back on the road, also with a flat tire but with another confederate posing as a passing motorist who had stopped and was changing it for her. Fifty-eight of two thousand passing drivers who saw someone helping a woman with a flat tire stopped to assist the next woman in need of help, compared with only thirty-five of two thousand who had not seen an example of helping.

The same influence has often been observed in sidewalk donations: More people will put money in a Salvation Army kettle, a blind beggar's cup, and the like if they have just seen someone else do so than if they haven't. Other experiments, employing news stories or broadcasts of altruistic acts, have likewise shown that there is a kind of contagion of benevolent behavior; people who have just heard about an altruistic act are more inclined to respond to someone in need than people who have not. Many of us can attest to that: We read of the outpouring of donations by other people to the victims of some flood, famine, or earthquake, and reach for our pen and checkbook.

But, of course, modeling works both ways. Not only cold, selfish, or harsh parents, but many other persons, can serve as models of hostile and inhumane behavior. If people children have any reason to admire are aggressive, cruel, or generally antisocial, the children are apt to learn from their example—and in most American homes children have frequent exposure to such examples in the form of violent television shows. Some of the violence, of course, is committed by the "bad guys," but some of it by heroic or charmingly picaresque "good guys"; in any case, violence is presented as a norm, not an aberration. The result, according to a wealth of evidence, is that children who view many violent programs are more unprovokedly aggressive toward their playmates than children who watch fewer such programs. The effect is neither temporary nor limited to play relationships. The long-term Cultural Indicators Project at the University of Pennsylvania's Annenberg School of Communications has for years been measuring both the content of television dramas and viewers' conceptions of social reality; its basic finding is that people who view a great deal of television—and thus a great deal of violence—are more likely to view the world as a mean and frightening place and to be fearful and mistrustful of others than light viewers. They are hardly likely, it seems obvious, to be altruists.

Discipline and Training

Almost all children experience some sort of discipline or training meant to make them less selfish and aggressive, more willing to share and to do things to benefit others. But some forms of discipline are productive, others counterproductive.

Many parents, like animal trainers, use techniques of simple conditioning—rewards for desirable acts, punishments for undesirable ones. They often claim that with the carrot-and-stick method they are able to get a child to stop beating up on other children and be "nice" to them.

There is good evidence, however, that children who experience primarily carrot-and-stick discipline will temporarily behave as parents want them to but without becoming altruistic on their own. Martin Hoffman and a colleague, Herbert Saltzstein, interviewed a large number of parents and their children about the parents' disciplinary practices, which Hoffman and Saltzstein classified as *power assertion* (spanking, yelling, and other forms of coercion), *love withdrawal,* and *induction* (explanations of how the child's actions would make the other person feel). The researchers then measured the children's moral development by having them make up the endings to incomplete stories about cheating or other wrongdoing.

The results were striking: Power assertion and love withdrawal often produced the desired behavior but not character change. The children complied reluctantly and with anger, anxiety, or guilt, but without internalizing the parents' (and thus society's) norms. Induction, on the other hand, especially by warm and loving parents, not only yielded the desired behavior but an awareness of others' feelings and needs, and began the internalizing of the parents' and society's standards.

Induction is only one way to explain behavior rationally to children; any form of reasoning with them about the value of unselfish and caring behavior furthers the development of altruism. It does so even if the child is too young to fully grasp the explanation; psychologists have noted that children respond to the process of reasoning, apart from its content. It is more effective, of course, when the child is able to understand the reasons.

Many children, in contrast, are taught altruism in the form of preachments or direct injunctions to be kind and unselfish by parents, ministers, and Sunday-school teachers. But using the kind of experiment in which children win something and then have an opportunity to share their winnings with the needy, researchers have tried a number of ways of influencing them to do so and found that preachment and exhortation are relatively ineffective.

Labeling

Most parents, when a child is spontaneously kind or helpful, will say something like "That was a nice thing you did" or "What a helpful person you are!" Labeling, as psychologists and sociologists call this, has considerable influence on behavior. People tend to live up to (or down to) their labels; when children hear themselves identified as, for instance, sissyish or brave, ladylike or tomboyish, they get an image of themselves that guides their future behavior.

A child whose parents take note chiefly of his selfish acts and label him selfish is likely to continue being so; one whose parents note his helpful acts and label him helpful is likely to be more so in the future.

This, too, has been experimentally verified. In a study by Joan Grusec and colleagues, a research assistant persuaded children who had won prizes to share some of their winnings with needy children and then said to some of them, "You shared quite a bit—you did what I expected you to do," and to others, "You shared quite a bit—you're the kind of person who likes to help others." Two weeks later, the children had another chance to share: Those who had been told they were helpful gave more, and more readily, than those who had been told they had done what was expected.

Learning by Doing

Children are greatly influenced in their development by the success or failure of their own behavior, both bad and good. Nursery-school children who act aggressively toward others are often "rewarded" in the sense that the other child yields up a toy, vacates the sandbox, and so on. As long as the aggression does not elicit superior coun-teraggression or is not controlled by adults, it is self-reinforcing; the child becomes even more aggressive. "Probably the most parsimoni-ous developmental answer to the question, 'Why aggression?',"writes the psychologist Robert B. Cairns of the University of North Carolina, "is that, for humans, 'Aggression works.' " But, fortu-nately, only up to a point: Parents, teachers, and society in general block this developmental tendency by a variety of methods ranging from moral suasion to sheer force. (Where that is not the case, in such socially chaotic situations as crack-ridden slums, or where a society condones and rewards brutality toward some despised mi-nority, aggressors learn from their own success and become mon-sters of brutality.)

Happily, the same principle holds true for altruistic behavior: Children's prosocial acts tend to be rewarding in one way or an-other, and they learn from, and are influenced by, their own behav-ior. When parents or other adults get children to take part in altruistic activities, it is the activities themselves, rather than paren-tal talk about them, that influence the children. Ervin Staub, who considers this a very important form of learning, says, "Change results from the experience itself. Children learn and evolve as a result of such experiences, especially if their actions have positive outcomes." He cites one of his own studies in which older children taught younger children; if the younger children were responsive, the older children tended to be more helpful to others afterward, but less so if the younger child were unresponsive. In another study he found that a child who was helpful to others got positive feedback from them—helping and sharing—and this, in turn, tended to form the first child's personality.

Similarly, in various experiments in which children have been persuaded to give part of their winnings in a game to unnamed poor children, to write letters to children in hospitals, and to help a teacher pick up spilled cards or paper clips, they later were readier to help and more generous with their help than comparable children who had not had such experiences. For they not only came to see themselves as kind persons, but vicariously experienced the other person's relief or pleasure and learned the importance to another of one's altruistic act.

Social Interaction

Outside the home, in play groups and school, children have a variety of other experiences that add to the foundation of altruism they have acquired at home. Exposure to other kinds of children and adults adds to their awareness of feelings and needs other than their own; this, plus their continuing emotional and mental maturation, increases their role-taking ability and, thereby, their level of altruism.

In the earlier years, however, their altruistic behavior is still largely self-serving. Younger children spontaneously teach each other the norm of reciprocity ("I'll be your best friend if you'll be my best friend") and quickly discover that to get favors it is necessary to do favors. In fact, at around six or seven, most children define friendship in terms of exchange ("He lets me ride his bike; then I let him ride my bike").

At the same time, they become aware from many sources— parents, teachers, other adults, and the media—of a larger cultural value: that it is right and good to help those who need it. Through both explicit teaching and unspoken implication and example, they gradually acquire a repertoire of "background expectancies"—the social norms of their society that specify how, when, and for whom altruistic acts should be performed.

By adolescence, these influences, interacting with the more developed intellect, bring about a shift to higher stages of altruistic thinking and a more thorough internalization of social norms. (Some of this, as we saw, takes place in early childhood, but most of it does so in adolescence.) When the norms become part of the person's mental and emotional structure, altruism is generated from within. Adolescents (and adults) tend to act altruistically to those in need because they feel a desire and need to; they feel good about doing so or guilty about not doing so, even if no one else knows how they responded.

Gender Roles, Sex Differences

There has been much debate about whether girls acquire altruistic patterns earlier, or in greater degree, than boys, and if so, whether this is due to biology or to their early recognition of what their society expects of them.

Twenty years ago, in the first flush of the new feminism, some researchers found little difference in the altruistic tendencies of the sexes. The traditional view that women were innately more nurturant than men was seen as a male chauvinist excuse for keeping women in the home and in the lesser helping professions. But more recently, most researchers who have looked at this issue have seen distinct differences appearing even in the early years of life. How much these are due to biology and how much to the socially prescribed gender roles that children begin to acquire in their early years is a moot point, but that differences do exist is beyond dispute. Some data:

- When nursery-school children are shown slides or told stories designed to elicit different emotions—happiness, sadness, anger, fear—girls react somewhat more empathetically than boys.
- Many studies of children ranging in age from three to nine have found boys more aggressive and less willing to share than girls.
- In experiments with fifth- and sixth-grade children, girls wrote many more letters to hospitalized children, made more toys for them, and donated more gift certificates for them than did boys in the same classes. (But letter-writing is apparently something girls do, boys don't do; boys are more

willing to pitch in and help when helping involves what they think of as boyish activities.)

As is often pointed out, however, boys and girls are treated somewhat differently from their earliest days—less so than a generation ago, but still enough to soon develop somewhat different expectations of themselves. This makes it hard to know how much the observed difference in altruism of the sexes owes to biology, how much to socialization.

In any case, by adulthood the sexes show somewhat specialized altruistic repertoires: Men help more in risky or physically strenuous situations (breaking up a fight, changing a tire), women more in situations traditionally thought of as requiring female ministrations (tending a hurt child, comforting a sick or emotionally troubled adult). The net conclusion is that males and females differ relatively little in their capacity for altruism but do differ somewhat in the kinds of altruistic behavior they exhibit and the kinds of situations in which they will offer help.

LATER DEVELOPMENTS

It is not only in childhood and adolescence that altruism gets built into us; at any time in adulthood, our beliefs or traits may lead us to do things that yield emotional rewards which further shape our personalities in the direction of altruism, a phenomenon Ervin Staub calls "self-socialization."*

A remarkable instance of this is the case of Bertha Pappenheim, a patient often discussed by Freud (under the name "Anna O"), although he himself never treated her. The self-absorbed, spoiled daughter of upper-middle-class Jewish parents in Vienna, she became a patient of Freud's early colleague Joseph Breuer when she developed severe hysteria, which rendered her at times partially paralyzed, unable to speak her native German properly, and subject to bouts of terrifying hallucinations. It was she who gave the name "the talking cure" to the soul-searching sessions—the forerunner of

*But so can self-socialization of the opposite kind: Ervin Staub, in his latest book, *The Roots of Evil*, shows how the people who committed the most horrific acts of genocide became capable of it by a series of steps, each of which reinforced and rewarded their tendencies in that direction.

psychoanalytic treatment—with Breuer that provided her with ca-
tharsis and relief.

But the relief was only temporary; when Breuer broke off treatment for personal reasons, she grew worse and was hospitalized for
several years. Eventually she recovered, and for a while toyed with
rather self-indulgent writing without much success or satisfaction.
But in 1895, at thirty-six, restless and looking for something meaningful to do, she accepted the post of housemother in a Jewish
orphanage in Frankfurt-am-Main. This changed her life: Over a
period of years her interactions with the children made her increasingly loving, selfless, and dedicated to their welfare.

After twelve years, she left the orphanage to pursue an even
more difficult altruistic goal: She organized and ran an institution for
illegitimate mothers and young prostitutes. As its chief administra-
tor for over two decades, she gave herself completely to the welfare
of her girls and women and to a prolonged public campaign for the
creation of institutions for "endangered girls." She had little or no
social life or pleasure other than her mission, and apparently needed
none.

A quite different example of the same phenomenon was the
transformation in middle age of a fearless explorer and scientist into
a great humanitarian. His name, now remembered by few, was
Fridtjof Nansen. Born in Norway in 1861, Nansen undertook a
series of Arctic explorations when he was a young man—tall, blond,
and an accomplished winter athlete—that made him a national
hero. At one point, he and one other man, cut off by extreme
conditions, spent over a year alone in the far North, surviving on
bear and walrus meat; once, when their two kayaks went adrift,
Nansen leaped into the freezing water, swam after them, and
brought them back, a feat that would have killed almost anyone
else. In his forties he became an oceanographer and, at the same
time, a statesman, serving as the Norwegian government's minister
to London.

By 1920, at the age of fifty-nine, he had had three distinguished
careers, none of which had anything to do with altruism. But in that
year the League of Nations, to which he was a delegate from his
country, asked him to head efforts to repatriate nearly half a million
prisoners of war from the former German and Austro-Hungarian
armies who were in Soviet POW camps. Nansen refused, but when

he learned of the conditions under which the men were living, he was overpowered by a desire to relieve their misery and accepted the post of high commissioner of the repatriation project.

Tall and bony, with snow-white hair and a huge, flowing moustache, he looked and played the part of humanitarian savior magnificently. The European powers and the new Soviet government refused to negotiate with each other, but Nansen, by virtue of his name, fame, and impassioned arguments, was able to deal directly with the Soviets, raise funds from a host of private sources, and overcome the resistance and hostility of the European governments. Soon he had mountains of food on their way to the prisoners; then, planning, traveling, pleading, and negotiating without respite, he organized their transport by a variety of means back to their several native lands. After two years, he reported to the League that the job was done: 427,886 prisoners of war had been returned to their homes. As Philip Noel-Baker, a British MP and a member of the League's Secretariat, said, "There is not a country on the continent of Europe where wives and mothers have not wept in gratitude for the work which Nansen did."

It had changed him. Even before the task was completed, vast Ukrainian crop failures in 1921 had brought starvation to millions in the Soviet Union, and the International Red Cross asked Nansen to head relief efforts; he wanted to decline and return to his scientific work, but was driven by an inner call to serve. A friend said to him, "If I know you rightly, you will never have peace of mind if you refuse," and, indeed, Nansen accepted. The League would have nothing to do with it, so he dealt directly with the Soviets, opened a headquarters in Moscow, raised funds by appealing to private organizations and the public in Western countries, and saved the lives of possibly millions.

Yet a third time need called him: An ill-fated Greek invasion of Asia Minor had ended in disaster, and vast numbers of Greeks in Turkey and Turks in Greece had to be relocated. Once more Nansen answered the summons and played an important part in the 1922–1923 exchange of more than 1.5 million Greeks and Turks. He was awarded the Nobel Peace Prize in 1922, and spent the entire 122,000 kronor on Russian famine relief and Greek-Turkish repatriation.

One more, and truly noteworthy, story of self-socialization has to do with the transformation of a self-indulgent and hedonistic

Nazi into a dedicated and extraordinary rescuer of Jews during the Holocaust.

Oskar Schindler, an ethnic German from Czechoslovakia and a Nazi party member from 1938 on, owned an enamelware factory in Cracow, Poland, which, during World War II, he changed over to the production of munitions parts for the German forces. Schindler, a fallen-away Catholic, was a fleshy, good-looking man in his thirties, a bon vivant and womanizer, and a close friend and drinking companion of Amos Göth, the sadistic Nazi commandant of the forced labor camp from which he got his Jewish workers. All in all, Schindler hardly seemed to have the makings of a great altruist.

But he was aware that his Jewish slave laborers, who under Nazi rules were not allowed to receive pay, could not survive on their meager rations, and he felt concerned about them. Although a Nazi party member, he had never been anti-Semitic, he had had satisfactory business dealings with Jews in the past, and sometimes he enjoyed long talks with one interesting intellectual Jew in his labor force. Learning from that man that certain of his workers were in acute need of food and medicines, Schindler bought supplies for them on the black market. This was to have been a one-time favor but soon Schindler was doing it again and again for an ever-larger number of the workers. Gradually, to save the lives of his entire labor force of over a thousand people, though it meant violating many Nazi laws and regulations, became his reigning passion.

Bribing SS guards and officers, spending his own money freely, and conniving and intriguing despite the risk to his own life, Schindler kept his Jews going until the Russian advance drew near. Then higher authorities ordered the entire complement of Jewish workers shipped to a death camp. Schindler was galvanized into action: Fiercely insisting to various officials that for the sake of the Fatherland he absolutely had to have these trained workers for his plant—which he was moving to safety in Czechoslovakia—he pleaded, swore, paid huge bribes, and in the end managed to send all 1,200 Jews to Czechoslovakia, where they survived. Schindler himself, bankrupted by his actions, lost the factory after the war and never succeeded in business again, but apparently had no regrets.

Bertha Pappenheim, Fridtjof Nansen, and Oskar Schindler were all transformed, in adulthood, not by the influence of outsiders but by their own acts, the resulting internal rewards, and their new perception of themselves. But while their stories are unusual, they are not idiosyncratic; self-socialization brings about an increase of altruistic tendencies in adulthood, though on a far smaller scale, in many of us, as the following kinds of research have shown:

Foot-in-the-Door Experiments

Salespeople and solicitors for charities have long known that if they can ask for even a tiny order or donation from a person and get it, they're likely to get a better one from that person later. They call this the "foot-in-the-door" technique.

The phenomenon was first experimentally tested by social scientists in 1966, when two psychologists, posing as volunteers, made a preposterous request of a number of California homeowners: Asking them for permission to install a public-service billboard on their front lawns, the researchers showed them a specimen photograph in which a lovely house was largely obscured by a huge, poorly lettered sign reading DRIVE CAREFULLY. Naturally, most of the homeowners refused, but a small minority acceded—nearly all of whom had had the foot-in-the-door technique used on them two weeks earlier. At that time a different volunteer had asked them to display a three-inch-square sign reading BE A SAFE DRIVER, and they had agreed to this innocuous request. Having done so, they were remarkably willing to agree to a much larger and far from innocuous request of a related kind the second time.

This principle, proven by experiments to hold good in a wide variety of situations, applies to altruistic acts: Those who give a little or help a little are more apt to give or help again and more generously the next time.

Bystander Research

A great many experiments have explored the conditions under which people will or will not offer help to a stranger in some sort of distress. (The study of seminarians in a hurry to talk about the Good Samaritan is an example of this type.) We'll look at such research in the next chapter, but for now it is worth noting that self-socialization can be a side effect of taking part in it: The brief, minor experience of helping in an experiment is enough to make participants more helpful when, months later, they come across another stranger in trouble. This is particularly surprising in view of the fact that such participants are "debriefed" after the experiment—that is, told that they had been duped and that the emergency was staged for the purpose of noting their reactions.

Some time ago, the social psychologist Shalom Schwartz, who was then running such experiments at the University of Wisconsin, grew concerned that the debriefing experience might be making the volunteers cynical and callous. Schwartz, who had grown up with a deep interest in ethics—his father was a rabbi—had gone to rabbinical school but had come to the conclusion that if he wanted to know why people do or don't behave ethically, and to have an effect on them, he should take up social psychology instead. He did so, but in the course of his own investigations grew uneasy at the thought that the experiments he was conducting might be making his volunteers less altruistic in the future. To see if this was the case, he told me, he conducted a special experiment with a number of his volunteers:

"We tracked down subjects an average of eleven months later," he said, "and invited them to what they thought would be a general discussion of their experiences in college. They came for an interview and filled out a questionnaire. Some of them were asked about their experiences in research on human behavior—this was meant to reinstate any negative feelings they might have had about the earlier experiment—while others were not. Then they got paid and left. Each of them had to go down a flight of back stairs where he came across a student in a neck brace and body brace lying on the floor. He seemed to have fallen and to be trying to get up.

"Those who had been reminded of having been deceived before were suspicious of the situation and few of them offered to help the fellow on the floor. But those who hadn't been asked questions that rearoused feelings of suspicion did offer help—and, surprisingly, more of them were helpful, and more helpful, than they had been in the experiment of nearly a year earlier! That earlier experience of helping had left them with a somewhat changed and more positive feeling about helping."

It wasn't the outcome Schwartz had expected but one that pleased him greatly.

Peace Corps "Returned Volunteer" Follow-ups

The experience of helping people in impoverished and undeveloped countries has had a powerful effect on many Peace Corps volunteers. Although it is impossible to know what they would have done with their lives had they not volunteered, many of them believe that their Peace Corps experiences confirmed them in their tendencies and steered them toward careers in public service and toward volunteer activities. One such former Peace Corpsman's story, as summarized in a recent Peace Corps publication:

> It took former Volunteer Timothy Carroll nearly ten years to make his idea fully operational to provide badly needed eye care to the poor people of Haiti. By 1984, Eye Care Inc.'s Haitian doctors and ophthalmologists were caring for 50,000 patients on a total budget of $800,000 (all of it raised from private sources). Carroll's effort was long-term, low-key, and received no media attention. Carroll, however, was satisfied. "Once you sweat for the poor," he said, "you can't get it out of your system."

A 1986 report on the Peace Corps and its returned volunteers says that three quarters of the staff of International Voluntary Services, half of the staff of Experiment in International Living, and substantial minorities of the staffs of CARE, Catholic Relief Services, and Volunteers in Technical Assistance, served with the Peace Corps.

Blood Donor Studies

Jane Piliavin, the psychologist who asked herself why on earth she or anyone would regularly, unasked, give blood, headed a series of studies designed to answer that question. (She, Daniel Batson, Shalom Schwartz, and a number of others have done their most important altruism research in areas related to some personal experience or private need to know.)

Piliavin and her team sent a detailed questionnaire to one-time, two-time, three-time, and habitual donors. They concluded, from the replies, that while many people, after the first donation, can think of reasons not to donate again, and do not, those who do go back begin to change as a result of their experiences:

> [They] begin to develop a sense of moral obligation to the collectivity [and] to incorporate the activity into their self-concept. . . . After the second donation, donors who return appear to have decided that they will continue as donors. They

are beginning to believe that significant others will be disappointed if they stop, that they themselves will be disappointed,
that they would think less of themselves if they refused, and
they are strongly motivated to give. The moral obligation that
has been developing now breaks through into citing "good
citizen" reasons for continuation—nearly three-quarters of the
three-time donors do so. Finally, after the third donation, the
majority (76%) of returning donors define themselves as "regular donors."

By that time, they have such good feelings about overcoming their
anxiety and reluctance, living by their personal norms, and fulfilling
a social obligation, that Piliavin et al. describe them as being "addicted" to their altruistic behavior.

THE ALTRUISTIC PERSONALITY

What kind of human being is created by the sequence of influences that we have just seen? Is any distinctive personality, any
recognizable pattern of traits, associated with compassionate behavior?

Given the disparities in the personalities of altruists we have
met thus far, the answer might seem to be no. What similarity could
there be between tormented, proud, contentious Florence Nightingale and tranquil, kindly, easy-going Marjorie Judge, the hospice
volunteer? Moreover, some people perform only certain kinds of
altruistic acts, others only different ones; the person who runs into
a burning building to save a child may be unwilling to spoon-feed
an aged stroke victim, and the one who donates bone marrow to a
dying stranger may drive past a stranded motorist waving for aid.

Still, psychological data and everyday experience attest that
certain personality types are linked with certain kinds of behavior:
impulsiveness with gambling, paranoia with hostility, and so on.
Why not, then, some set of characteristics one could identify as "the
altruistic personality?"

In the early years of altruism research, many researchers ignored this question. At that time, psychology was still dominated
by "situationalism," the behavioristic view that people act as they
do because of the situation they are in, rather than "dispositionalism," the psychodynamic view that they act as they do largely

because of internal forces. To be sure, a few Freudian and neo-Freudian psychotherapists ascribed altruism to such internal mechanisms as unconscious defense against one's own avarice, but they based this on what they saw in psychotherapy patients, a sample whose altruism might not be identical to that of nonpatients.

Those few altruism researchers who did try to identify the personality traits linked with altruism had little success. But this was because of the overly narrow way they looked for evidence. They tested people for specific traits and then subjected them to a situation where someone needed a particular kind of help; their data showed only that some traits seemed to produce altruistic behavior in some situations but not others, a not very enlightening finding.

By the end of the 1970s, however, a swing back toward dispositionalism was under way among social psychologists, and many altruism researchers were interested in the connection between personality and altruism. Furthermore, better research methods were coming into use: Researchers, instead of looking for correlations between single personality traits and behavior in a particular situation, began to look for correlations between groups of traits and behavior in a variety of situations. They also turned in part to "naturalistic" research methods such as observing children in school or at home, and staging situations in public places to see how normal people act in real-life circumstances.

From the evidence these better methods produced, a picture of the altruistic personality in childhood and adulthood has been emerging. Among the major findings:

- General mood: Happy preschoolers are higher in empathy and more altruistic than sad ones. (In adult life, too, mood is connected to altruism: As we will see in Chapter Six, adults are usually more helpful when in a good mood than when in a bad mood, which implies that happy people are more helpful than unhappy people.)
- Empathy: Whatever their mood, children and adults who easily sense what others are feeling and vicariously share that feeling are more likely to be altruistic than children and adults who do not.
- Emotional expressiveness: Preschoolers who readily express their feelings to teachers or peers when they are distressed are more likely than inexpressive children to be helpful when someone is in trouble.
- Popularity: Popular children and adolescents are generally

rather helpful; both popularity and helpfulness express a strong need to belong to or be connected with others. "Loners," presumably, are likely to be less helpful.

- Self-esteem: People high in self-esteem are more altruistic than people low in self-esteem.* The basic reason: A positive self-image makes for a positive connection between oneself and others, a poor or negative self-image for fearful or aggressive behavior. Moreover, high self-esteem makes for a sense of well-being, low self-esteem for the opposite, with consequent effects on one's response to another's need; Ervin Staub has shown that we weigh our situation against the other person's and tend to help someone we see as worse off than we but not someone we see as better off than we.

- Attitude toward other human beings: Adults who have a generally positive view of human beings are more apt to offer help to those in need than misanthropes. This is part of what Ervin Staub calls "prosocial orientation"—a combination of a positive feeling about other people, concern for their welfare, and a sense of responsibility for them. In a series of experiments, Staub and two graduate students gave volunteers a battery of tests measuring prosocial orientation, and later had each of them overhear and see a confederate who simulated severe stomach cramps and needed help. The results were clear-cut: People who scored high in prosocial orientation were more likely to help, and to give more help, than those who scored low.

- Internal moral standards: Some early studies of altruism, contrary to common sense, found little relationship between people's moral beliefs and how they act in laboratory experiments; they might profess altruism but not act altruistically. But more recent studies, using real-life situations, find that internal moral standards are usually an integral part of prosocial orientation and the altruistic personality. Three examples:

  1. Shalom Schwartz asked people to volunteer as bone marrow donors (not telling them that they would never actually be called on to donate); those who were

---

*On the average. But psychotherapist Bernice Hunt—my wife—comments that among her clientele she has seen some people with low self-esteem who seek out the helping role (e.g., caring for injured animals and human misfits) because this makes them feel superior, and therefore good about themselves.

willing not only had more humanitarian personal norms but a greater sense of responsibility to others than those who were not willing.

2. Several researchers compared the moral thinking of volunteers in hospitals, telephone crisis services, and the like to that of nonvolunteers; they found the volunteers to be more ethical, more concerned with the "rightness or wrongness" of behavior, and to have a stronger sense of responsibility to others than nonvolunteers.

3. Nechama Tec, a sociologist, interviewed Polish Christians who had rescued Jews from the Nazis during the Final Solution (she herself, as a Jewish girl, lived for three years in a Polish home under an assumed name, but her rescuers sheltered her for money and not out of compassion). Tec found that those who rescued Jews for altruistic reasons had a distinctly stronger sense of moral duty than those who did so for money.

The conclusion to be drawn from these and other similar findings is that people with altruistic moral standards are usually (though not invariably) altruistic in their behavior. Common sense was right after all.

Summing up the evidence, J. Philippe Rushton says:

It would seem there is a 'trait' of altruism.* Some people are consistently more generous, helping, and kind than others. Furthermore, such people are readily *perceived* as more altruistic, as is demonstrated by the several studies showing positive relationships among behavioral altruism and peers' and teachers' ratings of how altruistic a person seems.

People with particularly altruistic personalities are not, of course, unfailingly altruistic but only more often helpful, and helpful to a greater degree, than most other people. For personality is not the sole determinant of how we behave. In the view that reigns among altruism researchers today, both internal mechanisms and

*Rushton, with his current emphasis on genetics, says "trait of altruism" where most other social psychologists would say "altruistic personality."

the characteristics of the situation play a part. Even an altruist, if he is physically frail or has a bad heart, might not leap into a river to save a drowning child if other, sturdier people are on hand. Even a not-very-altruistic woman, if she came upon an infant abandoned in a corner of a parking lot, would almost certainly take it to the police or to a hospital.

How and why do different kinds of situation either elicit helping from or stifle the helping impulse in the altruistic personality? And in the not very altruistic personality? Let us see.

CHAPTER FIVE

"The Very Slave of Circumstance"

TWO TALES OF A CITY

Tale One

The scene: three A.M. on a chilly March night; a deserted city street in a slightly shabby middle-class neighborhood of fake-Tudor two-story buildings with ground-floor stores and apartments above. All is quiet, the upstairs windows are dark, no one is in sight. A young woman comes hurrying down the street, looking backward fearfully; when she parked her car in a nearby lot, she saw a man skulking nearby in the shadows, and she feared—

—and yes, oh God! The man comes running toward her out of the darkness, catches up to her under a street lamp, seizes her and makes a short violent movement. She screams, "Oh, my God, he stabbed me! Please help me! Please help me!" Lights go on above, windows are flung open, and someone shouts, "Let that girl alone!" The man disappears. The young woman is lying on the sidewalk, but no one comes to help her; one by one the windows close and the lights go out. After a while she struggles to her feet, staggers down the street and around the corner toward her apartment building—

—and he reappears out of the darkness, comes up to her, and stabs her again. "I'm dying!" she shrieks, "I'm dying!" Again the windows open and the lights go on; the man turns and walks away, gets into a car, and drives off. The young woman has collapsed; still no one comes to help her. Time passes; she starts to crawl slowly down the sidewalk toward her building. Above, some people watch her get as far as her doorway, when finally someone comes—

—but it is he, once more. He looks into one doorway, then the next, finds her there, slumped at the foot of the stairs, stabs her a third time, and vanishes. Only then, more than half an hour since the attack began, does someone call the police; they arrive within two minutes and find her dead.

In the following days the police query everyone in the neighborhood and are appalled—they, who are so inured to the sight of cruelty and callousness—to discover that a total of thirty-eight people saw and heard the attack but did nothing, not even telephone them, until it was too late. The explanations the people give for their failure to help are either unconvincing or chilling:

WOMAN: "We thought it was a lovers' quarrel."

HUSBAND AND WIFE: "Frankly, we were afraid."

WOMAN: "I didn't want my husband to get involved."

MAN: "I was tired. I went back to bed."

What manner of human beings are these? What place is this, what time in history, when not one of all those who saw what was happening would come to the defense of the woman being stalked and assaulted, or at least help her when she lay bleeding on the sidewalk, or at the very least pick up the phone and call the police? Is this some fantasy of the future, some pessimist's vision of what may become of humankind?

No, it is the true and well-known story of the murder of Catherine ("Kitty") Genovese in Kew Gardens, Queens (New York), on March 13, 1964, by Winston Moseley, a twenty-nine-year-old business-machine operator, who did not know her but told police he had similarly killed two other women and who was tried and convicted of the crime; a story that horrified citizens of the city, police, editorialists, and social scientists, many of whom saw it as holding up a mirror to modern urban humankind and reflecting a monster.

Tale Two

The scene: one A.M. on a raw March night in 1987; in a tiny, cramped apartment on the fifth floor of a dingy, six-story apartment building on East 97th Street in Manhattan, Timothy Mosher, a tall, slender man of thirty-five, is at the typewriter. Mosher, who studied film at New York University and hopes to become a film writer, has had no luck so far; he drives a cab part-time for a living and writes when he can.*

From the floor above, Mosher hears banging and thumping of some kind and a few seconds later a woman screaming. He is neither a powerful athletic man nor a scrapper, but without a moment's hesitation he races out his front door, up the stairwell, and in the direction the screams came from, the apartment of a woman he knows by sight but about whom he knows nothing else. (She is a forty-one-year-old nutritionist named Mana Mashoon.)

Why the instant response without thought of the danger he might expose himself to? Looking back today, Mosher, a mild-mannered and soft-spoken man, says, "Well, part of it was to help her, and part of it was that if something really bad was going on and I didn't do anything about it, I wouldn't be able to feel comfortable living with myself afterward. But I don't know if that was in my mind at the time or if I formulated that thought later." Nor did he consider whether anyone else might have heard the screams and take care of whatever was wrong. "I didn't think about it that way. In that part of the building most of the other people were quite elderly, or single women. It wasn't a matter of 'Who else is here?' but of 'Somebody's got to do something.'"

The door of Mana Mashoon's apartment was open a crack; Mosher pushed it further open and entered a narrow hallway. "As I did so," he recalls, "Mana came out of the bedroom with Jose Figueroa, the building super. He had his left arm around her waist. It was all very quiet, nothing was said, but she was all bloody about the face and neck and hands. I said, sharply, 'What the fuck's going on?' and he said, 'Someone stabbed her,' but he kept hanging on to her and it was obvious something was very wrong. I said, 'Let her go!' and he did, and as she ran out the front door, he and I started struggling hand to hand in that narrow hallway.

"I knew that he had a knife and that I had to get it away from him, but he was a short burly guy, very well muscled, and he had a lot of weight on me, and at some point he managed to raise the knife and stab me in the chest below the left collarbone. I knew it happened but I didn't feel any pain at first. The knife was wedged in my chest and I pulled it out and dropped it, but I kicked it into

*As of this writing, he is a production assistant in a firm that makes TV commercials.

the living room and he immediately ran out of the apartment. I was kind of dizzy, but I pulled myself together and went out into the hallway and took Mana by the arm—she had been banging on other doors but no one would open up—and led her down to my apartment and locked the door and called 911."

An ambulance arrived shortly and took the two of them to New York Hospital. Mosher was there a week, Mana Mashoon a little less; her neck had been slashed from ear to ear but not deeply, and she had cuts on her face and hands. (Figueroa had meant to rape her, not murder her; he pleaded guilty to all charges, and was sentenced, without trial, to eleven to twenty-two years in prison.)

How did Mosher, lying in the hospital, feel about what he had done? "I felt pretty good about it. And happy to be alive, damned lucky." Considering the danger, the injury, the pain, and the lost income—Medicaid paid his bills because his part-time cab driving left him below the poverty level, but he had lost two weeks' earnings—would he do it again? "It's hard to say," he says reflectively. "I don't cast myself in the role of a hero. I didn't give much thought to doing what I did; it was a situational thing, it was just something that had to be done. . . . I guess in the same situation I might do it again."

What accounts for the difference in the way the bystanders in these two tales behaved?

If there had been a single witness to each crime, we might suppose that one of them was unfeeling and self-centered, the other caring and altruistic. But it is extremely unlikely that all thirty-eight witnesses of the Kew Gardens assault were similarly unfeeling and self-centered.

As for Timothy Mosher, he is only one of more than seventy-two hundred persons who, since 1904, have been honored by the Carnegie Hero Fund Commission for risking their lives to save, or try to save, the lives of others; among these heroes have been men and women, children and adults, police officers and scholars, skydivers and nurses, athletes and invalids—an assortment most unlikely to have a single dominant personality pattern. However admirable Mosher's character, it cannot be the entire reason he acted as he did.

Personality is not a sufficient explanation of why anyone does or does not respond to someone else in distress; *personality in a given situation* is a more complete and better one. It may be that most of the thirty-eight at Kew Gardens and many or most of the seventy-two hundred Carnegie heroes had normally altruistic tendencies but that their behavior was partly or largely determined by specific features of the situation. Perhaps most of the thirty-eight might have behaved more admirably, and Mosher or other Carnegie heroes less so, under other circumstances.

And indeed, many hundreds of studies—the larger part of altruism research until recent years—have been aimed at discovering under what circumstances most people will or will not help others, especially strangers, in need of assistance. A single event, the Kitty Genovese murder, triggered all this investigation.

THE BYSTANDER EFFECT

The case of the thirty-eight passive witnesses to Kitty Genovese's murder was widely interpreted by news commentators, sociologists, and other pundits as indicative of the dehumanization of modern city dwellers, especially New Yorkers. In a spirit of this-hurts-me-more-than-it-hurts-you, critics accused them of apathy, alienation, callousness, inhumanity, and the gratification of unconscious sadistic impulses; some labeled them the Cold Society.

But two young social psychologists living in the city—neither of them native New Yorkers—found these glib condemnations of the character of New Yorkers unconvincing and troubling. Bibb Latané, an instructor at Columbia University, was a lanky, raw-boned, thatch-haired man with a jocular, country-boy manner. John Darley, an assistant professor at New York University, was a dark-haired, urbane, and distinctly Ivy League type. The two met at a party shortly after the Genovese murder and, though dissimilar in externals, found they had something in common: their professional disquiet at the public pronouncements about the Genovese murder and their intuitive feeling that there must be another and better explanation of the witnesses' passivity. They went back to Latané's apartment and talked half the night about the challenge this presented. Latané recalled that discussion for me:

"We commiserated with each other," he said, "about the problem of being identified as social psychologists at cocktail parties and being asked, 'What happened in Kew Gardens? How do you explain it?' We didn't know, and in fact we thought social psychology had nothing to say about it. But we also thought New York was getting a bad rap; we didn't feel that in our circle of friends and acquaintances in New York people were so callous and uncaring.

"Then we asked each other, 'What is it that's so important in this case?' That was easy to pinpoint: The newspapers, TV, everybody, was carrying on about the fact that thirty-eight people witnessed the crime and nobody did anything, as if that were far harder to understand than if one or two had witnessed it and done nothing.

"And we suddenly had an insight: Maybe it was the very fact that there *were* thirty-eight that accounted for their inactivity. It's an old trick in social psychology to turn a phenomenon around and see if what you thought was the effect was actually the cause. Maybe each of the thirty-eight knew that a lot of other people were watching—and *that* was why they did nothing.

"We talked for hours about how to set up an experiment to test that hypothesis by duplicating the situation. Not the actual event, of course, not the murder, but the central feature of what happened—an emergency witnessed by bystanders, either alone or in groups of various sizes—to see whether the mere knowledge that others were aware of the emergency would reduce each one's likelihood of helping."

Before they called a halt that night, Latané and Darley had devised their experiment. They would invite NYU undergraduates to participate in what was supposed to be a discussion of the personal problems of urban university students. Latané, Darley, or a research assistant would tell the participants that they would be working either in two-person, three-person, or six-person discussion groups but that to minimize embarrassment at revealing personal matters they would be in isolated cubicles, talking to each other on an intercom. This arrangement gave Latané and Darley total control over the situation; it also simplified the staging of an emergency—a faked, tape-recorded epileptic fit by another participant that would be heard over the intercom. In some cases a participant would think that he alone was talking to, and hearing, the person having the seizure; in other cases he would think that anywhere from one to four other participants also were hearing it over the intercom.

The following week Latané and Darley asked several graduate students to gather at Latané's apartment in the evening to tape-record the script. They played the parts of participants in the fictitious discussion, and with the help of a few beers each, they all tried out for the role of epileptic; a graduate student named Dick Nesbitt (today a professor of social psychology at the University of Michigan) was head and shoulders above the rest in his ability to sound as if he were in the throes of a seizure.

In the experiment, whether an undergraduate participant thought he was talking to only one other person or to as many as five others, the first voice he heard was that of Nesbitt discussing his difficulty in getting adjusted to New York City and his studies, then hesitantly mentioning that when he was under stress, he was prone to seizures. At his second turn to speak, he gradually became disordered and incoherent: "I—er—if somebody could help me out it would—er—er s-s-sure be—sure be good . . . cause I—er—uh—I've got one of the—er—sei—er—er—things coming on." As the attack grew worse, he began to choke, asked again for help, and finally gasped, "I'm gonna die—er—er—I'm . . . gonna . . . die—er—help—er—er—seizure—er." Then, after more choking sounds, he fell silent.

The results were electrifying: eighty-five percent of the participants who thought they and the epileptic were the only ones in the intercom discussion reported the seizure before he fell silent, while only 31 percent of those who thought four others were also hearing it did so. The supposedly sole auditors of the seizure also took action far more quickly than those who thought others too heard it happening. (When the students were asked afterward whether they had been influenced by the presence of others, they said no; they were genuinely unaware of its effect on them.)

Latané and Darley had thus solidly demonstrated what they called "the social inhibition of bystander intervention in emergencies," or, more succinctly, "the bystander effect." But to demonstrate it in the laboratory was not to explain it, so they put their heads together and came up with three hypothetical processes that might account for it: one, hesitancy about taking action in front of others until one knows what action is called for; two, the feeling that the inactive others may be behaving appropriately; and three, "diffusion of responsibility"—the feeling that if others also know of the emergency, one's own obligation to do something is lessened. In a series of subsequent experiments, Latané and Darley, and other research teams, showed that depending on whether bystanders see other bystanders, are seen by them, or merely know that there are others, one or another of these processes is indeed at work.

Latané and Darley concluded, with considerable satisfaction: "The results of our experiments show that situational variables such as the number of other people present are more important determinants of intervention in emergencies than apathy or alienation."

That first study of the bystander effect captured the imagination of many social psychologists and led directly to a good deal of other research on specific aspects of the phenomenon. In the psychology departments of dozens of universities, bright young Ph.D.s and graduate students carefully, yet often in a spirit of high jinks, contrived all kinds of seeming emergencies to test the power of the bystander effect: the sound of a falling ladder, chair, or bookcase in an adjoining room, followed by cries of pain; a fainting spell by someone heard on an intercom or seen on a video screen; the sound of a nearby explosion; the staged theft of someone else's books or money; the escape of a dangerous laboratory rat in the next room; a person overheard having an asthma attack; the sound or sight, via intercom or closed-circuit television, of someone being felled by an electric shock; and so on.

The volunteers in such experiments were always "naive"—unaware of, and carefully deceived as to, what was really going on. The researchers would invite them to take part in an experiment on perception, group decision-making, or something equally plausible, never revealing to them until afterward the real purpose of the experiment: to see how they reacted to the sight or sound of strangers in distress or danger, and how those reactions were influenced by the number and the behavior of other persons present.

By 1981, fifty-six studies, conducted in some thirty laboratories, had subjected over five thousand naive participants to many kinds of faked emergencies under conditions that led them to believe that they alone, or they and anywhere from one to a score of other people, were witness to them. In forty-eight of the fifty-six, the bystander effect was clearly demonstrated; since there was less than one chance in fifty-one million that this total of results was accidental, the bystander effect is considered one of the most thoroughly established hypotheses in altruism theory.

The Genovese case raised a second question: Is the bystander effect more common in big cities than in towns? Laboratory experiments couldn't answer that one; to do so, a number of researchers began conducting studies in urban and rural real-life settings.

In many parts of the country they arranged for pedestrians on a sidewalk to come upon a person slumped against a wall and moaning; for travelers in bus terminals and airports to see someone, possibly bandaged, slip and fall; and for drivers to see a stranded motorist by the roadside. Most of the time, however, researchers, mindful of the ethical problems of subjecting the public to simulated emergencies, used nonemergency helping situations: Shoppers in supermarkets would see someone drop and spill a bag of groceries; passengers in elevators would see a fellow passenger drop a handful of pencils or coins; pedestrians on sidewalks, in parking lots, and on campus lawns would come across dropped postcards bearing an important message and, being stamped, needing only to be mailed by the finder; and persons at home would answer their phone and find themselves talking to a distraught stranger who had apparently dialed incorrectly, had no more coins, and asked them to make a further call for him or her.

Out of this wealth of scientific flimflam the researchers extracted a number of findings. Some of the major ones:

- People in cities are, indeed, less helpful to strangers than people in towns, but dehumanization isn't the best explanation; the bystander effect is a more parsimonious and probable one, since in urban life it is quite likely that during most emergencies there will be other persons present. City people aren't necessarily less altruistic than town people, but are more often in situations that inhibit helping.
- City people learn to deal with many of the risks and uncertainties of urban life by avoidance or by assuming that the police or other services will take care of things; rural people have less reason to be cautious about getting involved, and have fewer helping services to depend on. Yet city people are not hard-hearted: If they see others rendering help—which clarifies the situation for them—they too will help; in fact, one experiment showed that they are more easily influenced to help by such modeling than rural people are.
- Even in large cities, people living in stable neighborhoods are relatively helpful; even in towns, people living in unstable neighborhoods may not be. It is not only the size of the city but the character of its community life that determines the extent to which the bystander effect prevails.
- In a close-knit society, people in larger cities may not be

deterred by the presence of others from intervening in emergencies: A study in the Netherlands found no difference in helpfulness between city people and rural people.

Thus, studies both of the bystander effect and of the influence of city size on altruism disprove the dismal interpretations of the Kew Gardens episode. New Yorkers and other urbanites are not inhumane monsters; they remain capable of, and inclined toward, helpful and caring behavior. Admittedly, in urban life circumstances often exist that inhibit the altruistic impulse, but in some cities and some situations urbanites can be as altruistic as anyone else.

As witness the case of Timothy Mosher.

TO HELP OR NOT TO HELP: THAT IS THE QUESTION

Two decades ago, the reigning view in altruism research was that external circumstances have more to do with whether or not a person behaves altruistically than his or her personality or moral norms, and that, in any case, they are the only influences on altruistic behavior that can be scientifically studied. As Latané and Darley expressed this outlook in 1970:

> It seems to us that many discussions of altruism have confused two basic questions. . . . [The first is:] "What is the underlying force in mankind toward altruism?" or "What motivates helping?" The second question is more specific: "What determines in a particular situation whether one person will help another?" The first question is a general one, of enormous social interest and importance, and of a semi-philosophic nature. It probably never will be completely answered by reference to data. The second question is more specific, more mundane, more amenable to research analysis.
>
> There is no reason to expect that principles used in answering the first question should also be important or even have much bearing on the second. It is possible, for example, that norms provide a general predisposition to help other people, but that whether someone will help in a particular situation is dependent upon other factors.

Today, most altruism researchers take a far more inclusive view of altruism research, since they now have techniques for exploring the internal events that are part of the decision to act or not to act altruistically. Still, the degree to which normal people are influenced in their decisions by external circumstances is much greater than most of us would care to admit; it is disagreeable to think that, like a mother bird stimulated by the sight of the chick's red gape to shove food into it, we, too, often respond mindlessly to external signals. But here are some of the humbling findings:

Ambiguity Versus Clarity

In the latter part of 1988 a great deal of newspaper space was devoted to the trial in New York of Joel Steinberg, a lawyer, on the charge of having battered his six-year-old adopted daughter to death. Testimony in court and statements to reporters indicated that neighbors had often heard sounds that might have been those of child abuse (but might also have been the sounds of more-or-less-normal punishment), and teachers had seen bruises and swellings on the child that might have been the result of beatings (but might also have been, as the child said they were, the result of falls and other accidents).

No one had intervened to help the child. TV commentators and letter writers to *The New York Times* railed against the heartlessness of those who hadn't wanted to get involved; the evidence of altruism research, however, suggests a less chilling explanation: They weren't sure what was going on.

Many incomprehensible stories of the failure of people to help someone in trouble make sense in the light of the evidence that most people are unmotivated to act if the situation is unclear and if there might well be an innocuous explanation for what they are hearing or seeing. What could be more callous than to witness a rape in progress and do nothing about it, especially when there is one rapist and twenty-five observers? Yet even that may not signify callousness, as this news story, carried by the Associated Press some years ago, indicates:

A 20-year-old woman who works for the Trenton [New Jersey] Police Department was raped yesterday in full view of about 25 employees of a nearby roofing company, who watched intently but did not answer her screams for help. . . .

[One of them explained], "Two people did that up there about a year ago but it was mutual. We thought, well, if we went up to them, it might turn out to be her boyfriend or something like that."

The watchers found the situation ambiguous; of two possible interpretations, it was natural that they should prefer the reassuring one to the disturbing one. A cynic might say that the explanation was only an excuse for their heartlessness or timidity, but studies have demonstrated that ambiguity strongly inhibits helping behavior. If people are not sure that help is needed, their altruistic impulses are blocked by the fear of doing something foolish, inappropriate, or hurtful.

To test this hypothesis, researchers Russell Clark and Larry Word devised an experiment in which a naive volunteer, aware that someone else was working on an electrical apparatus in a corner of the laboratory out of sight, would be busy at some task when from that corner would come a flash of light, a buzzing noise, and a shorting-out sound. When the unseen "victim" cried out, 75 percent of the volunteers came to his aid, but when there was no cry, only 13 percent did so; the cry clarified an uncertain situation.

In an even more startling experiment cited in *Psychology Today* by the psychologist R. Lance Shotland, volunteers either overheard what sounded like a rape in progress nearby or glimpsed a bit of struggle over closed-circuit television; those who only heard it were far less likely to intervene than those who saw something of the assault.

These were experiments with lone bystanders. But when there is a group of bystanders, especially strangers to each other, ambiguity is particularly inhibiting. As Robert Cialdini writes in *Influence: Science and Practice:*

> Because we like to look poised and sophisticated in public and because we are unfamiliar with the reactions of those we do not know, we are unlikely to give off or correctly read expressions of concern when in a group of strangers. Therefore, a possible emergency is viewed as a nonemergency and the victim suffers.

You may find it interesting to explore your own reactions to ambiguous emergencies seen in the presence of strangers by means

of a "thought experiment," as Einstein called a technique he used
to gain some of his most profound insights into physical laws. For
instance, he visualized a passenger in a box falling freely down a
very long vertical shaft and asked himself what would happen if the
passenger took coins and keys out of his pocket and let go of them.
(This was long before high-speed aircraft and space vehicles made
experiments in weightlessness physically possible.) Einstein correctly sensed that the objects would not fall to the bottom of the
box but would remain in midair alongside the passenger—a realiza-
tion that was an important step toward his development of relativ-
ity theory.

In somewhat the same way, you can experience the effect of
various circumstances on your own altruistic impulses by vividly
imagining each of the situations presented below and responding
not with a "correct" or socially desirable answer but with what you
honestly feel would be your own gut reaction and actual behavior.

Imagine you are driving on a busy highway, by day, when you
see the following situations:

1. An automobile parked at the side of the road with a young
   woman seated behind the wheel.
2. An automobile parked at a 45-degree angle to the road with
   a young woman slumped over the wheel.
3. An automobile parked at the side of the road with a flat tire
   and a young woman standing outside it with a jack and a
   spare tire.
4. An automobile parked at a 45-degree angle to the road with
   the driver's door open, a young woman slumped over the
   seat, and the flashers on.

And now perform the thought experiment again, this time
visualizing yourself driving on a quiet side road and seeing each of
the situations above.

If, on the busy highway, you would have stopped to offer help
in all four cases, you are either extremely altruistic or something of
a meddler; if you would not have done so in any of the cases, you
are either flinty of heart or extremely fearful. But if you would not
have stopped in the first two cases, might have done so in the third,
and probably would have done so in the fourth, you would be
average in your willingness to offer help when unsure that help is
needed. On the quiet side road, you should have been somewhat
more inclined to stop in all cases but the first.

This is not mere speculation. Some time ago two researchers, David Mason and Bem P. Allen, conducted just such experiments on both a busy highway and a quiet one in western Illinois. More drivers stopped in the two emergency situations (2 and 4) and the two unambiguous ones (3 and 4) than in the nonemergency and the ambiguous ones, and the highest rate of helping was in the one unambiguous emergency (4). But even in that case, considerably fewer stopped on the busy highway than on the quiet road: If there were many other drivers on the road, most passing drivers apparently either took the others' nonhelping to mean that help wasn't needed or assumed that someone else was bound to stop and take care of things.

Such findings have practical implications for any of us who ever find ourselves victims in an emergency, according to Cialdini:

> Even a resounding call for help is not your most effective tactic. Although it may reduce bystanders' doubts about whether a real emergency exists, it will not remove several other important uncertainties within each onlooker's mind: What kind of aid is required here? Should I be the one to provide the aid, or should someone more qualified do it? Has someone else already gone to get professional help, or is it my responsibility? . . .
>
> Your best strategy when in need of emergency help is to reduce the uncertainties of those around you concerning your conditions and their responsibilities. Be as precise as possible about your need for aid. Do not allow bystanders to come to their own conclusions because, especially in a crowd, the [general inaction] might well cause them to view your situation as a nonemergency.
>
> And request assistance of a single individual. . . . Pick out one person and *assign* the task to that individual. Otherwise, it is too easy for everyone in the crowd to assume that someone else should help, will help, or has helped.

Cialdini himself has had occasion to test the value of his own advice. He was in a rather serious two-car collision, and he and the other driver were both obviously hurt; the other man slumped over his steering wheel, unconscious, as Cialdini staggered out of his car bleeding and knelt in the road beside the car door. The accident had occurred in an intersection in full view of several motorists waiting at the traffic light; when it changed, they drove slowly past, rubbernecking but not stopping. Cialdini thought, "Oh, no, it's happening just like the research says. They're all passing by!" But then he rallied himself:

> By thinking of my predicament in terms of the research findings, I knew exactly what to do. Pulling myself up so I could be seen clearly, I pointed at the driver of one car: "Call the police." To a second and third driver, pointing directly each time: "Pull over, we need help." The responses of these people were instantaneous. They summoned a police car and ambulance immediately, they used their handkerchiefs to blot the blood from my face, they put a jacket under my head, they volunteered to serve as witnesses to the accident; one even offered to ride with me to the hospital. . . . Not only was this help rapid and solicitous, it was infectious. After drivers entering the intersection from the other direction saw cars stopping for me, they stopped and began tending the other victim.

Fear of Looking Foolish Versus Fear of Looking Bad

The presence of other people influences our behavior in yet another way, in situations where someone appears to need help: The wish to be thought well of by others, a major force in social life, sometimes strengthens and sometimes undercuts the altruistic impulse, depending on the circumstances.

On the negative side, helping behavior is inhibited by the fear that we will look foolish if we rush in to help and it turns out that helping was unnecessary or uncalled for. This is particularly apt to be our feeling if other bystanders look unconcerned and make no move to intervene. As Latané and two colleagues say, in a discussion of this effect:

> In order to help define a situation we look to other people, observe their reactions and behavior, and thus gauge our own actions on the basis of theirs. We are likely to find out how others interpret situations by watching their facial expressions and behavior rather than by talking to them, especially when among strangers in public places. If, in the midst of a crisis, a bystander is nonchalantly whistling or otherwise passively ignoring the situation, one would be likely to infer that there is no reason to intervene or that passive nonchalance is the socially appropriate behavior.

In Los Angeles, Eric Scott, an excavator and gatherer of fossils for the George C. Page Museum, recently had a nightmarish experience of this reaction. He knew that over the eons many animals have become stuck in the tar of the Rancho La Brea Tar Pits and sunk down into it, becoming fossilized. But last summer, when he noticed that someone had thrown a traffic marker over the chain-link fence surrounding the tar pits, he climbed over to remove it. "The asphalt looked crusted and hard," he told a reporter later, "but before I knew it, I was mired. The tar was soon up to my ankles and I was calling for help." Visitors to Hancock Park watched him from outside the fence without making any move to rescue him; evidently they took their cues from each other, each assuming that since no one did anything, the man stuck in the tar was in a ridiculous but not dangerous fix and heroically rescuing him would make the rescuer look equally ridiculous. (Eventually someone did help Scott who, but for that assistance, would himself have been fossilized.)

Conversely, in situations where help is needed, a bystander who thinks that other people know he is aware of the emergency will often feel compelled to lend a hand, even against his own wishes or inclinations, out of fear that failure to act will disgrace him in the eyes of the others. But if they don't see him, or can't know whether he did or did not try to help, he is much less likely to do so. This is true not only of emergencies but all sorts of situations involving acts for the common good: We are far more likely to do something to benefit our fellow human beings when they know of our actions than when they do not. Badges, pins, and armbands announcing one's participation in good causes are effective precisely because not wearing one makes visible one's failure to help.

Thus, while the presence of bystanders tends to inhibit helping, it can also promote it. This is the case particularly when the other bystanders at an emergency are our friends. Latané and Judith Rodin found, in an experiment, that when pairs of strangers heard an accident, one or both of them helped 40 percent of the time, but when pairs of friends heard the accident, one or both friends helped 70 percent of the time. The probable reasons: Friends are less likely than strangers to misinterpret each other's behavior or to feel embarrassed about acting foolishly in front of each other; they are more likely to communicate about the emergency and to be concerned that failing to help might damage the other's high opinion of them; and friends feel like a unit and therefore share responsibility, while a bystander and a stranger divide it. Similarly, people who work together are likely to help when they witness an emergency; apparently, members of close-knit work groups share responsibility, thus acting more like a solo bystander than a group of strangers.

The We and They Effect

Earlier we saw that human beings are helpful or benevolent primarily toward members of their ingroup but not toward members of outgroups. Many of us, however, like to think we are larger of heart than this. But how much larger? Researchers have found that even the most trivial clues to another person's identity can make a considerable difference in the bystander's willingness to help.

Not long ago, as I was driving through a parking lot in the town where I live, I saw a parked car with its headlights on. I stopped—as I assume most people would have done—and tried the doors, hoping to be able to turn the lights off and spare the unknown stranger the inconvenience of a dead battery; unfortunately, the doors were locked. But would I have done the same if I had seen a bumper sticker on the car advocating some political or social position I find obnoxious? The research evidence suggests not. In a study conducted on a university campus, far fewer students tried to turn off the lights of a car bearing a bumper sticker offensive to most of them, "America—Love It Or Leave It," than a car with no bumper stickers.

In a great many situations where help is needed or would at least be welcome, most people will more readily aid a stranger with whom they feel some kinship than one with whom they do not. If they come upon a lost letter, stamped and needing only to be mailed, and the names on it are of their own ethnic group, they are likely to mail it; if the names are those of members of an ethnic group they have an antipathy toward, they are likely not to. Voters leaving a polling place and coming upon a campaign worker who has just dropped a stack of campaign materials are more likely to help pick them up if the campaign worker is of their own party than if of the opposition.

So superficial a matter as differences in clothing are enough to diminish the helping impulse, even if the help asked for takes only seconds and costs nothing. In one such experiment, passersby were more likely to comply with the request "Can you give me two nickels for a dime?" when the person asking was dressed similarly to themselves than when he was not.

By extension, one can imagine such differences affecting the helping impulse in rather more serious situations. Many of us, if we were walking down a quiet side street and saw a respectably dressed man sitting on the steps of a building and grimacing, would stop and ask if he needed help. But how many of us would do so if he were wearing a fez and djellaba, or the leather-and-studs outfit of a Hell's Angels biker? Not many, to judge by the research evidence.

For in general, except for those who are unusually altruistic, most people are more inclined to be helpful to persons who hold similar beliefs, have the same kind of speech, dress like them, or are similar to them in any of a number of other ways than they are toward persons who are markedly different.

One would expect this to be especially true of race, since it involves not only highly visible differences but, quite often, cultural ones and deep-seated antipathies. And, true enough, some studies have found that whites will help whites, blacks blacks, more often and more readily than either will help a person of the other race.

But curiously, and hearteningly, other studies have found no such difference, and in at least six, whites helped blacks more in certain situations than they did other whites. This is particularly true when the situation is a serious one: There is much evidence that We-They bias is often transcended when the other person's situation is clearly grave and there is no good excuse, such as the presence of others, for failing to help. A pedestrian, seeing a person of different race whose grocery bag has just torn, spilling items on the sidewalk, might not stop to help pick them up; the same person, driving on a back road and seeing someone struck by a hit-and-run driver ahead, would be as likely to stop and help if the victim were of another race as of his or her own.

Other Inhibiting and Promoting Factors

Many other situational variables can either intensify altruistic responses or interfere with them. A striking example:

In a fascinating but little-known criminological experiment conducted some years ago, some inmates of New York City jails who had facial disfigurements were given plastic surgery, while others, similarly disfigured, were not. A year after their release from jail, far fewer of the convicts who had gotten cosmetic surgery than of those who had not were back in jail. The cosmetic surgery may have altered how the convicts felt about themselves but, more important, it altered how the outside world treated them after their release.

The power of visual variables to either arouse or to stifle compassion has been extensively studied by researchers. Several such factors were used in the notable series of experiments, mentioned in Chapter One, in which a young man fell down in a subway car and could not get up. In one variation, he was neatly dressed in denims and walking with a white cane; in another, he had a large "port-wine" birthmark on his face; in a third, he had no birthmark but, as he lay on the floor of the subway car, blood trickled from his mouth; and in a fourth, he carried no cane but smelled of whiskey and had a bottle in a brown paper bag.

These experiments, conducted twenty years ago, were among the most daring ever performed in altruism research in terms of the potential stress they imposed on bystanders; today, because of more stringent government controls over human research plus the increased litigiousness of our society, no researcher would be likely to try them. Jane Piliavin, a tall lean woman of fifty who exudes energy and enthusiasm, and whose nonstop flow of talk is punctuated with gusts of laughter, recalled those experiments for me not long ago:

"I got started on the subway studies," she said, "when I was teaching at the University of Pennsylvania and my husband, Irvin Piliavin, was doing postdoctoral work at Columbia under Bibb Latané and Philip Zimbardo. Irving was interested in the Latané and Darley bystander studies but he felt they were too abstracted from the real world. And one day he was on a subway and a drunk collapsed in the car and rocked back and forth on the floor trying to get up but couldn't. There were plenty of people on the car but nobody did anything. Finally my husband got up, went over to the man, and helped him to a seat.

"That started him thinking, and in a little while he, Judith Rodin, and I had designed our first subway experiment. We wanted to see whether the fallen man's being a drunk was what kept people from helping him. While we were at it, we thought we might as well see the effects of race. So we planned to have the man either sober and using a cane—to account for his falling—or drunk, and either white or black.

"Our first study was on the A Train in New York City. We asked the Transit Authority for permission and they said no, but we were ready to go, so we did it anyway." She laughed merrily, and went on, "We recruited confederates from Columbia—for each run we would have one victim, one helper (to help him up if no passenger did so), and two observers to record what happened.

"Given all Bibb's work on the bystander effect, we expected the victim to get little help. But it was amazing! When the victim was sober and had a cane, people helped him in sixty-two out of sixty-five trials, and very quickly—in an average of five to ten seconds. It made no difference whether there were a lot of people in the car or only a few; there just was no evidence of 'diffusion of responsibility' in that situation. Evidently, we human beings have built into us a propensity to help, as well as a predisposition to be selfish, and when people saw the man fall, that triggered off an immediate impulse to help that overrode the other—unless he was drunk.

"He wasn't really drunk, of course, but he acted it and we spilled some booze on his clothes to make him smell like a drunk." Again, she burst into hearty laughter, then continued, "The passengers were very slow to help—it took about a minute or more on the average—and at that he was helped only half the time.

"If our victim was using a cane, it made no difference whether he was white or black; people helped him. But if he was drunk, race made a great difference—almost always the only people who helped him were of the same race."

I'd read about the variation that involved the fallen man's having blood seep from his mouth; I asked how and when they tried that, and why. Jane Piliavin chuckled; that experiment had been notorious among altruism researchers.

"After the first study," she said, "my husband went on to other work, but Judy Rodin and I wanted to continue the subway studies. We wondered about aversive factors other than drunkenness. Would other things that repel people also make them reluctant to help? So we tried the large facial birthmark thing, and found that it reduced helping by a third and slowed it down a lot.

"And we decided to try the blood thing because blood is so strongly aversive to most people. We tinkered in the kitchen with mixtures of different things until we had it just right—Metrecal, for viscosity, mixed with red fruit juice of some kind. We did the study in Philadelphia on the Broad Street subway. The victim, who would always use a cane, would put an eye-dropperful of the mixture in his mouth just before getting on the train, and let a little of it trickle out after he fell, just a trickle, but people got *yucchh!* It reduced helping by a third, and slowed it *way* down. We quit after only forty trials because onlookers got so panicky at the sight of blood that we were afraid they'd overreact and pull the emergency cord.

"But by then we'd already learned what we wanted to know: Any aversive feature of the situation—blood, birthmark, drunkenness—adds to the 'cost' of helping and becomes part of the bystander's cost-reward calculations and decision-making."

The nature of those costs, however, varied somewhat. The cost of aiding the drunk was the need to be close to him when helping him, and the psychic effort of overcoming one's moral disapproval of him or fear of what he might do. The cost of helping, when blood was involved, was the chance of staining one's clothing and the effort needed to overcome one's revulsion. As for the birthmark, that, too, required that one be willing to pay the cost of coming close and enduring a sense of revulsion; it is generally true, in fact, that most of us find it easier to help attractive and unblemished persons than unattractive or disfigured ones.

A regrettable finding of many studies using both attractive and unattractive "victims" is that men are far more helpful toward an attractive woman in difficulty or need than toward an unattractive one. In the tales of chivalry that are part of our heritage of male-female relationships, the gallant knight is always envisioned as rescuing a beauteous maiden, never a toothless beldame; according to the current research, the tradition lives on.

More admirably, there is plenty of experimental and other evidence that when a stranger is in serious need of help or grave danger, many or even most of us are undeterred by that person's unattractiveness or other moderately aversive factors. But there are limits; in some cases the physical circumstances may be so horrifying as to immobilize us. Many photographs and TV sequences from Beirut have shown stunned bystanders staring aghast and unmoving at some bomb-blast victim whose legs have been blown off or whose viscera are spilling out through a rip in the abdominal wall. The bystanders, even if humane, are only human.

MY BROTHER'S KEEPER

Anything that makes the bystander feel responsible for the other person tends to overcome repugnance or other reasons for not helping. The sense of being responsible for others' well-being can range from the very limited, extending to only one or two other persons, to the virtually unbounded, extending to almost any other human being.

Most of us are somewhere between these extremes. We feel responsible for those close to us; as for strangers, our sense of responsibility extends to a limited set of them—most notably, small children and relatively helpless persons—and for others in need chiefly when certain external cues tell us that we are. Robert Cialdini's pointing his finger at individual motorists and telling them to help him was a way of assigning responsibility to them to produce helping.

Ervin Staub, in an experiment described earlier, found that most kindergartners and first graders, left alone by Staub's research assistant, did not try to help when they heard a little girl in the next room fall down and hurt herself. But in a simple variation Staub had his assistant say to children, as she left the room, "I will leave you in charge, okay? If anything happens, you will take care of it." That was enough to impel some of the kindergartners and many of the first-graders to go looking for an adult when they heard the accident or to try to help directly.

Not only children but adults can easily be made to feel and act responsible for a stranger. Several years ago, a young woman entered a cafeteria in New York City, placed her suitcase by a table where another person was eating, and went off to get some food. While she was away, a young man came by, picked up her bag, and walked off with it; the customer sitting at the table made no effort to stop him. If any observant customer saw that happen and was still on the scene half an hour later, he would have been thoroughly mystified to see the same young woman, carrying the same bag, put it down by a table where someone was sitting and, this time, ask that person to keep an eye on it while she got some food. Even more mystifying, while she was away the same young man came by and again began to make off with her bag, but this time was stopped by the person sitting at the table.

As you realize, this was an experiment. Psychologist Thomas Moriarty played out his scenario both in the cafeteria and on a beach, where the young woman spread out a blanket, left a radio on it, and went off, either saying nothing to the nearest bystander or else asking him or her to keep an eye on her things. At both locations, nearly all of the bystanders she asked to watch her possessions tried to stop the "thief," but of those she did not ask, only one in eight at the cafeteria and one in five at the beach did so.

* * *

As bystanders, our sense of responsibility is also strongly activated if we believe that only we, of the people who know about the situation, are capable of doing anything about it; if the other bystanders cannot help but we can, their presence does not diffuse our responsibility. To demonstrate this, researchers have concocted experiments in which the other bystanders were too far away to be able to help, or were children, or were wearing dark glasses and carrying white canes, and so on; in all such cases, the bystanders were very likely to feel as if they were solely responsible, and to act accordingly.

Special competence to help in a particular situation also makes a bystander feel responsible. The classic example, at least prior to the advent of monstrous malpractice suits, was the collapse of a heart attack victim in a public place and a voice from behind the onlookers calling out, "Let me through—I'm a doctor." And when a mugging or other violent crime is under way, it is the off-duty policeman who most keenly feels it his duty to rescue the victim. But conversely, when a bystander has reason to believe that someone else at hand is better qualified to help, the first one may feel relieved of responsibility. Similarly, someone who is not competent to help in a given situation will feel little obligation to do so; nonswimmers rarely leap into deep water to save drowning persons.

If situational cues could be relied on to produce altruistic helping by bystanders, ours would be a far safer and kinder world. But self-interest and other factors may blind many people to those cues; we have seen, for instance, that being in a hurry, or being cast in a special role such as that of a prison guard, can keep many people from noticing or reacting to the signs of distress in others that would normally trigger off altruistic responses.

But what if, as a society, we were to say that bystanders *must* notice and render aid to others, at least in emergency situations? Could we not pass a law to intensify bystanders' awareness of others' needs, heighten their sense of responsibility, and formally require them to assist strangers in grave danger?

As reasonable and obvious as this may seem, until 1971 no such law existed in any jurisdiction in this country. As recently as 1978, Professor John Kaplan of Stanford University Law School stated how things stood by means of a shocking fantasy:

You are sitting on the edge of a pier, eating a sandwich, and watching the sunset when the fisherman next to you leans too far forward and falls in. He screams to you: "Help! I can't swim. Throw the life preserver." You make no effort to get up to throw the life preserver, which is hanging only five feet from you, even though you could do this with absolutely no danger to yourself and with only the most minimal effort. Indeed, you sit chomping away at your sandwich and now, along with the sunset, you watch the fisherman drown.

Under the law of essentially every Anglo-American jurisdiction, you are guilty of no tort making you civilly liable to the family of the fisherman you permitted to drown, nor would you be criminally liable in any way for his death. . . . Neither our tort nor our criminal law concerns itself with the good that one does not do, but rather attempts merely to forbid the doing of harm.

With a very few exceptions, that situation still prevails. In 1971, Vermont enacted a law making it a crime for bystanders not to help a person exposed to grave physical harm if they can do so without danger to themselves or to others they are responsible for, and in 1985 Minnesota passed a similar law. Massachusetts recently enacted a very limited version of that statute requiring bystanders to report a crime of violence—that is, summon the police—as soon as possible, and Rhode Island followed suit with a similar law that applies only to sexual assaults. Other than that, the situation is still as Professor Kaplan pictured it.

The "Good Samaritan laws" of Vermont and Minnesota may seem radical, but such legislation has long existed in certain other countries. Such a law was passed in Mongolia in 1781; in 1845 the Russian Criminal Code made it a crime not to assist those in serious need of help; and similar provisions were added to the criminal codes of Tuscany in 1853, the Netherlands in 1881, Italy in 1889, France in 1941, and Portugal in 1982.

However, how effective those laws have been is not clear. They have not been widely enforced—in France, of one hundred thousand jail sentences in a recent year only sixty-two were for failure to rescue—but why they have not been, and whether or not they have changed citizen behavior, is unknown.

Even if they were known to be effective, such statutes would pose a number of problems in our legal system. For one thing, they conflict with our tradition of individualism and the right to be let alone. For another, unless they were to spell out a number of limiting conditions and exceptions, they might impose serious risks on innocent bystanders. Say an air traffic controller or someone in a similarly high-pressure job was on his way home exhausted after an extremely fatiguing day, saw a little girl drowning, and was legally required to try to rescue her; even though he could swim, in his fatigued condition he might lose his life in the attempt. Or what if a physician, much the worse for a long night in the operating room, came upon an accident victim, bungled the treatment due to exhaustion, and the patient died—would the physician be vulnerable to a malpractice suit?

The rationale for enacting Good Samaritan statutes—namely, that the law should require morality—is persuasive, and the need for such statutes was made obvious by the Kitty Genovese murder and the more recent 1983 rape case in New Bedford, Massachusetts, in which four men took turns violating a woman on a table in a bar while numerous onlookers did nothing (and some even cheered). But experts are divided about the feasibility of such legislation. A decade ago John Kaplan asked whether the increased prosocial behavior it could yield might not be outweighed by the costs in unfair and whimsical prosecutions and the like. However, sociologist Gilbert Geis of the University of California at Irvine has recently reviewed such limited evidence as exists, especially Portugal's relatively successful experience with such a law since 1982, and feels that it is only a matter of time before judicial decisions or new laws make it obligatory on passersby to help those in grave danger if they are "readily able" to do so.

"I DIDN'T THINK ABOUT IT"

Don't stop to consider this situation; give the first answer that pops into your mind:

You are walking down a sidewalk alongside an apartment building; you hear a cry, look up, and see that a small child is falling from a window several stories above. What do you do?

Almost surely, you said that you would try to catch the child (and in fact there have been actual instances of this occurring). And you would do so instantly and without giving the matter any thought.

Such immediate and automatic response to an emergency is a special form of altruism that many researchers call "impulsive" helping. What makes it special is that the altruist acts without stopping to appraise the situation or weigh the pros and cons of helping, uninfluenced by the presence or absence of other bystanders, the frightening or repellent aspects of the situation, or other inhibiting factors.

Not long ago, in an effort to extract the characteristics common to such situations, Jane Piliavin and three colleagues divided forty-nine existing studies of helping in experimental emergencies into those where helping could be considered impulsive—that is, in which at least 85 percent of the bystanders tried to help and did so in fifteen seconds or less—and those where it was nonimpulsive. When they looked for differences between the two groups, they found that the factor most strongly connected with impulsive helping was the clarity of the situation; bystanders had no doubt that help was needed.

But by itself that is not enough to cause impulsive helping; in some perfectly clear situations most bystanders do not rush in to help. From other existing findings, Piliavin and her colleagues concluded that impulsive helping is most likely to occur when, in addition to clarity, the danger to the other person is so grave and the need for action so urgent that the bystander cannot stop to consider the possible costs or risks of helping.

In experiments, those who have helped or tried to in apparently hazardous situations—seemingly "live" high-voltage wires, for instance—often say, when asked if they had realized the danger of what they were doing, "Yes, I knew but I didn't think about it." Piliavin and her colleagues conclude that certain emergencies narrow the bystander's focus of attention to the victim's predicament and blank out normal thinking.

Yet even in many a clear, and relatively grave and urgent, situation many bystanders do not immediately seek to help. But some do, and to explain why they do, we must, after all, go beyond the purely situational analysis offered by Piliavin and her colleagues. Ervin Staub argues, and offers experimental data to prove his point, that those who help immediately, when many others do not, have such strong and dominant prosocial values that in them the usual decision-making process is short-circuited. Staub prefers to call their behavior "spontaneous" rather than impulsive, because an instant response of this kind, unlike purely impulsive helping, stems not only from the situation but from deep-lying motivation.

Here is a prototypical story of spontaneous helping, told many years ago by the Japanophile journalist Lafcadio Hearn. A poor Japanese peasant, from his hilltop farm, saw the ocean rapidly withdrawing and knew that a tidal wave was in the making. His neighbors were working in low fields, too far off to hear him call out a warning. Without a moment's thought, he set fire to his own rice ricks and energetically rang the temple bell. The far-off neighbors looked up, saw the smoke, and rushed up the hill to help him, narrowly escaping death.

In situations that are extremely dangerous not only to the victim but to any potential rescuer, very few bystanders exhibit either impulsive or spontaneous helping. When someone is trapped in a burning car or is under attack by a criminal, the cues are present that should produce impulsive helping in most bystanders and spontaneous helping in some, but few bystanders help. What makes those few different? Why is a hero a hero?

The question has long puzzled altruism researchers. Most altruistic people are not heroic and do not instantly brave great danger to save others. Nor is all heroism altruistic (the flights of astronauts are not) or instant and unthinking (dangerous combat missions are performed after careful planning).

And yet nearly all of us consider the instant and unthinking rescue of someone in grave danger as the very epitome of both altruism and heroism. All of the heroic acts honored by the Carnegie Hero Fund Commission are of this type. Timothy Mosher's rescue of Mana Mashoon is one of them; here are three recent others, as described in the rather stiff prose of Commission reports:

Mark S. Wood rescued John J. Gehringer from two attacking dogs, Redford, Michigan, March 18, 1987. Gehringer, 55, was attacked by two 45-pound pit bull dogs that knocked him to the pavement and bit him repeatedly. Driving in the vicinity, Wood, 38, mechanic, saw the attack; he parked, obtained a club from a nearby business, and, shouting, approached the dogs. Both dogs turned on Wood, allowing Gehringer to regain his footing and escape into a nearby shop.

Wood fended the dogs off with the club as they charged from different sides, but then he fell and lost the club. One of the dogs bit him on the leg. After a motorist struck one of the dogs with his car, Wood jumped on the hood of the car and was driven to safety. The dogs were later captured and destroyed. Gehringer required three weeks' hospitalization and surgery for severe multiple wounds. Wood required hospital treatment for his wound, from which he recovered.

Rubin A. Vigil helped to rescue Luis G., Teresa G., Cesar G., and Susanna Lopez from burning, Westminster, California, May 25, 1987. The car containing the Lopez family was struck from behind by a pickup truck and immediately burst into flame. Driving nearby, Vigil, 28, a grocery store clerk, ran to the scene, where another man was attempting to remove Lopez, 31, from the driver's seat of the burning car. Vigil leaned into the car and freed Lopez's foot; then he and the other man pulled Lopez out of the car and guided him to safety. Returning to the burning car, Vigil and the other man leaned inside and removed Mrs. Lopez, 31. Despite flames spreading on the exterior of the car and heavy smoke filling its interior, Vigil entered the car for Cesar, 5, whom he and the other man removed from the back seat. After Vigil and the other man located Susanna, 6, and as they were removing her from the back seat, a burst of flame knocked them to the ground. Vigil required hospital treatment for first- and second-degree burns to his forearms, and he recovered. The Lopez family also required hospital treatment for their burns.*

Lucille Babcock rescued a woman from assault, Little Rock, Arkansas, July 29, 1987. A 22-year-old woman screamed as she was being assaulted [in a rape attempt] by a man outside her home. Miss Babcock, 65, writer, saw the assault from her nearby apartment. Although she was disabled, requiring back and leg braces, Miss Babcock approached the assailant and beat him with her cane. ["I whopped him upside the head," she told a reporter.] The assailant then turned on Miss Babcock, allowing the younger woman to escape. The

*The other man, a furniture mover named John Anderson Floyd, required hospital treatment for first- and second-degree burns to face, hands, and legs. He too received a Carnegie hero award.

assailant struck Miss Babcock, then fled. Men in the neighborhood captured the assailant and held him for police. The
younger woman was treated for multiple injuries, and she
recovered. Miss Babcock recovered from exhaustion.

Such situations have the characteristics that should produce
either impulsive or spontaneous helping, but they also have characteristics that paralyze the will to act in most people. Accordingly,
heroism of this type is rare and such heroes are highly esteemed. Yet
as the sociologist William J. Goode has pointed out:

> The heroic act has too small a practical effect to explain the
> great effect it arouses. . . . One therefore looks for its symbolic
> meaning: It represents an extreme conformity with the ideal of
> putting group interests ahead of one's own, and asserts dra-
> matically that the ideal is not mere rhetoric but lies within
> human capacities.

Heroism is esteemed, in short, because it is the quintessence of
altruism.

But it simply is not known, at this point, what impels impulsive
heroes to risk their lives for strangers; there is almost no research
information on the matter. As altruism researcher Lauren Wispé
points out, there are no data that show whether heroes are heroic
in general or only in specific areas; it is not known, for instance,
whether the person who rushes into a burning building would be
equally likely to jump into icy water to rescue someone.

There is, though, some recent data on one special kind of
hero—the person who intervenes in a violent crime. Gilbert Geis
and sociologist Ted L. Huston hypothesized, as others had, that
those who rush in to rescue the victim of a violent crime while it
is being committed are probably impulsive, reckless, self-destructive, accustomed to violence and on good terms with it, and motivated more by anger at the criminal than by compassion for the
victim. Geis and Huston interviewed thirty-one men and one
woman who had been awarded money by California under a special
state law that compensates people for losses and costs of injuries
incurred in intervening in a crime. They also interviewed a control
group of thirty-two Californians who matched the interveners in
age, sex, education, and ethnic background, but had never intervened.

Geis and Huston were taken aback by their results. They found the interveners somewhat different from the comparison group, but not in the ways they had expected: The interveners had had more training in first aid and lifesaving, more exposure to crime, and more of them had had police training; in addition, they were somewhat taller and stronger, on the average, and had more of a sense of general competence, than noninterveners. But that was all. As Huston, Geis, and two assistants concluded in a journal report of the study:

> The data showed, contrary to our expectations, that the interveners and the comparison group were virtually indistinguishable in terms of personality characteristics. None of the eight scales [measuring personality traits] differentiated the two groups, nor did any of the three subscales of Fischer's (1973) measure of humanitarianism.

Of the psychological traits the researchers looked at, only the interveners' greater sense of competence—perhaps based on special training and physical characteristics—seemed significant.

But Geis and Huston add that beyond these moderate advantages, the interveners may possess one other crucial, but unmeasurable, trait. As Geis has written:

> Our study can be taken as a celebration of unusual people who, for whatever reason, took a courageous step in a society not commonly given to such behavior. . . . What can be stressed finally though is an existential point: the point that each of these interveners had, if only this once, done something thoroughly decent. . . . In their own way, this is what our Samaritans told us. You may, as you wish, take it as a poignant commentary on the quality of contemporary life, or as an invigorating and inspiring text about the potentialities of the human spirit.

Or both.

CHAPTER
SIX

Altruism Anatomized

INSIDE THE BLACK BOX

A crucial question about altruism remains: Why does one person pass by the stranger in trouble and another stop to help?

Even when volunteers in controlled experiments have generally similar cultural backgrounds, upbringing, and personality profiles, some will rush off to aid a presumably injured person in the next room, others will not. What we have seen tells us what the most *likely* response by members of a homogeneous group will be in any helping situation, but not whether any particular member of the group will respond that way.

For while innate tendencies, culture, upbringing, and personality all interact within us, we are decision-making creatures with a fair amount of control over how we use those data in our deliberations. We weigh each situation in the light of our feelings, our judgment of what helping will mean to the other person and entail for us, our sense of right and wrong, and a great deal more, and having done all that, *choose* either to help or to pass by; behavioral science cannot predict with certainty what that personal choice will be.

We ourselves are aware of only part of this complex process; by far the larger part takes place in the unconscious. We saw earlier how abbreviated and incomplete are the explanations altruists typically offer of their own behavior, and that is true even of those who are unusually thoughtful or insightful.

For example, Marion van Binsbergen (today Marion van B. Pritchard, a psychoanalyst practicing in Vermont) was a Dutch college student when the German Army invaded her country in 1940. The Germans instituted, one by one, a number of measures restricting the movements of Jews and depriving them of their civil rights. When they finally began deporting Jews to the concentration camps in 1942, Marion and a handful of her friends created their own informal rescue organization: They found hiding places for Jews, helped them move there, and supplied them with food, clothing, and ration cards—acts for which they themselves, if apprehended, would have been sent to concentration camp or even shot out of hand.

Van Binsbergen, in addition to taking many such risks, moved into a large country house belonging to an elderly friend of her parents in order, at the request of underground workers, to shelter there a Jewish father and his three small children. For two years, until the war ended, she housed the family, obtained food and clothing for them, and when Germans searched the house, placidly sat with her feet on the floor beneath which the family was hiding in a dug-out space. Had the Germans looked there, she probably would have been summarily executed.

Today, as a psychoanalyst, Marion van B. Pritchard surely has more self-understanding and insight than most people. Yet her recollection of why she decided to rescue Jewish strangers at the risk of her own life (as told to the editors of *The Courage to Care,* a documentary film and book about rescuers of Jews during the Holocaust), while moving and admirable, portrays only the ripple on the surface, not the currents beneath it:

> One morning on my way to school I passed by a small Jewish children's home. The Germans were loading the children, who ranged in age from babies to eight-year-olds, on trucks. They were upset, and crying. When they did not move fast enough the Nazis picked them up, by an arm, a leg, the hair, and threw them into the trucks. To watch grown men treat small children that way—I could not believe my eyes. I found myself literally crying with rage. Two women coming down the street tried to interfere physically. The Germans

heaved them into the truck, too. I just sat there on my bicycle, and that was the moment I decided that if there was anything I could do to thwart such atrocities, I would do it. . . . I could not have done anything else. I think you have a responsibility to yourself to behave decently.

Even skilled researchers, probing what went on in the hearts and minds of people who have performed major altruistic acts, generally come up with simplistic explanations of what must have been highly complex decision-making processes.

Over a decade ago, Carl H. Fellner of the University of Washington School of Medicine and John R. Marshall of the University of Wisconsin Medical School interviewed a number of kidney donors in depth. Prior to the development of immunosuppressive techniques that permit the transplanting of organs from cadavers to unrelated persons, most kidney transplants were from living relatives of the recipients. Such donations were major acts of altruism: For the patient it was the gift of life, but for the donor it was a major sacrifice, involving not only a serious operation, with all its attendant pain, trauma, and disfigurement, but, if the donor's remaining kidney ever failed, the same short and grim future the recipient had faced. But such considerations hardly came to light, for all Fellner and Marshall's searching; instead, they got answers like these:

A 60-year-old woman: "People say to me what a brave thing to do. I say, there was no bravery connected. It was just a thing I had to do." A 22-year-old man: "I had never done anything like this before. Just drifting with the tide. First time I did something worthwhile. Something that had to be done." . . . A 31-year-old man: "I had to do it. I couldn't have backed out, not that I had the feeling of being trapped, because the doctors offered to get me out. I just had to do it." A 27-year-old man: "I never was particularly close to my sister (the recipient), but I had to do it anyway." [And a donor not identified by the authors]: "How could you live with your conscience if you had done nothing and the poor fellow died?"

It is apparent, from all that we have seen, that such explanations, though correct as far as they go, leave out most of what must have taken place in the minds of the speakers. Not that they were being reserved or coy; they probably were not conscious of the rest.

This is characteristic not only of the mental processes that result in altruistic behavior but of all cognitive activity, partly because much of it takes place in the unconscious, and partly because even the conscious part is the outcome of preconscious processes of which we are rarely cognizant.

Were you aware, for instance, of how you put together the last sentence you uttered—how you formulated the thought, fine-tuned its nuances to suit the relationship between you and the other person, retrieved the words you needed from memory, and assembled them in the form of a grammatical sentence? Hardly; no more than you were aware of all that went on in your mind when you buttoned your shirt, caught a high fly ball, signed your name, or brought your car to a halt at a red light. This relegation of most "overlearned" material to the unconscious, cognitive scientists say, is essential to efficient functioning; we would speak haltingly, at best, and spend an hour buttoning our shirts, if we had to give conscious thought and attention to every word and movement.

So it is with the thoughts and emotions that lead to altruistic acts: The materials of which they are formed are so well drilled into us as to no longer require conscious thought but exert their influence from the vastly roomier unconscious.

In the early years of altruism research, none of this was of interest to most altruism researchers; they were concerned with the influence on behavior of external circumstances, and considered what took place in the mind, whether conscious or unconscious, either unimportant, unknowable, or both. This was the outlook of behaviorism, which still dominated psychological research and theory, as it had since early in the century, and which held that the attempt to study what goes on inside the mind is as unscientific as guessing what kind of machinery is inside a sealed black box on the basis of what it does when you push its buttons.

In any case, they said, speculating about mental processes is unnecessary: Since we can experimentally determine which stimuli, under what conditions, produce certain responses, we know all we need to know; it is needless and pointless to ask what goes on in between, in the black box.

But by the early 1960s psychologists were beginning to realize that while behaviorism could explain much about how animals and human beings acquire simple forms of behavior, it could cast no light on such complex cognitive phenomena as language, love, reasoning, problem-solving, creativity, philosophy—and altruism.

They realized, too, that although they could not directly observe what takes place inside the black box, they could deduce it from indirect evidence, somewhat as physicists infer the characteristics of invisible nuclear particles from the tracks they leave in a cloud chamber or on photographic film.

If, for instance, volunteers are given a very easy memory task—remembering a set of three consonants—and as soon as they have seen them have to count backward by threes in time to a metronome, they will forget the three consonants willy-nilly within seconds. Why? The counting procedure preempts their attention and prevents "rehearsal" (repeating something over and over to oneself, as one does an unfamiliar phone number); from that, one can infer that attention is necessary to rehearsal, and rehearsal necessary either to holding data in short-term memory or registering it in long-term memory. Thus it is indeed possible to experiment with the black box in ways that reveal the nature of its unseen machinery.

When this cognitive approach to psychology began displacing behaviorism, it broadened and deepened altruism research; investigators started trying to deduce the unseen mental and emotional processes involved in the altruistic act, and have been doing so, piecemeal, ever since. In the past several years, a few ambitious altruism researchers have assembled these many findings into complete "models" of what goes on in the mind, step by step, between a person's first perception of someone in need of help and the decision to help or not to help. While their versions are not identical, they agree on the general sequence of events. How do they know what that sequence is? By deduction from empirical data, much as in the three-consonant memory study just described.

An example: We have seen that when experimenters deliberately use ambiguous situations in helping experiments, many participants fail to realize the victim's need and so do nothing. From this one can infer that the early part of the sequence of events leading to a decision to help or not help is something like this—

awareness of situation → *interpretation* → *recognition of other person's need*

—but that absence of the first step, or an error in the second step (an incorrect interpretation of the situation), will result in inaction rather than lead to the third and later steps.

What follows are the major points on which the various models are in general agreement as to what takes place within the black box.

WHAT'S GOING ON?

I start with a specimen of a very trifling altruistic act that I will dissect, step by step, to show the sequence of mental processes involved. I choose it because I was the altruist in the case and therefore feel free to speculate about what went on in my mind. And to be honest, much of what I say took place there is, indeed, speculative, since most of the mental processes involved were unconscious. But I have used free association and reverie to bring them to light; anyway, it happened in *my* mind, which I like to think I am reasonably familiar with.

On a sunny fall day I am walking up Central Park West, a residential avenue in Manhattan, lost in thought, mulling about a good way to begin the next chapter of a book I am writing. I am vaguely aware of a quite good-looking, nicely dressed young woman coming in my direction. As she nears me, I notice, startled, that she is crying.

She sees me looking at her; she comes over to me and hesitantly says, "Sir, could you possibly help me? You look like the kind of person who—" and breaks off, covering her face with her hands and sobbing. I ask what kind of help she needs. She says that she came to the city this morning for a job interview and that her pocketbook was stolen; she is frantic because she has to get back before her two young children come home from school. Panicky and deeply embarrassed, she asks if I could possibly lend her cab and train fare—fifteen dollars—which she will return by mail the next day.

I hesitate a moment, and then say, "Yes, I can do that." I give her the money; she asks my name and address, writes them down on a slip of paper, thanks me profusely (I wave away the thanks), and hurries off.

Altruism researchers used to be of two minds as to whether the mental processes leading to altruistic behavior are primarily cognitive (aspects of thinking) or affective (emotional). Of late they have more or less concluded that the two kinds are thoroughly inter-woven in the train of mental events preceding a helping act. But the essential first step is purely cognitive: Awareness of the situation. Without that, nothing else takes place.

Here is that step, as exemplified in the first seconds of my little specimen episode:

> On a sunny fall day I am walking up Central Park West, a residential avenue in Manhattan, lost in thought, mulling about a good way to begin the next chapter of a book I am writing. I am vaguely aware of a quite good-looking, nicely dressed young woman coming in my direction. *(Mmm . . . I like that long-legged body, that swinging, clean blond hair . . . What was I thinking about? Yes—how* am *I going to get that chapter off to a fast start? I might use the anecdote about—)* As she nears me, I notice, startled, that she is crying. *(Hey! What is this? This nifty-looking young woman crying openly on the street, in the middle of the day, where anyone can see? What could be wrong? Has she just lost her job? Broken off with her lover? Been raped? Learned of a parent's death?* She sees me looking at her; she comes over to me and hesitantly says—

Let's stop there briefly to examine what happened.

Like Darley and Batson's seminarians in a hurry, if our attention is totally preempted, we may fail to notice someone else's distress and so never take even the first step toward deciding whether to help or not.

It is not only major concerns that can keep us from noticing someone else's need of help; anything, however trivial, that clutters up our attention can do so. In one experiment, researchers subjected participants, who were carrying out a routine but demanding cleri-cal chore, to various levels of noise, in the middle of which a female confederate of the researcher dropped her books and papers. The more noise, the less altruism: At forty-eight decibels, 72 percent of the participants helped her pick up her things, but at eighty-five decibels, only 37 percent did so.

Notice that the distracting influence—in this case, background noise—need not be something to which we are *paying* attention. It is simply that too many sights and sounds pouring into the senses create "stimulus overload" or "input overload"—in effect, a kind of static that makes us unable to see or hear someone else's distress.

Psychologist Stanley Milgram suggested some years ago that it might be input overload, and not just the presence of bystanders, that makes people in large cities unhelpful. A research team in the Netherlands tested Milgram's hypothesis in twenty real-life settings that had varying levels of traffic, street noise, pedestrian density, and numbers of public establishments along the street. In each locale, confederates manifested a need for help in such ways as dropping a bicycle key without noticing that they had done so. The finding: The greater the total barrage of city stimuli, the fewer passersby who helped. Latané and Darley's bystander effect accounted for part of that result, but noise, traffic, and number of public establishments were responsible for the rest.

The role of attention also explains another puzzling phenomenon, namely, the effect of mood on helpfulness. In many experiments like one mentioned in Chapter One, researchers have induced a good mood in some of their participants by having them imagine happy events, giving them unexpected small sums of money, or having them take tests and reporting to them (falsely) that they had done excellently. When these people then saw someone in need of help, or were asked to donate to a good cause, they were far more giving than participants who were in a neutral mood. Researchers had a number of explanations of this "feel good, do good" effect: it was due to a "glow of good will," an increase in outgoing feelings towards others, an impression of oneself as an effective person, a lessened need to think of one's own interests, and so on.

They expected, naturally, that negative moods would have the opposite effect, and, indeed, when they induced sadness, shame, or embarrassment in their volunteers by having them imagine that a friend was dying of cancer or making it appear that they had accidentally ruined an experiment, the volunteers were less generous and helpful than people in a neutral mood. That is, in *some* experiments. In others, perplexingly, negative moods made them *more* altruistic. It was easy to see that sad moods might create pessimism, generalized anger at the world, or a feeling of helplessness, any of which could dry up kindly impulses. But how could negative moods sometimes do just the opposite? The most plausible thesis was that participants were trying to lift their spirits or improve their opinion of themselves by doing something admirable.

But last year, two teams of investigators separately reviewed the accumulated data of various mood studies and came to similar conclusions: The reduction or increase in altruism is due not to the mood itself so much as where it focuses our attention. When we are in a good mood, we become expansive and outgoing, and able to notice the needs of others. When we are in a poor mood due to depressing thoughts about others, we are sensitive to their needs; when we are in a poor mood due to depressing thoughts about ourselves, we become self-absorbed and half-blinded to what is happening to others.

WHAT A PITY! (ETC.)

.... She sees me looking at her; she comes over to me and hesitantly says, "Sir, could you possibly help me? You look like the kind of person who—" and breaks off, covering her face with her hands and sobbing. *(I'm uncomfortable, I feel awkward at being witness to her loss of control in public. But I also feel sorry for her. Whatever her trouble is, I'd like to comfort her. Is it, I wonder, because I find her attractive? Or is it because I sense her genuine pain?)* I ask what kind of help she needs. She says that she came to the city this morning for a job interview and that her pocketbook was stolen; she is frantic because she has to get back before her two young children come home from school. *(How awful for her, to be stranded in the city with no money and with two children coming home in a few hours to a locked house, a missing mother. No wonder she's so upset . . . and I feel upset for her.)*

Having noticed that someone needs help, we react with arousal—an emotional response ranging anywhere from mild discomfort or concern to overwhelming pain or alarm. Several factors determine the kind of arousal produced and how strongly it motivates us to consider helping.

The Characteristics of the Situation

To recapitulate what we know:

- We are less aroused when others are present—unless they are friends or close acquaintances, in which case we are as strongly aroused as if we were alone.
- The nature of the problem varies in emotional impact: If we see a stranger drop a sheaf of papers, we may pass by with a rueful smile; if we see a stranger fall from his bicycle and

lie in the road, we feel powerfully impelled to help him.

- Some situations arouse us so intensely—the child about to fall out of the window—as to bypass the rest of the mental processes of altruism and propel us instantly into an effort at rescue.
- Particularly gruesome and repellent situations, such as an accident in which someone has had an arm cut off, may paralyze us or cause us to turn away, sickened.

The Characteristics of the Victim

Some of the more important parameters we have seen:

- We feel more disturbed by distress in attractive persons than in unattractive ones.
- We are strongly moved by distress in someone we see as one of Us; we may be little moved by distress in someone we see as one of Them.
- We may not be aroused at all if the victim is drunk, filthy, disfigured, or disgusting in some other way.
- We almost always are much stirred by such helpless victims as infants, aged persons, and the handicapped.

Why do certain characteristics of the situation and of the victim arouse us? The question may seem to need no answer: If you see a child wailing over the body of a pet dog killed by a car, or read of the Armenian mayor who lost all fifteen members of his family in the 1988 earthquake, you may feel that any normal human being would be distressed for them.

Still, the question does need an answer. Why do the sorrows and miseries of others, especially strangers, affect us? If the basic drive of all life is self-preservation, why do we have emotions that lead us to act against our own interests to relieve others' pain?

Two mental processes, both already mentioned, are responsible.

Role-taking is the ability acquired during the years of growing up to *see* things from the perspective of others.

Its primary function is information-gathering: It is a way of judging how the other person must be feeling and what that person wants someone to do for him or her. The information may motivate us, in any of several ways, to give some thought to helping. One way: We may believe that if someone feels as that person does, it is only right and proper to help him or her. Another: It engenders sympathy for the other person—pity and compassion based on intellectually understanding that person's feelings even though we may not empathically share them. Two examples:

- During the 1984 Olympics, when runner Mary Decker collided with runner Zola Budd and fell, tearing a leg muscle, millions of us, watching on TV, saw her cry and flail about in despair and anguish; we could comprehend her feelings and sympathize with her—and even wish we could comfort her—but only someone who has trained for years for such a competition and lost the chance of glory through a sudden accident could actually come close to understanding what she felt.
- Hermann Graebe, a German engineer, managed to save the lives of more than three hundred Jews in Poland, the Ukraine, and Germany during the Holocaust by getting them work papers and employing them in his firm, which was doing work for the German army. Aside from all other influences in his life that led him to do so, a critical experience was his involuntary witnessing of a massacre in Dubno. He recently recalled part of that experience for the editors of *The Courage to Care:*

> One of the most terrible things I remember seeing was a father, perhaps in his fifties, with his boy . . . maybe ten years old, beside him. They were naked, completely naked, waiting for their turn to go into the pit. The boy was crying, and the father was stroking his head. The older man pointed to the sky and talked quietly to the young boy. They went on speaking like that for a while—I could not hear what they said because they were too far away from me—and then it was their turn. . . . The boy cried and the father talked to him and stroked him. How do you explain that?

Graebe, his words suggest, could not share the father's feelings—the situation was too bizarre, too unlike anything he had ever experienced—but could understand them, and, in consequence, was overwhelmed by sympathy and moral outrage ("How do you see such a thing without being stirred into action against whatever or whoever caused it to happen?" he says), and became an outstanding rescuer of Jews.

Empathy, the other mental process that causes us to be aroused by someone else's misery, does so by making us *feel* what the other person is feeling. This is a puzzling phenomenon: How and why would Nature cause us to feel emotions like those of someone in need or distress—emotions appropriate to that person's situation but not to our own? Inappropriate emotions may lead to acts against our own best interest; empathy thus is at the heart of the mystery of altruism.

The answer, as we have already seen, is in part that empathy has survival value and so is selected by evolution: It makes for mutual understanding and help, and thereby confers a greater chance of survival on groups that are genetically predisposed to it. And in part the answer is that empathy is created by socialization: We learn, as we grow up, that empathic responses are rewarded by friendship, loyalty, and social approval. Hence, children, in the course of their development, increasingly empathize with others in distress. By adulthood, nearly all of us often and automatically share the feelings of others in distress and are moved by those feelings to consider helping.

Imagine, for instance, that it is a raw, windy, rainy day; you hear your elderly and frail neighbor get into her car and try again and again, in vain, to start it. As the battery runs down and the starter strains and falters, what would your reaction be? Wouldn't you get the same sinking feeling you know she has? And wouldn't you think about hurrying out to offer her assistance?

The evidence of several kinds of studies verifies that most people do, indeed, have empathic reactions to others in distress (or at least to certain others in certain situations). One kind is self-report: People are asked how they feel in response to stories or pictures of other persons who are in difficult situations; most often, their feelings tend to match the feelings of those persons. Or participants may be exposed to simulated crises, as in so many of the experiments already described, and then asked how they felt; both their visible reactions and their answers indicate a general tendency toward empathic arousal.

Finally, in search of more objective evidence on the matter, some researchers have been studying the facial expressions, taking the pulse, and measuring the skin conductance (due to perspiring) of volunteers who, in experiments, see or hear others in distress. Such data, tied in to how participants say they feel and how they actually behave, support the theory that empathic responses are a major factor in helping behavior.

But the decision to help or not to help is still some steps away. While we may often feel that our decision follows instantly upon emotional arousal, it is actually the product of several further, and more complicated, mental processes. These may take minutes, days, or longer, but most often seconds, or even only a fraction of a second. But research, like a high-speed stop-motion camera, can capture even the highest-speed mental acts and hold them up for our inspection.*

SHOULD SOMEONE TRY TO HELP?

. . . . She is frantic because she has to get back before her two young children come home from school. *(She looks so helpless, so stricken, so alone, and so fearful for her children. If she's telling the truth, if this isn't a con, she's really in a fix. What should she do? Phone someone back where she lives? But she hasn't even got money for a phone call, and maybe there's no one she could call who could drop everything and be there to meet the children. In any case, she has to get home, but how can she? Should she go to the police?—no, she can't spare the time, and even if she could, they wouldn't give her cab and train fare, they'd refer her to some other source, Travelers' Aid, most likely. But Travelers' Aid is probably downtown, and without money how could she get there—and do so in time to get cab and train fare from them and get to the station and be home before her children? . . . Someone should help her, but who?)*

Having become aware of someone else's distress and been aroused by it, we appraise the situation by bringing to bear our accumulated knowledge of the world we live in. One reason children become increasingly altruistic as they grow older is that they

---

*The mental activities generated by arousal may take place in sequence but more likely many of them go on simultaneously; the human mind, cognitive scientists say, does a great deal of parallel processing. Since I cannot simulate that with words on paper, I must ask you to imagine it as you read the following sections.

have more experience to draw on and can better evaluate another person's problem and give a more realistic and sophisticated answer to the question, "Should someone try to help?"

The answer, in most of the cases presented throughout this book, is obviously yes; look back at any of them and it will be apparent that had you been present, you would have made that judgment.

But sometimes the answer is no, because helping would be either inappropriate, embarrassing, costly to no good end, or even life-threatening. For instance:

- On a downtown street, two plainclothesmen shove a neck-lace-snatcher against a wall, frisk him, and then lead him away in handcuffs. The suspect, a skinny black teenager, is bleeding from a split lip, gasping for breath, and obviously terrified. Should someone try to help him? Clearly not—at least, not a bystander and not then and there; if help is in order, it should come from a public defender in the court-room.
- During a major storm at sea, a small boy is swept off the deck of a cruise ship. The captain has been keeping its bow to the wind because any other heading, in these mountainous seas and high winds, would probably cause the ship to broach and founder. He dare not turn around to search for the boy, nor could a lifeboat be launched in time to save him or make it back to the mother ship. Should someone try to help? Alas, no.

SHOULD I TRY TO HELP?

. . . . *(Someone should help her, but who? Someone she knows—but she probably doesn't know anyone around here, and she hasn't got money to phone anyone elsewhere. Someone passing by who sees her crying—whom she sees looking at her—and whom she begs for help—*Me! *Now wait a minute! Why me? Just because I'm the only one around at the moment? Or because she saw something in me? She said, "You look like the kind of person who—" and burst into tears. The kind of person who what? Who would help a stranger in trouble? How could she know that about me?—I myself don't even know if it's true.)* Panicky and deeply embarrassed, she asks if I could possibly lend her cab and train fare—fifteen dollars—which she will return by mail the next day. *(Fifteen dollars! No ordinary panhandler, this one!—but why should I call her that? I don't think she is one; I think she's just what she seems to be. And she's in real trouble. Can I trust a total stranger? Should I? I like to think I'm a good judge of character, and looking at her and listening to her, I don't think it's a scam. And she really needs help. Things have gone well for me this year, and I can afford to take a chance, and she might not easily find anyone else around here—how many other people on the street would believe her? Yes, I think I ought to lend her the money, I think it's the right thing to do.)*

If real-world knowledge and good judgment yield the answer yes to the question, "Should someone try to help?," the next question is "Should *I* try to help?" At this point a number of the influences we have seen earlier come into play:

- Here again, *the presence or absence of others* who might help, or who might be better able to help than you, affects your judgment.
- You take into account the *needy person's dependency on you.*
- You factor into the equation *your own competence* (or lack of it) to help in the specific situation.
- You predict the *social consequences of helping or of not helping* by drawing upon your experience and your knowledge of what is expected in your society. If, in a given situation, you know that most people would think well of you for helping and ill of you for not helping, the answer to the question "Should *I* try to help?" is probably yes.
- *Your personal norms* may have even more influence than social norms on how you appraise the situation and, ultimately, how you act. Social norms specify what other people expect you to do, personal norms what you expect of yourself—often, a more rigorous standard. You obey a social norm of helping in order to be seen as a good person but a personal norm of helping in order to see yourself as a good person. Which is why many a person who has performed some costly or dangerous altruistic deed will say, like the kidney donors, "I had to do it" or "I couldn't have lived with myself if I hadn't."

AND I WANT TO HELP BECAUSE—

> *. . . . (Yes, I think I ought to lend her the money, I think it's the right thing to do. But do I really feel like doing so? Yes and no. I might lose fifteen dollars—and feel like a fool; I'd be ashamed to tell friends that I fell for a run-of-the-mill con. But look at her—she's staring at me like an animal in a trap—eyes wet with tears, miserable, in pain, hoping against hope that I'll rescue her. It makes* me *feel miserable. I hate feeling that way. If I give her the money, I'll feel as much better as she does, and good about myself, I'll feel I'm a fine person—unless I start thinking I was a sap and get angry with myself for—No, that's petty of me to think only of what it will do for me, or to me, if I give her the money. What matters is what it will do for her. She'll be so relieved, all will be well—that's the reason to help her— and, yes, I* do *want to.)*

The conclusion "I should help" is like a course plotted on a map showing which way to go, but one still needs some form of propulsive power, or, in psychological terms, motivation.

Here, finally, we come to the very heart of our subject: What is the primary motivation to do something that will benefit another person at some cost to ourselves? If there is a solution to the mystery we have been investigating—how altruism can exist although it conflicts with self-interest—it is here that we must find it.

Throughout the centuries, as noted earlier, philosophers puzzled over the question as to why anyone would behave altruistically to his own disadvantage; many, finding no good reason, concluded that true altruism does not exist and that we are benevolent only when it benefits us in some way to be so. In modern times much the same view is widespread among social scientists, especially psychologists, most of whom assert that all altruism is self-serving in one way or another.

In what way can it serve us? They offer a variety of answers. Those with a psychoanalytic orientation say we act altruistically to relieve guilt over wrongs we have done. To test this concept, altruism researchers have induced guilt in volunteers by making them think they caused an assistant to spill a box of sorted file cards, spoiled an experiment, and so on—and found that afterward these volunteers were readier to help, and more generous with their help, than volunteers in whom no guilt was induced. But while guilt may account for such "compensatory helping," it does not explain why participants help in all those other situations where no guilt is created. Evidently, guilt can account for only part of helping.

Psychoanalyst Anna Freud offered a different explanation based on self-interest: Because givers enjoy the act of giving—because it is pleasure-producing—it is selfishly motivated. This has the ring of truth; we often anticipate, before doing kindness, that it will make us feel good. There is some research support for this idea: Studies have shown that people with low self-esteem are more likely to help than persons with a normal degree of self-esteem, probably in order to feel better about themselves. But the same studies show that persons with high self-esteem are also more altruistic than normal. Obviously, improving one's self-image cannot be the only motive or even the chief one for altruistic behavior.

Most altruism researchers prefer to state the self-interest theory in more general terms: We are altruistic only when the benefits it yields us, whatever they are, outweigh the costs of benefiting others. Altruism thus does obey the fundamental law of reinforcement, namely, that we do what rewards us and avoid what does not.

It is certainly true, and obvious, that many acts we call altruistic are motivated by self-interest. Some, perhaps most, philanthropists give chiefly because they desire applause and fame. Much corporate giving is intended to improve the company's public image and to better its community relations. Political leaders work to improve the lot of the poor and ailing at least partly to strengthen their own hold on office.

And nearly all of us will admit, if we are honest, that self-interest lies behind some or many of our own benevolent acts. We give to a program that finds jobs for ex-convicts partly out of compassion but partly because it may reduce recidivism and the level of crime in our city. We support the United Way because many of the activities it funds will improve our own community. We back the costly expansion of the city's shelters partly out of pity for the homeless but largely to keep our public places from becoming their dormitories and latrines. As that most acerbic of social commentators, the Duc de la Rochefoucauld, said, "We would often be ashamed of our finest actions if the world knew all the motives that produced them."

Still, many of us also do kindly deeds that bring us no such practical benefits, as examples throughout this book attest. When we stop to help a stranded motorist, send a check for Sudanese famine relief, or volunteer our time and effort in any good cause, where is the self-benefit so many psychologists believe motivates all benevolent acts?

Psychologists have an answer that we have already heard, based on ample evidence of the close connection between empathy and altruism. When we see someone in distress, empathy causes us to share that distress; we try to rid the other person of it in order to make ourselves feel better. Thus, helping someone else rewards us.

Yet if this selfish aim were the major reason for altruism, why would we not prefer simpler and less costly ways of ridding ourselves of distress? The Piliavins and Judith Rodin, in their first subway study, suggested that there are, in fact, four alternative ways of relieving empathic distress: helping, getting help, escaping from the scene, or telling ourselves that the victim doesn't deserve help. They hypothesized that we weigh the costs and rewards of each alternative and select the one that is best for ourself. "Note that the major motivation implied in the [Cost-Reward] model," they concluded, "is not a positive 'altruistic' one, but rather a selfish desire to rid oneself of an unpleasant emotional state."

Fairly often, however, helping seems the alternative with the greatest payoff for the helper in terms of relief of inner discomfort. Robert Cialdini has been one of the most vocal proponents of this wholly egoistic explanation of altruism for the last fifteen years. Cialdini, an affable and good-natured man, told me how he came to this seemingly Scrooge-like view:

"In the early 1970s," he said, "some studies had shown that people who had been made to harm others were more helpful afterwards, and it looked as if guilt-relief must be the reason for altruism. But the guilty people were just as extra helpful to others they hadn't harmed as to those they had. That didn't make sense to me.

"I began to think that not just guilt but a more general mood state—sadness—must be responsible. We say, 'I helped because I was sorry for this individual,' but what that means is that *we* were feeling discomfort as a consequence of *his* discomfort. That led me to think that the motive behind altruism is to rid ourselves of our own empathic distress rather than to aid the victim, and that's what I've tried to demonstrate experimentally. A number of my colleagues have said that this is an unduly cynical view, but I don't see it that way at all. It's an extremely adaptive and highly commendable feature of human nature."

Altruism is thus, in Cialdini's cheerfully unsentimental view, a form of hedonism: We're good to others when we're feeling rotten because it makes us feel better. Any negative mood can motivate us to be altruistic, but the most important source of such negative moods is empathy. As Cialdini puts it in formal terms, "The Negative State Relief model of helping . . . suggests that by responding empathically to someone in need, the potential helper is saddened and is therefore motivated to help in an effort to elevate his or her own mood."

Cialdini's strongest evidence for his hypothesis comes from an experiment that he and two graduate students at Arizona State University conducted a few years ago. They reasoned as follows: If we create a condition in which our volunteers *can't* change a sad mood they're feeling, they won't help anyone else because they won't have any reason to—if our theory is right.

But how could they make volunteers believe their sad moods couldn't be dispelled? The team thought up a fanciful device: They told volunteers that they were to take part in a test of Mnemoxine, a new drug that temporarily improves short-term memory; half would take the drug, half would not. (The "drug" was nothing but half an ounce of flat tonic water.) The experimenters also told them that it had an odd but harmless side effect: For about half an hour it would freeze whatever mood they were in; if they were happy, they'd stay happy, if sad, sad. (There was, of course, no such effect, but the participants thought there was.)

One member of the team then asked each participant—each went through the experiment alone—to perform a preliminary memory exercise by recalling either a happy experience, a sad one, or a neutral one; the real purpose was to induce a happy mood in some, a sad mood in others, and a neutral mood in still others.

Then, reminding the participant that the mood-freezing drug had now taken effect, the experimenter left the room, ostensibly to get some supplies. As he did so, a confederate wearing a badge of a local nonprofit blood organization popped in and asked the participant if he or she would be willing to make some brief phone calls to help gather additional information about local blood donors.

"If we were right that relief of sadness is the crucial motive in altruism," Cialdini told me, "then those who thought their sad mood was frozen shouldn't have been any more helpful than the neutral-mood group, because helping wouldn't make them feel better. But those who hadn't taken the drug and thought their sad mood *could* be dispelled *should* have been more helpful than the neutrals. And that's exactly what we found." Adding to this confirmation of his hypothesis were the results with the happy participants: Since they had no reason to want to change their mood, those who had taken the drug should have been neither more nor less helpful than those who hadn't—and they weren't.

That makes a strong case for the egoistic theory of altruism, to which most behavioral scientists concerned with the subject subscribe. But certain leading altruism researchers and theorists, among them Ervin Staub, Dennis Krebs, and David Rosenhan, disagree. Even though much altruistic behavior is motivated by self-interest, they say, there *is* such a thing as true altruism: behavior aimed at meeting the other person's needs rather than one's own. That can be the case even if the altruist does benefit in some way, says Martin Hoffman. He distinguishes between the consequences of an act and its aim: "Because a person has a satisfied feeling afterwards does not necessarily mean that he or she acted in order to gain that feeling."

The most articulate and vocal believer in true altruism is Daniel Batson, he of the Good Samaritan experiment fame. After completing that study, he spent some years working on the psychology of religion, a natural outgrowth of his previous training at the Princeton Theological Seminary. But his central interest was in morality, and he eventually came to focus his efforts on the topic that has engrossed him for the past fourteen years and with which he is now identified by his peers. Batson told me how it came about:

"In about 1975," he said, "when I was teaching at the University of Kansas, Jay Coke, a graduate student of mine, wanted to do a thesis on the cognitive aspects of altruism. We set up an experiment in which participants heard a bogus radio news broadcast about a female student whose parents had been killed in a car crash and who as a result might have to put her siblings up for adoption.

"We meant to study how the participants cognitively appraised this situation, but what surprised us was that they had two distinct kinds of powerful emotional response to it. One was an anxious-disturbed reaction that did not generate any desire to help. The other was an empathic response that did.

"That finding, it seemed to me, contradicted the Piliavin Cost-Reward model. Helping, it showed, wasn't determined by a calculation of costs and rewards but by the particular kind of emotional response you have to someone else's distress. To me, that meant that empathic emotion—not just distress, but a sharing of the other person's feelings and viewpoint—is the mechanism behind true altruism. That's a finding with radical implications about human nature."

Ever since then, Batson and various colleagues have been doggedly testing and advocating the empathy-altruism hypothesis, which these days he formally states as follows:

> The magnitude of altruistic motivation is assumed to be a direct function of the magnitude of empathic emotion. Of course, reducing the other's need is likely also to bring social and self-rewards, avoid social and self-punishments, and reduce the helper's own aversive arousal. But it is proposed that feeling empathy for the person in need evokes motivation to help in which these benefits to self are not the goal of helping; they are simply consequences of helping.

While Batson agrees that much prosocial behavior is selfishly motivated—he calls most of this pseudoaltruism—he says that true altruism seeks the good of the other person without any thought of self-benefit. But how can one show that such true altruism exists?

He and four of his students at the University of Kansas carried out an experiment, several years prior to Cialdini's, to do just that. If all helping, they reasoned, was aimed at relieving one's own feelings, people would always choose between helping and escaping, and take what was the easier way under the circumstances; if, however, some helping was aimed solely at relieving the other person, people would help even when helping was painful and escaping was easy.

To create those conditions in the laboratory, they had to resort to an unusually intricate scenario. First, the team member who dealt directly with the participants—female undergraduates—and who said her name was Martha told each one that she would take part in two experiments at the same time, one on memory, the other on the effects of unpleasant conditions (electric shocks) on task performance, where she would be only an observer.

About half an hour before the memory experiment, Martha said, the participant would take a tablet of Millentana, a memory-improving drug (actually, a placebo capsule containing cornstarch). While waiting for the memory drug to be fully absorbed, she would act as an observer at the second experiment, in which a young woman named Elaine would try to perform a memory task while receiving electric shocks at random intervals.

Martha also alerted each participant to a temporary and harmless (but purely fictional) side effect of Millentana: She told half of them that for twenty-five minutes they'd have a feeling of warmth and sensitivity such as they might feel when reading a touching novel, the other half that for twenty-five minutes they'd have a feeling of uneasiness and discomfort such as they might feel when reading a distressing novel.

Having taken the capsule, each participant began observing the electric-shock experiment on a video screen; what she was really seeing was a videotape in which a confederate acted the part of Elaine without actually being shocked but portraying anxiety, physical discomfort, and mounting emotional anguish. Martha, acting as if she were troubled by Elaine's reactions, went to talk to her, then returned and explained to the observer that as a child, Elaine had been thrown from a horse onto an electric fence and was finding the experiment extremely upsetting.

This scenario was troubling to all the observers, but, as postexperiment interviews verified, those who had been told that Millentana would make them feel warm and sensitive assumed that their emotional response to watching Elaine was personal distress. While those who thought the drug would create feelings of personal distress took their emotional reaction to her to be primarily empathic concern.

These differing interpretations, the researchers hypothesized, should produce different reactions to what happened next—an opportunity either to escape from the situation or to take Elaine's place. Half the participants were told that Elaine would undergo two trials but that they could leave after the first one; that offered an easy out. The other half were told that they had to watch both trials; for them, the alternative to not helping was the pain of continued watching. All participants, after hearing about Elaine's childhood trauma, were given an opportunity to take her place for some part of the remainder of the experiment. (Of course they never did have to do so.) Thus, they could choose between helping, at considerable cost to themselves, or not helping; and whichever they chose, some of them could escape easily, while others had to remain.

If there were such a thing as true altruism, those who took their emotional reaction to be due to fellow feeling for Elaine would offer to take her place, whether or not they could easily escape. But those who took their emotional reaction to be one of personal distress wouldn't be strongly motivated to relieve Elaine's suffering if they couldn't escape, and, if escape were easy, inclined to get out. Batson told me, beaming, what happened:

"Because of the complexity of the manipulations," he said, "I told the students that I didn't think it would work. I said, 'Don't expect too much.' But lo and behold, it worked! The manipulations had exactly the effect we wanted—and so did the pattern of helping. The people who thought they were feeling personal distress were much more likely to choose to escape rather than help, if escaping was easy, but the people who thought they were feeling empathic concern were just about as willing to take Elaine's place whether escape was easy or not. I regard that as an extremely important result."

Thus, empathy, at least in this experiment, did not lead to the choice of the least costly way of relieving one's feelings, as it should have if the egoistic view of altruism was correct, but to actions intended to benefit the other person rather than oneself, as it should have if there was such a thing as true altruism.

Which theory of empathy-based altruism is correct?

Probably both. Some leading altruism researchers and theorists, Nancy Eisenberg, Martin Hoffman, and Dennis Krebs among them, say that Cialdini and Batson mean different things by "empathy" and in their experiments have demonstrated two distinct and different mental processes, each of which results in altruistic behavior.

The Cialdini theory and experiments concern empathy in its elementary sense: an emotional state similar to another person's. If a basic human motive is to avoid pain and to seek comfort, people sharing another person's distress will weigh the costs and the rewards of various ways of relieving their feelings and will help only when helping seems the cheapest or least unpleasant alternative.

The Batson theory and experiments concern empathy in a more advanced sense: an emotional state in which one takes the other person's viewpoint and therefore feels sympathetic, compassionate, and concerned with that person's welfare. Batson calls this "empathy," but other researchers call it "sympathetic distress" or simply "sympathy."

Although we saw above that sympathy can be generated by role-taking, a wealth of evidence shows that it is most powerful when it is the outgrowth of empathy. Little children experience empathy but don't know what to do about it; as they learn more about the world and other people, their response is transformed into feelings of concern and sympathy. Mature adults possess both capabilities: We often react to another's distress with empathic distress and weigh our alternatives egoistically, but sometimes we react with empathy-based sympathy and respond with true altruism.

One question, philosophic rather than scientific, remains: Is selfishly motivated benevolence only pseudoaltruism, as Batson says? Does only selfless, sympathy-motivated benevolence qualify as altruism?

My own answer (with which you may or may not agree):

- Altruism is not a single entity; like love, beauty, and pleasure, it is many related things.
- Different kinds of altruism are the outcome of different motivations and hence have different degrees of moral value. True altruism is the most admirable and the most inspiring kind, but even if one is partly motivated by the desire to gain some inner reward, the resulting benevolent act is admirable and moral, though somewhat less so than pure altruism.
- Acts of helping or benevolence motivated by crass self-interest and external rewards, as in the case of rescuers of Jews who did it for money, are not altruistic. We can be grateful for them, since they have good consequences, but they are not instances of human compassion.

—BUT CAN I AFFORD TO?

. . . . *(She'll be so relieved, all will be well—that's the reason to help her—and, yes, I do want to. But—)* I hesitate a moment. . . . *(—maybe it is, after all, a con. Or maybe it's not my responsibility. What do I have to lose if I just say no and walk on? Well, it might hang over me for hours. Or days. I'd worry about her kids, I'd feel bad that someone in such a state had asked for help and I could so easily have given it but didn't. I'd dislike myself.*

As against that, what do I stand to gain if I say no? Not much: fifteen dollars, and a sense of having been street-smart.

Suppose I help her, what do I have to lose? If it's a con, fifteen dollars. Wouldn't kill me, but still that would buy me a book or pay for a bottle of wine in a restaurant. And I'd feel naive, foolish, stupid, and disillusioned.

And what do I stand to gain if I help her? I'd feel relieved, I wouldn't be bedeviled the rest of the day or longer by thinking that I should have helped her, that maybe some awful thing will have happened to her kids. And I'll feel good about myself, I'd like who I am—

do that." I give her the money; she asks my name and address, writes them down on a slip of paper, thanks me profusely (I wave away the thanks), and hurries off.

Once we are motivated to help, whatever the reason, we perform a kind of problem-solving: We use our accumulated experience and knowledge to predict the benefits and the costs of the various kinds of help one might offer—and of not helping.

This does not contradict Batson's findings on selfish versus selfless altruism: Each kind of motivation leads us to calculate the outcomes of the various alternatives, but in different ways.

Empathic Distress

When we are selfishly motivated to reduce our own discomfort, we reckon the costs and rewards of both not helping and of helping, and choose the alternative best for ourselves.

Weighing all the many factors involved calls for a kind of intuitive mental calculus; in most cases, and especially in emergencies, we do this almost instantaneously. But that is not surprising; we do it all the time—when, for instance, we decide in a fraction of a second how to answer an awkward question someone has asked us, or how best to return a tennis ball speeding toward us.

When the costs outweigh the rewards, we prefer not to help, but we are all creatures of conscience; to enable ourselves to choose not helping without suffering guilt and self-dislike, we often use any of several mental defenses against helping. Some of the major ones noted by researchers:

- "Nothing's really wrong."
- "There's nothing anyone could do to help."
- "I can't do anything about it." (Sometimes a legitimate reason for not helping, sometimes a self-deceptive excuse.)
- "It's not my responsibility"—the police (or the government, the United Nations, etc.) will take care of it; or, I didn't get him in that fix, so why should I shoulder the burden?" (Though sometimes valid, this is often a way of negating the moral norm of responsibility for others.)
- "He doesn't deserve help"—he brought it (drunkenness, addiction, AIDS, poverty) on himself by being immoral, lazy, perverted, etc. When helping seems too costly, many of us

- "He doesn't deserve help"—he brought it (drunkenness, addiction, AIDS, poverty) on himself by being immoral, lazy, perverted, etc. When helping seems too costly, many of us resort to the "Just World" rationale, namely, that good, hardworking people do well while sinful, lazy ones bring their sufferings on themselves and deserve no sympathy.
- "Helping them doesn't really help them." Recent examples of this defense: Sending food to starving Eritreans only benefits the totalitarian Ethiopian regime; if we didn't give to panhandlers, many of them would find work.

Sympathy

In contrast, when we are motivated primarily by concern for the other person we reckon which course of helping will be most advantageous and least costly—to him or her—and yet not excessively costly or ruinous to ourselves.

We may be aware of the potential rewards to ourselves such as relief of distress, feeling good about ourselves, or winning social approval, but these are not part of the equation. Most kidney donors, for instance, have said that before the operation they expected to feel inwardly compensated (as indeed they were), but from their accounts of their decision-making, it is clear that this played little or no part in the calculations.

As for tangible (external) rewards, altruists not only don't weigh these in but if they know there is to be such a reward, the very thought may interfere with their motivation. In a recent study, participants who had been rated as to altruism by a personality test were asked by a graduate student if they would help her with a research project she was having trouble with; she told some of them that she would compensate them in the form of course credits, and others that she could give them no compensation. Students who ranked high in altruism were nearly twice as willing to help her when they did not expect compensation as when they did; students who ranked high in egoistic motivation were twice as willing to help when they would be compensated as when they would not.

Estimating the feasibility and the value *to the other person* of each kind of help we might give, we weigh against each of them certain kinds of cost: our own health and our own life, which are as worth preserving as the other person's; and the harm to those who depend on us of our doing something ruinous to ourselves or our fortunes.

These, rather than personal rewards, are what we balance against the good we can do by helping.

Only exceptional people, in exceptional circumstances, give no thought at all to such costs and consider only what is best for the other person—as in the almost incomprehensible behavior of Arland Williams (the man who, in the icy Potomac after an airline crash, helped others to safety until it was too late to help himself) or that of the soldiers who committed altruistic suicide by throwing themselves on top of a live grenade.

But altruism of that order need not be our model or goal; each of us is a human being, with as much right to life and health as any other. There are no absolutes to altruism; each case has to be weighed on its own, and the feasible ideal is to reach a decision based on what is good for the other person and not grossly harmful to ourselves. Helping the waylaid stranger cost the Good Samaritan money, time, and effort but not his life, his fortune, or his health. He remains as good a model for us as he was nearly two thousand years ago.

A postscript: I never got my fifteen dollars back—but, happily, it did not change my outlook; I felt I had learned something good about myself, and that I had made the right decision. I was not a loser in the transaction.

CHAPTER
SEVEN

"O Brave
New World"

A BALANCED VIEW OF HUMANKIND

Despite the abundant evidence that compassion is a basic human trait, the view has long prevailed that human beings are either heartless or brutal toward most of their fellows. Every compendium of familiar quotations has an abundance of statements like "The greatest enemy to man is man" (Robert Burton) but almost none like "Precious is man to man" (Thomas Carlyle). Altruism research attests that kindness is as integral to human nature as cruelty, yet in the news and in the historical record cruel acts vastly outnumber kind ones.

Why are we keenly aware of the despicable in us but largely insensible of the admirable? Not, I suggest, because the despicable is common and the admirable rare but the very reverse. Prosocial behavior of all sorts, including altruism, is so normal and expected that we scarcely notice it but are struck by its absence or opposite. We see nothing unusual in a passerby's helping a fallen elderly person to his feet but are surprised and disturbed if the passerby ignores him. We expect people to be kind and helpful to a stranger in distress; we are startled and troubled when they look away and hurry past. Cruelty is attention-getting, kindness unremarkable, and so we agree with Seneca that "man delights to ruin man" and with William James that "of all the beasts of prey . . . [man is] the only one that preys systematically on its own species."

The evidence of altruism research, however, shows us ourselves in truer perspective. Like Miranda in Shakespeare's *The Tempest,* we have long known of the Caliban in us, but when we see that there is also a Ferdinand, we may have an epiphany like hers:

> How beauteous mankind is! O brave new world,
> That has such people in 't!

Familiarity with the research data might transform even an embittered misanthrope into a believer in the human potential for decency. That, at any rate, was the experience of one social scientist who had overpowering personal reason to regard humankind as vile but whose own research findings, a major contribution to the field, transformed his view, and him.

This is the story of his research and his life.

Samuel Oliner, tweedy, bespectacled, and silver-haired, is a professor of sociology whose gentle and thoughtful manner conceals a dark truth: certain horrendous experiences of his childhood that are central to his real identity. Oliner rarely speaks of them to friends or to his colleagues at Humboldt State University, a small institution in the logging country of northern California, but he recounted them in *Restless Memories,* a memoir published in 1979. It begins with the event that led him, forty years later, to undertake the major work of his life, an ambitious study of the psychological and social factors that engender human altruism.

That motivating event, paradoxically, exemplified the diametric opposite of altruism. Before dawn on Friday, August 14, 1942, a convoy of trucks roared into the fetid ghetto of Bobowa, a town in southeastern Poland. In the ramshackle houses lived a thousand Jews recently uprooted by German soldiers from their homes in nearby towns and villages; their forced relocation was the first phase of the Final Solution, the Nazi plan for the extermination of the Jews, which went into effect beginning in late 1941 in Poland, and later in other Nazi-controlled countries. As the trucks pulled into the marketplace, German *Einsatzgruppen* leaped out, firing into the air and bellowing, *"Alle Juden raus!"* ("All Jews outside!"). Terrified men, women, and children ran into the dark alleys and streets crying and screaming, and the soldiers, beating them with rifle butts, herded them onto the trucks, which, as rapidly as they were filled, pulled away into the night.

In one house a young woman named Ester Oliner, clutching her two young children, whispered to her twelve-year-old stepson, Shmulek, "Run away, my child, and save yourself! Hide, hide, hide! They're killing us all!" Shmulek ran outside in his pajamas, climbed onto the low flat roof of the house, and covered himself with loose boards and rubbish piled there. For hours he heard shrieking, weeping, shouting, gunshots, and the sound of trucks grinding in and out of the marketplace. All day he lay motionless under the sun-baked boards, often drifting into a daze only to wake again and again with a madly beating heart when there was a nearby noise. Finally, as the memoir recalls:

> By late afternoon the ghetto was quiet. The people had stopped crying, the Nazis had stopped shouting, and the trucks had stopped roaring in the streets. The ghetto was like a ghost town. . . . A feeling of great loneliness filled my body, and I wondered if I were actually dead. Maybe I was dead and my lot through eternity was to lie under these boards and listen to the breeze in absolute stillness.

At last he ventured to emerge. The ghetto was deserted; except for Shmulek, all its inhabitants, including his father and stepmother, grandparents, half-brother, and half-sister, were gone. As he would learn a couple of days later, they and all the other inhabitants of the ghetto had been marched into a huge pit in a forest at Garbacz, half a dozen miles to the southeast, and machine-gunned down, along with the inhabitants of another nearby ghetto, among them his other grandparents, his brother, sister, and other members of his family.

Still clad only in pajamas, Shmulek went back into his family's house to put some clothes on. But it had been totally looted by Poles from the Christian part of Bobowa; nothing was left. He searched in other houses until he found some old patched clothing that more or less fit him, and then spent the night hiding in a closet, each noise made by the wind causing him a paroxysm of fright. In the morning he made his way through Bobowa, terrified that he'd be noticed and seized, but because he was blond, with hazel eyes and a short straight nose, he looked more Polish than Jewish, and no one paid any attention to him. Having no plan, he automatically headed for Bielanka, the tiny village some five miles to the southeast where his family had lived before being forced into the ghetto.

The next two or three days are a blur of images in his memory: bare feet on cold muddy roads, barking dogs, fields of grazing cows, nights in ruined barns, constant gnawing hunger. At one point he begged a weathered old farmer for a piece of bread (Shmulek's speech did not betray him; unlike many segregated city Jews, the Oliners, living among Poles in a farming village, had spoken Polish without a Yiddish accent); the farmer gave him some and told him, chuckling, what the Germans had done with the inhabitants of the Bobowa ghetto, never noticing that the small boy's face turned deathly pale under its dirt.

Shmulek realized that at Bielanka he would have to seek help from a Gentile, since no Jews were left. He knew that any Pole he revealed himself to could get a bounty for turning in a Jew who had left the ghetto; he knew, too, that under a Nazi edict anyone who aided or hid him could be shot or hanged. The only person he could think of on whom he might take a chance was Balwina Piecuch, a peasant woman in Bystra, a village near his former home; she had done business with his father and been on good terms with him. Making his way to the Piecuch house after dark, Shmulek timidly knocked.

"Who's there?" a man's voice called out.

"Shmulek. Shmulek Oliner," he said, "Aron's son."

A moment later he was in the warm whitewashed kitchen, sobbing out his story to Balwina and her husband. Balwina, aghast, drew him to her ample bosom and sought to comfort him. "Don't cry," she said, "don't cry, my child. The Lord will help you." She assured him that she would shelter him for a while, but warned him to remain hidden, since if any neighbor saw him it might be the end for him—and the Piecuchs. Balwina then set out bread, butter, and milk; after Shmulek had eaten his fill she sent him to the attic to sleep in her son Staszek's bed, while Staszek, a boy Shmulek's age, came downstairs for the night.

Shmulek remained in the Piecuch house for over a week while Balwina mothered him and readied him to live as a Gentile. She renamed him "Jusek Polewski," taught him the catechism and a few prayers, and warned him never to be seen naked, since his circumcised penis would betray him. Then, because he was known in this area, she devised a long-range survival plan for him: He was to make his way northward from village to village, posing as a boy whose family was hard up and who was seeking work as a stable hand.

He found just such a job with a childless couple, Marion and Anna Padworski, in Biesnik, several miles to the north. (At that time, even a few miles in the backward and hilly Carpathian countryside was enough to separate him from anyone who might recognize him.) The Padworskis had acquired a farm whose Jewish owners had been forcibly removed to a ghetto; having no one to help with the cows, they were glad to take the boy on. They believed he was Jusek Polewski of Lyrzna, whose widowed mother would come some day to negotiate his wages with Mr. Padworski. Jusek/Shmulek continually made excuses for her failure to arrive (he usually said she was ailing), and Padworski never seemed suspicious.

Still a mere boy, Jusek/Shmulek led a bitter life: Totally isolated, without family or friends, he worked all the time, slept in the stable, and came inside only at mealtimes. Even those moments of respite were less than welcome, since he constantly feared that some slip of the tongue or reaction to things the Padworskis said—Mr. Padworski was pleased that the Nazis were exterminating Poland's Jews—would give him away and bring a swift, fearful end to his misery.

His only support came from Balwina Piecuch, who from time to time sent Staszek to see how he was and to bring him a message of encouragement. "Staszek would stay out of sight in the bushes until I came near, tending the livestock," Oliner recalls. "He'd wave to me and I'd sneak away and we'd talk. Sometimes he'd bring a warning from his mother like, 'Be extra careful, there's going to be a search for Jews in the next few days.' Once I had a dream in which my mother warned me that Balwina was going to inform on me, so I told Staszek I didn't like my job and was going to leave it; I wanted Balwina to think I would be gone. But the very next day he came back and said, 'My mother said to tell you, "I'm keeping an eye on you. You're well adjusted there, and I don't hear any rumors about you. You're safe. Stay." ' And I believed her, and I stayed."

He endured this slavelike existence for over two and a half years; at times it seemed the only life he had ever known. Then, in March 1945, Russian troops advanced through Biesnik, and shortly Balwina sent Staszek to get him. Shmulek told the Padworskis that Staszek had brought word that his mother was very ill, and left. He proceeded with Staszek to the Piecuch house, where Balwina wept over him, hugged and kissed him, and said, "You're safe. You don't have to be afraid anymore."

Dazed and totally unprepared for freedom, Shmulek was taken in hand by a Jewish survivor, an old friend of his father's who helped him reclaim his father's land (which he turned over to the Piecuchs) and found him a place to live with a group of young Jewish survivors in a nearby town. For a while, Shmulek earned his keep by doing odd jobs for Russian occupation officers, but it was a life with no rewards and no future; he was an illiterate, ignorant, lonely, and emotionally traumatized fifteen-year-old whose most formative experience had been the slaughter of his entire family and the abrupt end of the world he had known.

After a while, however, he heard that he might be eligible for sponsorship as an orphan immigrant by the Jewish Refugee Committee of England. He applied, and in time was accepted, shipped to England, and for three years lived with other orphaned youths at a small academy near Canterbury, where he got the rudiments of an education. Then for three more years he eked out a barren, lonely existence as a cabinetmaker's apprentice in London, where he lived in a shabby rented room. Meanwhile, with Committee help he tried to locate any relative in the United States who would sponsor his immigration. Eventually a Brooklyn businessman named Saul Oliner, a distant cousin he'd never heard of, agreed to do so, and in December 1950, Samuel Oliner—he had by now anglicized his first name—arrived in New York.

There, for the first time since the day of wrath at Bobowa, he was among friends. But it did little to change him; although he worked in Saul Oliner's hairnet importing firm and occasionally socialized with distant cousins, he remained deeply traumatized, bitter, often darkly moody, and without a goal. But after being drafted and serving for two years in Korea, he was entitled to educational benefits under the GI Bill of Rights and enrolled at Brooklyn College; there he discovered sociology and a sustaining interest—the scientific study of what makes people behave as they do. But it did not occur to him then or for many years that through social science he might see humankind in a kinder light and come to terms with his past.

By his mid-twenties Oliner had married a young graduate student in education, moved to San Francisco, started a little drapery business while pursuing graduate studies in sociology at the Berkeley campus of the University of California, and fathered three sons; still, he remained, in his own understated words, "wary of people," "mistrustful," and "disillusioned." His wife Pearl, a tall, amiable woman with a faintly schoolteacherish manner, recalls the Samuel Oliner of those years: "He had put the past on hold. He told me very little about it or about his feelings and hardly ever talked about those matters with others. But it was always there inside him. For many years he would often have nightmares of being chased and would shout in his sleep, and I'd have to wake him and calm him. He didn't really encounter his past and deal with it until he began teaching the Holocaust at Humboldt."

That did not take place until Oliner was forty-eight. In 1971, at forty-one, he had completed his Ph.D. requirements, been appointed to the faculty at Humboldt, and sold his business. With so late an entry into the field, he did not expect ever to do any major research nor did he have an overpowering interest in any subject needing investigation. But after half a dozen years of teaching at Humboldt, all that changed.

"When some people began denying that the Holocaust had ever happened," he told me when I visited him, "I felt I had to start teaching the facts. The department chairman agreed and I began giving the Holocaust course in the fall of 1977." In so doing, Oliner could not help reliving his past experiences. Week after week the lecture material he prepared brought back excruciating memories: of his peaceful boyhood on the farm so abruptly ended by the German invasion of Poland; of his beautiful teenage sister weeping as she came home from a Gestapo station where two officers had raped her; of his white-haired grandfather being shoved against a hot stove and then knocked to the floor by a Nazi officer; of the crying and screaming the day of the exodus from Bobowa; of the pit in the forest at Garbacz that he had forced himself to visit after his liberation.

Oliner had expected teaching the course to cause him personal misery but had not foreseen that it would create despair in his students, most of them non-Jews. "Sam would come home and sit in the recliner by the window, silent and sunk in gloom," Pearl Oliner recalls. "After a while he'd tell me how students had cried as he spoke, and he'd wonder if he were doing the right thing."

One spring day in 1978, at the end of a lecture, a young woman student came up to him, tears welling from her eyes. Speaking with a German accent, she said, "Professor Oliner, I'm quitting the course. I can't stand the guilt over what my people did."

Oliner, pained for her, said, "But it wasn't your *people*, it was *some* of them." He drew a distinction between Germans and Nazis, and assured her that in the midst of the Holocaust, some Gentiles, including Germans, heedless of danger, had hidden and cared for Jews. After hearing him out, she felt able to remain in the course, but the incident, he told me, had a profound effect on him:

"I recognized that it distorts the image of humanity to focus only on the negative," he said. "Millions couldn't or wouldn't help, but others risked their lives to save Jews, as Balwina Piecuch saved me. I hadn't been bringing that into the picture. I saw that I had to deal with the Holocaust from a different perspective. I had to give my students a balanced view of humankind. And I had to have such a view myself.

"So I applied to a small foundation administered by the university for a minor grant to develop a project I called 'Altruism in Nazi-Occupied Europe.' I got the grant, and at the end of the academic year I took my sabbatical and went to Berkeley, where there was an institute devoted to the study of the Gentile rescuers of Jews. It was called The Institute for Righteous Acts—in Israel, the rescuers are known as 'the righteous among the nations'—and in the 1960s it had sponsored research on the rescuers and then become inactive. In 1978 the Institute was only two file cabinets full of research materials, but it was a good place to start my work."

The Institute for Righteous Acts had been the idea of Rabbi Harold Schulweis of Oakland, California. Schulweis had read in historian Philip Friedman's *Their Brothers' Keepers* that some Christians had risked their lives to rescue Jews from the Nazis. (Later research established that there were at least fifty thousand such rescuers, who saved some two hundred thousand Jews from death.) Schulweis urged the director of the Judah Magnes Memorial Museum, Seymour Fromer, to create an institute to do research on rescuers, a subject he said had great potential value for moral education. Fromer was persuaded; the Museum and several other donors provided funds for a pilot study by a psychologist named Perry London who, in the course of four years, gathered material and located and interviewed twenty-seven rescuers and a number of rescued persons. Then the funds ran out, London ended his study, and the Institute went into hibernation.

Oliner spent some weeks reading his way through the Institute's files; then he began seeking out and interviewing rescuers who had emigrated to the United States and Canada. His interviews with aging Danes, Poles, Germans, and others elicited tales of compassion and succor that sometimes made him choke up. But as a social scientist he wanted much more than deeply moving narratives; he wanted to find out, through research, what psychological and social influences had caused the rescuers to behave as they did.

To do so he needed hypotheses that would generate the right questions to ask them. In the Institute files he had found three, tentatively offered by Perry London in a brief final report: Rescuers tended to have a spirit of adventurousness, to identify strongly with a highly moral parent, and to feel socially marginal—like outsiders—in their own communities. Oliner wasn't satisfied: "I couldn't see how he came to his conclusions except impressionistically," he says. "There weren't any real data, nor was there any statistical analysis showing how likely it was that the results were real and not due to sampling error." Nor did the hypothesis of adventurousness ring true to Oliner; it seemed a trivial and unconvincing explanation of the kind of benevolence he had personally experienced.

In search of other and better explanations he began reading his way through hundreds of studies of prosocial behavior. He found in them a bewildering but exciting profusion of hypotheses and made copious notes of those that dealt specifically with altruism: that it is the socially determined outgrowth of a natural empathic reaction to others' distress; that high self-esteem and a strong sense of autonomy make people so secure that they can rise above self-interest to do what is good for others; that altruism is either elicited or inhibited by external circumstances such as the absence or presence of other people; that it stems from social norms internalized during childhood; that it is a conditioned response children learn through example and praise; that it is a largely inherited trait, the product of specific but as yet unidentified genes; and so on and on.

After a year or two, Oliner's immersion in the scientific literature of altruism had not only familiarized him with the field but begun to alter his view of humanity and, with it, his personality. Various acquaintances found him becoming genial, gentle, fun to be with, and even, says one colleague, lovable. Friends of long standing, dining at the Oliner house, were surprised to learn that Sam himself had baked the bread they were eating, and equally surprised when, in the course of animated conversation, he would illustrate a point by telling a joke, often of the genre in which the village fool proves wiser than the rabbi.

His reading had also turned him into a man possessed—no

longer by the demons of the past but by the dream of doing a major study, before time ran out, of altruism as personified by the rescuers, now an aging and waning group. To do so, however, he would have to solve two problems.

The first was that he had compiled a list of over forty hypotheses about altruism, far too many to test at one time, particularly by means of a questionnaire. The genetic hypothesis he could exclude out of hand as being outside his real interest: "All the evidence," he says, "indicates that whatever our inherited predispositions, we can be made either more or less altruistic by experience and psychosocial factors—and since these are potentially within human control, they're what interested me." He also excluded many other hypotheses as not central to his concern: "Many of the situations in laboratory experiments last perhaps half an hour and induce only shallow levels of distress and minor altruistic acts. I wanted to test hypotheses relevant to the profound altruism of those who risked their very lives, often for years, to help others who were unrelated to them and often strangers to them." In the end, he had winnowed the list down to thirteen.

His second problem was to obtain a research grant. By pure luck, his name came to the attention of a man who had some money at his disposal and who wanted to back just such a project. Dr. John Slawson, formerly a social psychologist at Columbia University, had been executive vice president of the American Jewish Committee for many years. In 1944 he had proposed what became a classic study of prejudice, *The Authoritarian Personality,* the work of a team of social scientists, and he had long wanted to set in motion a study of the obverse phenomenon, the altruistic personality. When he retired in 1981, the AJC honored him by putting at his disposal a fund for a research project of his own choice. He drew up a memo outlining his ideas for a "Good Samaritan/Rescuer Project," the gist of which he summed up in a letter to another foundation executive:

> Perhaps we can obtain a portrait of the Altruist—the motivations for his acts of mercy and willingness to face the risk of torture and certain death by taking this action. What was the rescuer's character structure, personality pattern, early socialization influences? . . . Hopefully, we may be assisted by our findings to say something of value, in general, about this type of altruistic behavior in our daily lives.

Looking for a research director, Slawson sounded out a number of well-known social scientists, but none seemed to him to have a passionate interest in the project. Then he heard about Oliner from Rabbi Schulweis and William Helmreich, chairman of the sociology department at City College, and invited him to come to New York to talk. Although Oliner had no name in sociology, Slawson found him intensely dedicated to the subject, and after much discussion of methodology decided to give him $150,000 for what Oliner was by then calling the "Altruistic Personality Project." Slawson wangled another smaller grant for him from the Revson Foundation, and Oliner raised some additional funds by contracting with The Free Press for a book about the project.

In late 1982, Oliner plunged into frenetic work on research design and staffing. He told me about these phases of the project in some detail:

"First," he said, "I and my advisors, and several colleagues at Humboldt who agreed to help, discussed what kinds of rescuers to include. Nechama Tec, a sociologist, tells in her book *Dry Tears* how she and her parents, Polish Jews, lived in hiding for three years with Polish Christians who took them in only because they could pay. That's not altruism. Our definition of altruism is: helping someone who will benefit from your help, which involves risk and cost to you but for which you neither expect nor want external rewards. I specify 'external' rewards because feeling good about what you're doing and about yourself is a reward, an internal one. But many rescuers didn't think about even that kind of reward when they undertook to save someone.

"My original plan was to gather a sample of rescuers and interview them, asking them to tell their story in their own words and also asking about what kind of childhood they'd had, what kind of role models they grew up with, how well they thought of themselves, what kinds of experience of Jews they'd had before the Nazi era, and so on. Of course, relying on such interviews involves terrible methodological problems—after so many years people may have forgotten much, or come to see things differently from how they were, or they may want to make themselves look good. But I meant to use only cases authenticated at Yad Vashem, the memorial center in Israel that collects and verifies cases of rescuers. Also, I planned to collect rescued-rescuer pairs whenever possible, to see how reliable the rescuers' stories were. I did eventually gather about a score of such pairs, and in every case the survivor's story confirmed what the rescuer said, so it looked as if we could have a good deal of confidence in what verified rescuers told us.

"My first informal proposal didn't call for a control group, but fairly early on, several people I talked to urged me to have controls and to look for factors differentiating rescuers from others. The controls weren't to be *evil* people, just people who were demographically similar to the rescuers and who could have helped but didn't. I knew the value of using controls—and I also knew the serious problems involved in finding them and getting their cooperation. But I decided it was worth trying. As things turned out, I believe the rescuer-control comparisons are the central and most valuable aspect of the study.

"Then there was the problem of what questions to ask in order to elicit the data we needed. We racked our brains over that. I visited survey research centers in Michigan and Berkeley and got advice about the questions, and about survey and questionnaire design, from a lot of people, including my former professor at Berkeley, Neil Smelser, a distinguished researcher, who agreed to be our chief methodological advisor. In the end my team and I decided on a combination of closed-end questions for all the points on which we needed concrete information, plus an open-ended narrative in which the person would ramble on, telling his or her story. We based our questions on the thirteen hypotheses I had selected. These fell into three clusters: situational factors that might have influenced the person to act or not to act as a rescuer, the person's attitudes and values, and his or her personality traits.

"In most cases we thought up, worked out, and pretested the questions ourselves. But for certain important hypotheses involving traits of personality, there already existed excellent 'scales'—well-validated sets of questions measuring those traits. So we included questions from four such scales: on self-esteem, social responsibility, empathy, and sense of autonomy or control over one's life.

"The final version of the questionnaire ran to sixty-six pages and included some four hundred questions, though not everybody got asked all of them. The interviews took anywhere from two to twelve hours to complete. Even so, we had to leave out a great many questions we wanted to ask, because for economic reasons the questionnaire had to be manageable in a single interview."

In March 1983, while the questionnaire was in the early stages of development, Oliner went to Europe to seek the help of social scientists in France, Germany, and Poland in training and supervising interviewers in those countries. (In America, he and his team did their own interviewing.) His goal being manifestly worthy and his pleas impassioned, he found willing associates in all three countries and the United States, and, later, in Italy, Holland, and Norway. Like Oliner and his wife, who, also a professor at Humboldt, worked on the project with him and coauthored the book, neither the European supervisors nor his Humboldt colleagues received any pay for their work; the subject motivated them to donate their time and effort. As Paul Crosbie, a sociologist at Humboldt, told me, "Sam asked my advice, and in order to answer him I had to read some of the questionnaires. That hooked me. It was inspiring." He ended up donating seven months of his leisure time to working out the computer program for compiling and analyzing the question-naire data.

From Poland Oliner went to Israel, where he spent a week in the archival vault at Yad Vashem reading through a substantial portion of the 5,700-odd cases on file there and selecting some five hundred names as possible interviewees. Later he gleaned others from the files of the Institute for Righteous Acts and by means of a letter he sent to 5,500 American rabbis, asking them to help locate rescuers. In the end, his staff completed interviews with 406 rescuers, 126 controls, and 150 rescued survivors.

"Of course," he says of this sample, "it isn't ideal from a methodological point of view—it's not a random sample. But since only a small fraction of rescuers are known, there's no way to get a random sample. Still, in many respects it's pretty good because it includes people from all walks of life, all kinds of educational and economic background, and all kinds of families.

"As for the controls, each of our foreign supervisors studied the demographic characteristics of our sample of rescuers in his or her own country and then, using directories and such devices, went out and gathered a sample of nonrescuers who came from the same places and were of comparable age, sex, and education. Again, our 126 controls aren't a random sample, but they're a *matched* sample— they match the rescuers in major demographic traits. How they *differ* from them is what we wanted to find out."

For five years Oliner, outside his teaching duties, was an early-rising, late-working, seven-days-a-week chief executive officer, that being the role of the principal scientific investigator of such a research project. He wrote countless letters advising, cajoling, and directing his supervisors and interviewers; made innumerable phone calls to them to discuss scientific procedures and to urge haste; chaired frequent staff conferences on all sorts of issues; reviewed and critiqued the computer printouts, analyses, and rough drafts of the findings written by others; and, usually in the middle of the night, wrestled with the practical and theoretical problems of the project.

"Sam was an incredibly driven person," Paul Crosbie told me. "And he expected everyone else to be as dedicated and driven as he. That made him tough to work with, but you couldn't get mad at him—his intentions and his motives were so obviously good." Jack Schaffer, a professor of psychology and close friend of Oliner's, says, "I've often wondered why Sam drove himself the way he did. My guess: Many Holocaust survivors have a sense of mission because they ask themselves why they're survivors while so many others died. Part of Sam's answer, I think, is to *contribute* something valuable."

Oliner's intimates say that his research healed him. As Rabbi Schulweis puts it, "His work on rescuers was for him the therapy of knowledge. He found the spark of decency in human beings. It was a morally educative experience." Douglas Huneke, a Presbyterian minister who knows Oliner and has himself interviewed rescuers and written a biography of Herman Graebe, says, "Sam had a sense of absolute urgency, of the great importance of the work. It was a compelling passion with him, and a great fulfillment for him."

Fulfillment began to come to Oliner soon after the interviewing of rescuers got under way in late 1983. As batches of completed and translated interviews and questionnaires arrived on his desk, he read them with a growing sense of excitement and exaltation. He could see bits and pieces of evidence supporting many of his hypotheses and, intriguingly, refuting some others. He also found many of the interviews moving, and reading through them often became somewhat tearful; to show me why, he pulled a number of manila folders out of a drawer in a cluttered little office and invited me to sit down and read for a while. It didn't take long to see what he meant. From my notes:

File 310: Young Warsaw housewife during the war. Q: What got her started as a rescuer? "At the beginning there were these miserable Jewish children in the streets. They sneaked out of the ghetto through the sewers and sat motionless near shops. Legs thin as sticks, covered with ulcers. One could only cry. What crime did they commit to be so punished?" Q: Why did she continue to help? "Pity, just that. I was sorry for them, sorry to see them suffering."

File 274: Was nearing ordination as a priest in 1943 in northern Italy. Jewish acquaintance asked him to help him make his way through Alpine valleys to Switzerland. "I said I needed some time to think about it. The next day I agreed to take him." Q: Why? "Friendship and charity for people who were being persecuted." Having helped one person, he felt like helping all who heard about him; made a hundred trips; was arrested, jailed for months; was released when a cardinal intervened and got him to promise not to do any more rescuing (but when released, he promptly went back to doing so).

File 314: Was a middle-aged Oslo housewife during the war. Made many hair-raising trips across the border to help Jews escape from Nazi-controlled Norway to Sweden. Q: Did she think about the risk she was taking? "It was quite clear what it was. I didn't even think about it. It didn't prevent me from doing what I thought was right."

File 336: Dutch insurance clerk, in his 30s during the war. When Nazis began sending Jews to death camps, he started hiding them in his home and sending them on to more permanent safe addresses. Q: Did he think about risk he was taking? "Didn't stop to think about it. It just had to be done. These people had to be kept from the hands of the Germans."

As the cases poured in, Oliner was struck by the complexity and variability of the phenomenon of altruism. Some rescuers had acted instantly, others had had to think it over; some had been afraid, others not; some had acted out of pity, others out of a sense of duty. Some had done nothing until a haggard, desperate fugitive begged them for help, others saw such a person in the streets and said, "Come home with me." Some sheltered a single person for a brief period, others housed and fed entire families for months or years.

Oliner could see, too, that analysis of the data was likely to yield some surprises. "One rescuer I myself interviewed," he told me, "was a Swiss Seventh-Day Adventist whose father wouldn't send him to school on the sabbath and was jailed as a result. I figured he became a rescuer because he was socially marginal, had suffered, and was religious—but discovered that in fact he was a highly self-confident fellow who didn't feel at all marginal, didn't feel he'd suffered, and wasn't particularly devout. Again, while the prosocial research literature laid a lot of emphasis on high self-esteem, some of the rescuers in the interviews I was reading had distinctly little self-esteem."

But these were only early and subjective reactions to Oliner's reading of the questionnaires; what was far more exciting and fulfilling was the computerized tabulation and analysis of the data. For only analysis could yield statistical proof or disproof of the hypotheses. First, it would show which experiences and traits were predominant among the rescuers. Second, it would compare these data with a similar analysis of the controls: If nonrescuers, though like the rescuers in most other ways, lacked certain experiences or traits common in rescuers, those experiences or traits were probably crucial to altruistic behavior.

Of course, any such differences between rescuers and controls might be the result of chance selection, just as bridge hands differ purely by accidents of distribution. But since rescuers and controls were alike in major ways, Oliner could feel fairly certain that the differences in their behavior weren't due merely to the luck of the draw.

Fairly certain, however, isn't good enough. The scientific criterion of credibility is called "statistical significance"; it's determined by subjecting the data to such tests as chi-square analysis, ANOVA (analysis of variance), multivariate analysis, and discriminant analysis. These procedures, carried out for the project by psychologists Donald Bowlus and Mary Gruber at Humboldt, deduce from the size of the samples, the average size of the differences between them, and so on, how confident one can be that any correlations are due to real connections among the factors and not to mere accidents of sampling.

If the computations were to show a 50 percent chance that a particular difference between rescuers and controls was due to accident, Oliner could have no confidence that the difference meant anything. But if the computations showed a 95 percent chance that it was real and only a 5 percent chance that it was due to accident, the difference would be "significant" and he could be fairly confident that it pointed to a causal connection. And if there was only a 1 percent chance that the difference was accidental, he could be highly confident that he had found something meaningful.

* * *

Not until mid-1986, after three and a half years of unremitting work, were the data in good enough shape for statistical analysis to get under way. But then, as the university computer began spitting out page after page of calculations, the shape and scope of the findings of the Altruistic Personality Project emerged. It was clear at once that they were of major importance. No less an authority on altruism than Ervin Staub would say two years later, in a review of *The Altruistic Personality: Rescuers of Jews in Nazi Europe,* the 1988 book in which Samuel and Pearl Oliner reported the results, that the work is "the most extensive, most in-depth study [of the rescuers] to date," and that its findings "confirm, importantly extend, and add to, previous findings on rescuers and in the study of altruism; a few of their results conflict with or disconfirm the results of past research."

While the book was still in preparation, I spent much of one afternoon in Pearl Oliner's office with both Oliners discussing the results of the data analysis. (Pearl Oliner, with a doctorate in education, is very much at home with the methodology and results of the study.) Oliner began by speaking about the hypotheses the data had disconfirmed:

"When I first came upon the marginal-man thesis," he said, "I thought, 'Wow! There *must* be something to that.' It sounded highly plausible. But when the computer runs started coming out, it simply didn't hold up. The overwhelming majority of our rescuers—eighty percent—contrary to the marginality hypothesis, had a sense of belonging to their communities, and were no different in that respect from the controls.

"Nor did London's hypothesis that rescuers were adventurous pan out. You could always cite this or that case to make a point, but the data tell the truth: We found that there simply was no significant difference between rescuers and controls as to adventurousness.

"An even bigger surprise was what data analysis revealed about religiosity. Many people have claimed that religious ethics played a major role in rescuer behavior. The Danes saved nine tenths of their Jews by ferrying them to Sweden in fishing boats, and some say that's because of the Danish religious ethic. And there was the famous rescue work done by Pastor André Trocmé and his Protestant parishioners at Le Chambon in France. But those are exceptions, not the rule. We were astonished to find that although ninety percent of our rescuers had had a religious upbringing, only fifteen percent cited religion as the main reason for what they did, and that there was no significant difference between rescuers and controls as to religiosity.

"And self-esteem—now there was a real surprise! We had originally felt sure, based on early altruism studies, that it would make a hell of a lot of difference, but analysis showed that it didn't seem to matter. Some people with high self-esteem didn't help the Jews, some did; some nonrescuers had low self-esteem, but so did some rescuers. Overall, there was no difference between the two groups. But that ties in with recent suggestions by some researchers that both high self-esteem and low self-esteem can motivate people—for different reasons—to help others."

Pearl Oliner, thumbing through a foot-deep stack of computer printouts, added that two other hypotheses had not been borne out by data analysis:

"We expected, naturally, that how people felt about the Nazis would be highly correlated with rescuing or nonrescuing," she said. "It wasn't. Nearly the same proportion of controls as rescuers had been opposed to them; being anti-Nazi wasn't enough to make people rescuers.

"And generally, circumstances made far less difference than the laboratory research would seem to suggest. By circumstances I don't mean the presence or absence of other people but the overall life situation of the individual—where the interviewees lived, or how many people were in their household, or whether there were children in the home who would be endangered by rescue activities. Neither these nor most other circumstances made any difference. Not even their resources seemed to matter. You might think that having an extra room in the house would make them more likely to take people in, but it didn't; if they felt the urge to rescue someone, they did it under the most difficult circumstances."

Then what factors *did* matter, I asked. Pearl Oliner started by mentioning two that had moderate statistical significance:

"Having a network of people—family or friends who could lend them emotional and practical support—made some difference," she said. "So did having lived near Jews earlier in life; some rescuers had had Jewish friends, but many others had merely known Jews who existed on the peripheries of their social world in schools, gymnasiums, and universities. Both of these findings, which we had expected, were weakly confirmed. And we had hypothesized that rescuers would have a sense of autonomy—of being in control of their own lives—and nonrescuers a sense of powerlessness. That was somewhat more strongly confirmed.

"But it's the highly significant differences between rescuers and controls that are most interesting. We found that rescuers were definitely more empathic and more easily moved by pain than non-rescuers, and 37 percent of our rescuers attributed their first helping act to an empathic reaction. Rescuers also generally had a strong sense of personal and social responsibility for others—a norm-based belief about how they should act—and that moved more than half of them to perform their first helping act."

Oliner then got to the central issue: "The most important question," he said, "is how the rescuers got to be that way. We hypothesized, based on many studies in the literature of child development, that the way parents disciplined rescuers and nonrescuers would prove to be one of the crucial factors. And it was." He asked Pearl to cite the data from her printout; she leafed through it and announced what she found:

"Just as many rescuers as nonrescuers were disciplined by their parents for bad behavior—but the parents of rescuers depended significantly less on physical punishment and significantly more on reasoning or explaining than the parents of nonrescuers did. The difference is great enough to make us 99.9 percent confident of that finding. That's confident!

"Praise by parents for good or kind behavior is another significant factor in creating the altruistic personality. So is modeling: Closeness to the parents was very important, and being close to a parent who was a good role model of caring behavior was *extremely* significant—it reached the level of *total* confidence, that is, we feel one hundred per cent certain that the difference is real rather than accidental."

I had been wondering how all these findings tied together, if indeed they did, and as if reading my mind, Oliner spoke up about a finding he'd been saving for the last:

"The most exciting thing coming out so far," he said, "is a dimension that combines traits of personality, internalized values, and how the person was socialized in the home—the most strongly correlated, strongly positive factors we've been talking about.

"It also incorporates attitudes towards others who are different from one's self—how far outside one's own group one still sees people as being like one's self, as fellow people and not 'them.' We measured that trait with a string of questions such as, 'Before the war, did you think Turks—or Gypsies, or Jews, and so on—were very much like you, somewhat like you, not very much like you, or not like you at all?'

"We invented this dimension, which we call 'extensivity.' It's the extent to which caring goes—how far it reaches out to include outsiders and not just the intimates in your ingroup, and how strongly you feel that justice is not just for yourself and your own kind but for others beyond your group. We tested the idea: We compiled extensivity ratings for our cases and then, using only those ratings, we found we could correctly identify individuals as rescuers or controls 73 percent of the time. Extensivity is the essence of the altruistic personality—and the data give every reason to believe that it's teachable."

These days Samuel Oliner is no longer driven; work continues, but at a relaxed pace, on an additional 150 questionnaire-and-interview protocols that have trickled in and on detailed analyses of the data by gender, nationality, and other factors. Such findings will be of value to specialists, but Oliner is confident that it is the broader conclusions of the Altruistic Personality Project that can be put to use by teachers, parents, and policy-makers to promote and increase the extent of altruism throughout society. He himself, however, does not offer prescriptions as to how to do that; he spoke about this on the last night of my visit to him:

"I'm certain that we can incorporate the implications of the study in the classroom and the home, but I'm not clear about exactly how to do it, or at what grade level," he said. "Nor have we tried to spell out the specifics of applying the findings to child-rearing, or to social policies. The *what* of altruism is our work; the *how* to use that knowledge is for others—educators, developmental psychologists, and applied sociologists—to work out.

"For me, however, there is one clear implication. I believe very strongly that the Holocaust has to be taught not only in colleges but in high schools, and understood as part and parcel of Western history—not in order to wallow in morbidity but because it is a lesson in how humanity can lose its direction, its humanness.

"But a course made up only of horrors and bad news about humanity is terribly discouraging and leaves students in a state of desperation. Our findings make it possible to teach the course constructively. If you say to the students, 'Humanity is not all bad.

Look at the empirical evidence,' and offer them some examples and some of the findings about altruism, it makes the Holocaust material tolerable. It gives them a balanced view of humanity.

"I think many people are desperate for that balanced view and the hope that it makes possible. They need proof that humanity has not totally lost its soul, they crave some good news about human nature. And there *is* some good news."

I asked, as a last question, how much the project had done for his own outlook on humanity and life. Perhaps afraid to sound treacly, he answered slowly and with caution: "The project has made me feel . . . better," he said. "I find myself feeling grateful to the people who cared. It's because of some of those people that I'm here. It's because of many others that many of us are here. There *are* such people in the world—and we can teach our children to be like them."

He was silent for a moment, then added, "I have found this type of research fascinating because it gives us insight into the variety of human behaviors, the possibility of people's behaving in so many different ways—including caring, giving, loving ways. It's inspiring, really."

Again he said nothing for a moment, then added, "I haven't had a nightmare for months."

KNOW THYSELF

Having read this far, you have already applied the research findings in one important and effective way: By learning about them, you have changed yourself. For as people come to know what underlies their responses, whether positive or negative, to the needs and distress of others, their new self-knowledge alters their attitudes and, thereby, their behavior.

Some will dispute this, arguing that attitudes, even when based on knowledge, do not determine how people actually behave. Many whites, for instance, who claim to be unprejudiced against blacks will flee their neighborhoods if blacks begin moving in. But recent psychological research has shown that while general attitudes (such as being unprejudiced against blacks) may not translate into specific behaviors, specific attitudes (such as willingness to have black neighbors) do; whites who have no objection to black neighbors don't flee them.

Other people may argue that behavior is determined mainly by existential forces; attitudes only link those forces to behavior. Marxists maintain that the means of production and its ownership dictate both our ideology and our behavior. Sociologists name as the determinants not only the means of production but class, occupation, the power structure, ethnic affiliation, culture, and many other social phenomena. Economists and geopoliticians stress such influences as geography and natural resources, climate, drought, and famine; historians, still others.

But while all of these play a part in the end result, history bears ample witness to the power of knowledge and the attitudes it begets to alter the way human beings act. One need only recall the vast changes in human behavior resulting from the development of clocks, calendars, and the alphabet, the Copernican view of the solar system, the germ theory of disease, birth control, the light bulb, electric motor, and computer.

Similarly sweeping changes in our culture have been brought about by psychological knowledge, particularly within recent decades. Among the educated, most people no longer regard emotional disorders as the result of sin or weakness of character or deal with them on that basis, most men no longer consider women mentally inferior or treat them as if they were, and most parents no longer regard children as little beasts whose unruly spirits need to be tamed or rear them on that assumption. In each case, knowledge has modified attitudes, and, through them, behavior.

We can therefore reasonably assume that knowledge about the altruistic impulse and the forces that inhibit or elicit it will affect our attitudes and, through them, our behavior.

And indeed we have already seen proof of this. Many studies cited in early chapters have shown that when children or young adults see examples of altruism, are told about its results in reasoned terms, or have hands-on experience of helping, their attitudes and their behavior become more altruistic.

Recall, for instance, Shalom Schwartz's follow-up study of undergraduates who had taken part in bystander studies and afterward been debriefed (told of the purposes of the study). When Schwartz, a year later, rigged a situation in which these same students came across a man in a neck brace and body brace lying on the floor in a stairwell, more of them offered help and were more helpful than in the experiment a year earlier; their previous experience and the explanations they received at that time left them with

a more positive attitude toward helping and made them more helpful than formerly.

Thus, it appears that whatever makes for altruistic attitudes
makes for altruistic behavior. That is why most of the altruism
researchers I talked to believe that wide dissemination of their findings would increase the readiness of people to be helpful to those
in need of help. When people learn what makes them indifferent,
callous, or unhelpful to specific others or in particular situations,
they will be less inclined to follow the impulse to pass by or ignore
the person in need; their knowledge frees them to overcome that
tendency and to act in accordance with their empathic and sympathetic feelings, and with their ideas of right and wrong.

I asked Bibb Latané, the doyen of bystander research and the
codiscoverer with John Darley of the bystander effect, what social
changes he thought might reduce the tendency of bystanders to do
nothing to help someone in distress if other people are present. "The
simplest and most direct change," he said, "would be an increased
awareness by the general public of the inhibiting effects of other
bystanders. To the extent that people become aware of the fact that
the presence of others may inhibit their acting as they would want
to act, they will better see the situation as it is and act the way they
would like to. What can make them aware? Books. Articles. TV
documentaries. Education in general. I don't think it will take place
immediately and directly, but I do think it can and probably will
happen."

Ervin Staub, in a letter replying to the same query, made the
same point:

> The spread of information about what inhibits helping
> would be extremely useful. Awareness of how the presence
> and behavior of others may inhibit us from responding to
> people in need and of our tendency to devalue those who suffer
> will reduce the power of these inhibitory forces. My belief in
> this is fortified by my own impression of greater sensitivity in
> students exposed to such information and by research findings.

He cited a study conducted by psychologist Arthur Beaman
and colleagues at the University of Montana. In it, unknowing
participants attended a lecture on emergency helping behavior in
which they learned about Latané and Darley's analysis of the causes
of the bystander effect. The participants later attended a second

lecture, but this time each was notified to come at a different time and arrived alone (the researchers did this so as to have control over the conditions of the experiment). When the students arrived, an instructor redirected them to a different building; as they left with another student who had just arrived—actually, the researchers' accomplice—they came upon a young man who had apparently just had a bicycle accident and was hurt. Although the accomplice played the part of a nonhelping bystander, two thirds of the participants went to the aid of the bicyclist. But in a control group of students who had not heard the helping lecture and who also came across the victim in the presence of the nonhelping bystander, only a little over one quarter offered help.

Staub's letter continued:

> Frequently, people do not even pay attention to others' needs or avoid getting engaged with those needs as they hurriedly pursue their own goals. As they become aware of this tendency, and of the intensity or urgency of others' needs, they are more likely to attend to and feel concern for the suffering of others. The end result is that at times their prosocial goals will outweigh their self-related goals.
>
> Altruistic behavior is also increased when people become aware of their own potential power not only to help but to induce others to help. I found in some of my own research that what one bystander (actually a confederate) said to another about the meaning of sounds of distress, or what should or should not be done, greatly increased or decreased helping by the other bystanders (Staub, 1974). Other research and many real-life examples from the Holocaust also show the great power of bystanders to influence each other; those who are aware of this will use their influence.

One more testimonial to the influence of knowledge-created awareness comes from *Emergency Intervention* by Jane Piliavin et al:

> In our society, we are trained from an early age to see the problems of other people as "none of our business," to close our feelings off from others' experiences. . . . We filter out— before we ever really "see" them—most of the problems, crises, and even the real emergencies occurring around us. . . . [But] students in classes we have taught that have gone into

helping in any detail always report an increased incidence of seeing emergencies.

Enough of these expert opinions; make your own experiment and see for yourself. In Chapter One, on pages 36–39, I invited you to take an altruism test and calculate your own altruism score; if you did, you may find it interesting to turn back now and take it again. You may well find that your consciousness of altruism has been raised and that your score is higher this time than the first.

REARING SAMARITANS

In the sandboxes of every public park, the same scene is played out time and again: One toddler tries to take another's toy, the second yowls and hits the first; the first hits back; and the two mothers intervene, crying "No, no!" and exhorting both children to "be nice" and to share with each other. Their intervention is all right as far as it goes, but it doesn't go very far; research data show that neither admonition nor exhortation does much to discourage selfishness and promote generosity. Most parents know very little about how to influence their children in this direction, but altruism research shows how they could do so effectively.

But a caveat is in order: Unlike the laboratory mouse, the human infant is not a purebred creature of known proclivities, and does not live in a controlled environment. Our children come into the world with varied predispositions and capabilities; furthermore, as they grow up many unpredictable random influences affect them—TV, neighbors, playmates and classmates, the vagaries of the economy, and others. As a result, no research-based program of parenting could unfailingly produce altruistic people; it could, though, help them become more that way than they would otherwise be.

Here are some of the elements of such a program:

Reinforcement

While many parents believe that both punishment and reward will train children to behave altruistically, the facts are otherwise.

As we have seen, forcing children (by threat or punishment) to desist from selfishness and to be helpful or generous doesn't change their character in the direction of altruism; they behave as told to only while the threat is hanging over them.

But, surprisingly, materially rewarding them for spontaneous kindness or helpfulness is little better: Studies have shown that children given concrete rewards for friendly and cooperative play are more friendly and cooperative as long as rewards are being given, but not afterward. In fact, children who are remunerated for being spontaneously kind or helpful are less likely to be so when the remuneration is no longer forthcoming. The reward undermines their incentive; they think they were behaving that way for the concrete benefit, not for its own sake.

But one kind of reward—self-approval—does strengthen and promote the altruistic impulse. When children are kind or helpful, praising them for it and telling them they're kind and generous— *labeling* them and their behavior—leads them to see themselves that way and to feel good about themselves; that leads to continued altruistic behavior.

Reasoning and Induction

We have also seen that preachments and exhortations to behave altruistically have relatively little effect. Reasoning with the child works better, even when the child is too young to fully grasp the explanation, and much better when the child is able to understand why caring and helping behavior are desirable.

Induction—explaining how both uncaring and caring behavior make the other person feel, and what their practical effects are— helps the child to see the event from the other person's point of view (role-taking) and, even more important, to vicariously feel the other's feelings (empathy).

But sometimes children's comprehension is too limited, or their self-centered desires too strong, for reasoning or induction alone to succeed; control of some sort—nonpunitive—may be needed. Martin Hoffman told me how he first gained insight into this component of the induction process: "One day, in the bathroom with my two-year-old daughter," he said, "I wanted her to stop doing something and do something else. I explained it inductively, I did just exactly the right thing, but she totally ignored me. So I took her by the shoulders and said firmly, 'Jill, I want you to listen to what I'm saying.' And she did. That's when I realized the value of power assertion in making a child listen and attend—it's the heart of my theory of induction."

Modeling

To recapitulate: The way parents treat their children is children's first and most important model of behavior. If their parents are kind and giving toward them, that becomes their idea of how to behave toward other people; harsh and ungiving parents teach the opposite.

Again, how parents treat people outside the family has considerable influence on children; the sons and daughters of widely altruistic people tend to be altruistic. The effect of such parental modeling, however, is deep and lasting only if the parent is warm and loving toward the child; only then does the child internalize the parent's values and behavior and make them its own. The same is true of reasoning.

Marian Radke-Yarrow, Phyllis Scott, and Carolyn Zahn-Waxler, of the Laboratory of Developmental Psychology (at the National Institute of Mental Health), conducted an experiment in which teachers were either cool or warm toward their pupils, and either told them about altruistic behavior or actually modeled it (toward figures in a diorama). Their conclusion:

> To extrapolate from the findings of this study to child rearing . . . the parent who is an altruist in the world but is cold with his child reaps a small harvest in developing altruism in his child. Further, the parent who conveys his values to the child didactically as tidy principles, and no more, accomplishes only that learning in the child. Generalized altruism would appear to be best learned from parents who not only try to inculcate the principles of altruism but who also manifest altruism in everyday interactions . . . [and whose] practices toward their children are consistent with their general altruism.

Hands-on Experience

Just as children learn from firsthand experience how to behave in company or in the classroom, so they can learn to be altruistic by having opportunities to be so. Ingenious and concerned parents can find or create learning-by-doing experiences for their children such as having them spend an hour or two a week visiting and socializing with residents of old-age homes, writing letters to or making toys for hospitalized poor children, taking food to a bedridden neighbor and serving him or her, and so on.

Says Ervin Staub, "Just as the ancient philosophers had proposed, moral behavior is learned through engagement in moral conduct. A prosocial behavioral tendency develops, in part, through participation in prosocial behavior."

ALTRUISM IN THE CURRICULUM

Can altruism be taught in the classroom? Or to be more precise: Can teaching it in the classroom actually make children altruistic?

Burlington, New Jersey, is a largely blue-collar town of about ten thousand people on the east bank of the Delaware River, less than an hour's drive northeast of Philadelphia. Just off the river in an area of shabby old row houses is the Elias Boudinot School, a flat, one-story building of modern design, all green-enameled panels and aluminum-framed windows. Inside, in spacious classrooms, 130 children from five to ten years old attend classes ranging from kindergarten through fourth grade. About 40 percent are black or Hispanic, and 20 percent come from families on welfare.

Boudinot is not an inner-city school by any means and most of its children are decently dressed and reasonably well-behaved, but it is hardly a place where one would expect to see altruism being taught in the classroom. Yet on a bright fall morning when I visit Boudinot, that is just what is happening in several of the classrooms.

"We're going to work on our character education today," Mrs. Olive Holmes, a slender, attractive black woman, tells her twenty-five fourth graders. Despite the formidable name of the topic, the children look delighted; they have found character education fun. And for good reason: It involves talking about themselves, listening to stories, playing guessing games, and play-acting, among other things. "How did you feel this morning when you woke up?" Mrs. Holmes asks. Hands shoot up; nearly everyone wants to tell.

"Grumpy" (the class giggles).

"Tired" (sympathetic groans).

"Cranky" (more giggles).

Mrs. Holmes asks Cranky, a handsome, snub-nosed black boy: "How did your mood affect your family?"

"I told my sister to get out of my room or I'd hit her!"

"How do you think that made her feel?"

"Um . . . um . . . bad, I guess—she cried."

"Was there another way to handle that? Let's all talk about that." And they do, for a few minutes, some in hesitant and uncertain whispers, others proudly stating answers they feel sure of, as does one pigtailed white girl: "You could tell her you're feeling cranky and you're sorry but please let you alone for a bit."

"Very good!" says Mrs. Holmes. Then she goes on, "We have two students in this class who were new here last week. I want all of you to think for a minute about how you would feel if you came to a new school and you didn't know anybody there or where to go." Silence, while everyone thinks about it. Then Mrs. Holmes reads aloud a little story about Janet, a fourth grader, who, with her little brother, is standing outside a new school, feeling alone and bewildered. Robert, a fifth grader, comes over to them, smiling, and offers to help them; he leads them to the principal's office, introduces them to the secretary, and tells them he'll meet them at lunch break and show them the cafeteria.

"Janet was impressed," Mrs. Holmes reads, "by . . . what was she impressed by?" The hands shoot up again.

"His personality."

"How nice he was."

"How kind he was."

Mrs. Holmes: "And how does it make people feel when someone is kind?"

"Comfortable."

"Happy."

"Warm."

"Very good," said Mrs. Holmes, "and now think about this: Would you do that? Would you be like Robert?" After letting them ponder that for a moment or two, she says, "Let's try it, now," and asks who would like to play the part of the new kids in school and who would like to be Mr. McNamara (the principal). Picking three out of the nearly unanimous show of hands, she has them step out outside; then "Mr. McNamara," a plump black boy, grinning proudly, brings the other two in and says, "Mrs. Holmes, I have two new students here, Michele and Bill," and leaves.

"Now," says Mrs. Holmes, "who will show us what to do?"

A girl: "Hi, Michele, I'll take you to your seat." (Mrs. Holmes: "Good!")

A boy: "Billy, make yourself comfortable here." ("That's good, too.")

A girl: "On be—, uh, uh, be—be*half* of the class, we welcome you." ("Very good!")

And so on.

In another classroom, third graders are getting a half hour of character education from Mrs. Elizabeth Piechowski, a stocky young white woman with a pleasant but no-nonsense manner. After having the class discuss what "generosity" means—their answers start with "kind" but, deftly steered by Mrs. Piechowski, become more focused, ending in "sharing" and "giving stuff to people"—she reads them a little story. Paul, Terry, and Kenny, the story goes, liked to play together, but whenever they played in Paul's backyard, he wouldn't let the others play with his toys. He'd snatch them away from Terry and Kenny, saying that they were his and he wanted to play with them. "Little by little," Mrs. Piechowski reads, "Terry and Kenny played with other boys until at last Paul found himself with no friends, all alone."

She closes the book and says, "Now, at each one of your six tables"—their desks are grouped into six clusters or "tables" of four or five each—"I would like you to spend five minutes discussing how you think this story could have had a different ending—what you would have done if you were Terry and Kenny, and maybe what you would have done if you were Paul. You have to think about both sides."

For the next five minutes the scene resembles an adult workshop or seminar: At each table, the children (who have done this before in previous weeks) intently and seriously debate what other things the three boys could have done to make things turn out better. Then Mrs. Piechowski says it's time to hear what ideas they've had. "Table One—Steven?"

Steven: "Help one another share."

Mrs. Piechowski: "All right, but how are you going to do that? Table Two—Nicole?"

Nicole: "If I was Paul I'd start by apologizing."

Mrs. Piechowski: "But if Paul doesn't, and you were Terry or Kenny, what might you do? Table Three—Danny?"

Danny: "One or both could visit Paul and talk to him, and maybe he'll change his mind."

Mrs. Piechowski: "Maybe that would work, maybe not. What else might they do? Anybody now, from any table."

Patricia: "Terry and Kenny could talk it over with Paul and then he might start to share with them."

Mrs. Piechowski: "What do you think they would say to Paul that would get him to do that?"

Keesha: "We want to be friends, so please share."

Steven: "If you don't share with us, we won't want to share with you."

Tammy: "They could say how it made them angry when he wouldn't share, and then he might change his mind."

So it goes for about ten minutes, moving from the vague to the specific and from empty pieties to emotional realities. Then Mrs. Piechowski sums up what they have discovered in their discussion: "We learned from our story that because of Paul's behavior, he lost his friends and was all alone. But he hadn't realized how his behavior made them feel. Maybe he didn't feel good about himself, and if you don't feel good about yourself, it isn't easy to share or to know how others feel. But when they told him, that helped him realize, and change."

At all grade levels in the Elias Boudinot school, children get character education once a week; so do the children in 40,000 other classrooms in 1,318 schools in 427 cities, all of which use curriculum materials developed by the American Institute for Character Education.

The AICE, a small nonprofit foundation based in San Antonio, was started twenty years ago by a retired college professor in an effort to introduce into classrooms the teaching of such basic moral and social values as honesty, generosity, tolerance, freedom of speech, the rights of others, and responsibility for one's own behavior. A second aim was to raise children's self-esteem in order to make them better able to resist peer pressure and to be aware of others' feelings.

With a grant of over $2 million from the Eli Lilly Endowment, a small staff signed up a sizeable cadre of classroom teachers to develop curriculum materials, based on research findings in education and psychology, by which to teach these values in kindergarten and the elementary grades. (Recently, the curriculum has been extended to higher grades.) The AICE, which today has a staff of four and several times that many volunteers, publishes and sells the materials and provides teacher-training seminars. The curriculum materials have been available to schools since 1980.

The term "character education" has right-wing and religious overtones, but the AICE's curriculum materials and the values they impart are not based on partisan ideology or religious doctrine. To be sure, the AICE materials have been most widely adopted in conservative and middle-of-the-road communities—in many of which Kiwanis Clubs have sponsored and paid for the materials and seminars—but they are now making their way into other areas as liberal teachers and parents become aware of the program's basis in research.

The growing use of the AICE materials is only one facet of a recent movement by educators across the spectrum of political opinion to include character education—or, as some prefer to call it, education in social behavior—in public school curricula. This reverses a long-term swing in the opposite direction. Moral education in the form of moralistic stories and pious precepts had been long been part of schooling in this nation, but by the turn of the century, as the population became a mishmash of subcultures, educators and the public became increasingly unsure that teaching morality in the classroom was appropriate. By the 1930s many educators were arguing that in a pluralistic society the schools had no business trying to foist the dominant group's morality on pupils. As a 1932 National Education Association report on character education asked, "Who are we, that we should attempt to tell you what you should do in order to be good?"

By the 1960s this view was dominant; educators, minority groups, and many elements of the general public believed in "value-free" education, and only conservatives still sought to have moral education—of the old type—included in public schooling. But in the 1970s, with the increase in crime and delinquency, the dropout phenomenon, and other social ills, educators, social scientists, and community leaders of all hues of political opinion began to rethink the matter.

And with the advent of research findings on prosocial behavior, the view began to emerge that the schools, microcosms of society, were the ideal place in which to develop children's social skills and promote their social development by teaching them cooperation, perceptiveness, empathy, and specific behaviors based on these traits. As J. Philippe Rushton wrote in 1982:

> Perhaps it is in the educational system . . . that society can most readily make a significant and active contribution to increasing prosocial competencies and motivations. It is time we turned to a far more intensive and disciplined program of prosocial education, in the widest sense of the term. How a child behaves and reasons and how he clarifies and acts on his values are all important and might be attended to more completely in schools than they are today.

This was character education of a new sort: not preachment and dogma but classroom experiences that could induce personal growth and social development; not based on political or religious ideology but on scientific knowledge of how prosocial feelings and behavior are acquired.

In the 1970s, the first of what would eventually be scores of experimental programs were begun in schools in many parts of the country. The new view of educators and behavioral scientists began filtering down to the general public, and by 1987 a Gallup survey found that 62 percent of adults felt that it was possible to develop character education courses acceptable to most people in the community, and 56 percent said that either the schools alone, or the schools as well as parents and churches, should teach such material.

Altruism is one of the most important components of character education, although it is rarely mentioned in the curriculum materials. They name, instead, responses and behaviors on which altruism is based; for instance, lessons like those I witnessed are labeled "Generosity, Kindness, Helpfulness and Politeness."

Do the AICE methods work? Principal William McNamara of the Boudinot school is convinced that they do: "I can see the changes in children's behavior," he told me. "There has definitely been a decrease in scuffling and fighting in the halls and the lunchroom. We haven't formally evaluated the results of the program in our school, but all of us feel certain that we're getting something of value across to our pupils."

Similar encomiums have come from many schools. Among the effects reported by a number of school principals: Better attendance, cleaner buildings and grounds, better feeling between teachers and pupils, improved classroom discipline, decreased vandalism. A few years ago the AICE sent a questionnaire to a sample of teachers who have used the materials and to the principals of their schools: Ninety-three percent of teachers who replied said that students' self-concept had improved, 85 percent that behavior in the classroom had improved, and large majorities that behavior in the lunchroom and the playground had improved. Majorities of the principals said the same thing, and 64 percent reported a decrease in vandalism.

All of which sounds almost too good to be true. But comparable results have been reported by many other sources.

Several dozen programs of empathy-training, using role-taking and other techniques, have been tested in schools in communities of various kinds; almost all have had positive results.

Other programs, using group discussions of various Kohlbergian moral dilemmas, have resulted in distinct gains in altruistic attitudes.

Still others have tested cooperative learning techniques on standard curriculum subjects; students work together in small groups to solve problems together and help each other. Both the research data and the testimony of teachers attest that such techniques increase prosocial and helping behavior.

The results of the AICE programs and of the many experiments and demonstrations just referred to make it seem probable that within the next decade or two prosocial education, in one form or another, will be a part of the curriculum in a great many American public schools. Conceivably, this may be the most effective application of the findings of altruism research.

One other note on the teaching of altruism in the classroom: In 1987, for the first time in this country's history, courses in philanthropy, funded largely by half a dozen foundations, were introduced into the undergraduate curricula of nine colleges and universities, and seven more began offering such courses in 1988. Some of the courses deal chiefly with philanthropy as a cultural phenomenon, but others come far closer to offering vicarious experience in altruism. Chapman College in California, for instance, calls its course "Self-Fulfillment and Service to Others," and students not only read the biographies and autobiographies of people whose lives were dedicated to voluntary service but examine the psychological, sociological, and philosophic bases of caring, benevolence, and generosity.

SOCIAL SUPPORTS

We have seen some ways in which the research findings can be used to promote the development of the humane personality. But the findings imply that in addition to building altruism into individuals, we can build it into our social structure—that is, modify the social environment so that it will foster altruistic behavior.*

Here are some suggestions toward that end by altruism researchers and other social scientists.

Creation of Incentives

Since the decision to help or not to help often involves cost-reward calculations, it would make sense to increase the rewards our social institutions offer for altruistic behavior. Altruism motivated by the hope of reward is not the purest kind, but the results are often as good as if it were.

At present, societies of physicians, teachers, lawyers, scientists, and other professionals have, as part of their general ethic, pious but vague statements about the public service that members ought to perform. They could do much better: They could spell out in detail the kinds and amounts of public service they expect or even require of members—and offer valuable credit for it. Such service might be a prerequisite to certification or membership in such societies and an ongoing requirement for the maintenance of good standing. Or it might be made the equivalent of other kinds of achievement; academic faculties, for instance, could give it as much weight toward tenure or promotion as the publishing of academic papers.

Pro bono service might also be given a cash value: To encourage top-notch surgeons and lawyers to give up valuable hours to altru-

---

*This nation's many social programs oblige society as a whole to help the poor, the ailing, the elderly, and others who need it. I am interested here, however, not in society's legal obligations to those in need but in those changes in custom and law that might increase the motivation of individuals and corporations to perform altruistic acts.

istic work, the income tax law might be revised to give substantial credit for it; conceivably, hours spent in that way might even be credited at the donor's usual per-hour rates.

Speaking of tax law, the recent changes reducing the tax benefits of philanthropy were in considerable part responsible for a marked dropoff in the growth of philanthropic giving of all sorts. In 1987 total giving was up 6.5 percent over the previous year— nearly twice as much as the inflation rate for 1987 but the smallest rise in a dozen years and only half as great as the rise in six of those years. Lawmakers would do well to restore the incentives to giving.

Citizen Crime-Reporting Programs

A number of experimental projects have been shown capable of counteracting the tendency of witnesses to a crime to do nothing if other witnesses are present; any or all of these programs, implemented on a large scale, could prevent future Kitty Genovese tragedies.

One is WhistleStop, in which witnesses blow a whistle to alert residents in their homes to call the police. Another is Radio Watch, in which citizens with two-way radios and members of CB clubs report crimes, fires, accidents, and other emergencies to the authorities.

Neighborhood watches and block projects bind neighbors together and promote mutually defensive and helpful activities.

State and federal laws making it an offense to fail to report a crime in progress might also help counteract the bystander effect.

Bystander Laws

Laws could oblige bystanders to give aid to accident victims or others in danger of harm or death. As noted above, they would have to be carefully drawn in order not to put an unfair burden on anyone and not to require anyone to risk his or her life to save another. Assuming such safeguards were built into the laws, they would be society's way of assigning responsibility to the bystander, thereby strengthening the motivation to help and counteracting the bystander effect.

Public Recognition of Corporate Altruism

Our society currently relies on regulatory agencies to keep business from polluting the environment, marketing noxious products, or performing other socially harmful acts. But all too often the agencies intervene only after substantial harm has been done. Social responsibility on the part of business—corporate altruism—would be a better answer, writes economist David Kennett of Vassar College:

> In some grey areas of particular sensitivity (for example, the marketing of potentially carcinogenic products) regulation cannot adequately perform the task without a greater degree of voluntary disclosure and restriction than at present. This is an area where altruistic behavior in the producer can achieve an end that regulation cannot, or only at great social cost.

Can management be truly altruistic? Adam Smith thought it unlikely: "I have never known much good done by merchants who affected to trade for the public good. It is an affectation, indeed, not very common among merchants and very few words are needed to dissuade them from it."

But perhaps systems of awards honoring socially responsible actions by businesses—and thus indirectly winning the honorees additional market share—might motivate them. Consumer organizations, Chambers of Commerce, and business and professional organizations could establish their own seals of approval for the products, services, and brand names of socially responsible businesses.

But it is necessary to draw the line at such overt commercialization of philanthropy as the current fad for "cause-related marketing," examples of which are MasterCard's reaching for extra business by advertising that a fraction of its receipts will go to six charities, and Miller Brewing Company's giving a penny to United Cerebral Palsy for each case of certain beers purchased. Maurice G. Gurin, chairman of the American Association of Fund-Raising Counsel Trust for Philanthropy (but speaking for himself), warns that such promotions damage the integrity of the philanthropic ideal: "A philanthropic gift should cost the donor something; it should not provide the donor a profit. If commercially based funding becomes widespread, it will seriously affect motives for philanthropic contributions—gifts that mean sacrifice and a desire to share."

Organ Donation Request Systems

About twenty thousand persons die each year under circumstances that would make their organs useful to others in need of transplants. But according to a recent estimate, less than 15 percent of this potential harvest is made use of; the rest go into the grave, while people with kidney disease, liver disease, and heart disease who could be saved continue to sicken and die.

Our present policy, embodied in state laws, is one of total voluntarism; no one is obliged to donate his or her organs at death. Yet as long ago as 1968, a Gallup survey found that 90 percent of Americans said they would be willing, if asked, to donate their organs at death. The problem is that there is no system in effect to ask more than a small percentage of them.

Medical ethicists and others have suggested several possible mechanisms for gathering a larger harvest without infringing on individual rights. The two most feasible:

- Adopt laws providing that unless deceased persons, while alive, had explicitly refused to consent to the donation of their organs, they are presumed to have given such consent. With presumed consent in effect, doctors would be free to remove usable tissues and organs at death without having to obtain other permission.
- Enact and put into effect a system of "required request" in which all citizens would be obliged by law to indicate whether or not they were willing to donate their organs; the requests could be efficiently administered through a mandatory checkoff on driver's license applications or tax returns.

Controls over TV Programming

Any proposal to control TV content or viewing hours beyond the present limited guidelines raises serious questions of censorship and of interference with the rights of viewers. Yet in the past dozen years there have been over a thousand articles in psychological journals about the effects of TV on behavior, especially its potential for inciting aggressive and antisocial behavior in children, plus a number of articles on the potential of prosocial TV to induce prosocial behavior. The present diet of TV violence is undoubtedly a powerful force interfering with the development of humane personalities and a humane society.

One possible answer: The Federal Communications Commission could strictly limit the broadcasting of violence to the late evening hours. It could also promote the use of prosocial content by expanding the definition of required public service programming so as to include dramas and entertainment with such content.

Alternatively, broadcasters might create their own rating group, as filmmakers did long ago, to weigh the kind and quantity of violence included in TV shows and to require each show to be prefaced with a statement to parents as to its rating.

Intergroup Activities

Projects in which persons of different social subgroups work together to achieve a common goal have been shown to dissolve intergroup hostility, increase awareness of common humanity, and enlarge the population of those toward whom we are able to feel altruistic. Examples: sports teams made up of members of different faiths and races; classroom cooperative study groups made up of students of different backgrounds; neighborhood and community projects of all sorts; and intergroup political or humanitarian drives, rights movements, and reform campaigns.

As Ervin Staub says in a letter to me:

> Creating a feeling of community among the inhabitants of cities would result in a view of others as Us rather than Them, and increase caring and bystander response. The media, elected officials, influential citizens, and public and religious organizations can all play a role in this.
>
> They can set examples for others to follow, initiate activities that bring inhabitants together, and appeal to values that promote helping. They can create pride in the city and the opportunity and desire to come together in pursuit of shared goals. They can induce the inhabitants to help each other by joining in community projects, working and playing together, helping each other across subgroup lines.
>
> Since people learn by doing, one result will be a more

positive evaluation of other inhabitants of the city, and greater concern about their welfare. Another result will be a changed perception by individuals of themselves, as people who care and are willing to help.

A Committed Leadership

If there is, as I think there is, a widespread yearning to believe in the decency of humankind, a call to altruistic action by a committed leadership might trigger a national response. Recall again how America was galvanized when President Kennedy said, "Ask not what your country can do for you; ask what you can do for your country"; recall our national pride in the Peace Corps concept and the dramatic response, when it was announced, of so many who found in it a way to serve and to give rather than to demand and to get.

Perhaps it is time for another call to arms. Perhaps a challenge from the President or some other national leader to serve in a Helping Corps or a Samaritan Service would bring us to our feet cheering, sensing that our inner desire to do good to our fellow human beings can transform and ennoble us, and that when we ask not how we can be served but how we can serve, we ourselves are well served.

That is the ultimate paradox of altruism.

EPILOGUE

As I come to the end of this examination of the compassionate side of human nature, I would like to say what researching and writing this book has meant to me. I hope reading it has meant something similar to you.

It now seems indisputable to me that human beings are not essentially or wholly selfish, uncaring, cruel, or brutal. They can be and often are all those things, but they also can be and often are generous, caring, kind, and gentle.

Most of us, alas, extend our benevolence only to a narrow circle of our fellows and are indifferent or potentially hostile to others, especially those who do not look like us, eat like us, talk like us, smell like us, or worship like us. We often turn our eyes away from their suffering and, if we have reason to think of them as our enemies, are willing to incinerate tens of thousands of them at a time by firebombing their cities or, with a single blinding atomic blast, turn a hundred thousand of them into charred corpses and doomed, purulent walking dead.

But we need not be so, and are not always so. Many of us are helpful not only to family members but to friends, acquaintances, and even strangers; many of us give our money, our time and effort, and our blood to benefit people in need whom we do not know and will never meet; and a few of us will, on occasion, risk our own lives to save the life of a neighbor or even a stranger. Such behavior, though it does not fit the picture of human nature drawn by self-styled realists and pessimists, is neither abnormal nor freakish; it represents what almost all of us sometimes are capable of, and perhaps, thanks to behavioral science, may often or usually be in the future.

I will not see that in my time; I am not even sure it will ever come to be; but I believe that it *could* come to be as a result of our learning that we are made of better stuff than we have been told we are.

How can I believe this, I who have lived through World War II, the era of the Vietnam War, the times of the Khmer Rouge and the PLO terrorist attacks on civilians in buses and children in schoolrooms? Don't I see reports in every day's news of rapes, arson, drug-war executions, beatings to death of children by their own parents? Am I blind to the campaigns of extermination being waged in Ethiopia, Sri Lanka, and Sudan? Don't the police, the doctors on the emergency wards of the city hospitals, the survivors of the Central American torture chambers and the Nazi extermination camps, see and know the truth about human nature?

Of course they do. Part of the truth.

But altruism researchers have another kind of vision; they see farther and know better. Some of them, like Samuel Oliner, have personally experienced the worst side of humankind, yet through scientific research come to see that the compassion of a Balwina Piecuch was no accident or oddity but as much a part of human nature and its potential as the brutality of a storm trooper. Others, without having endured such traumas, have been motivated by a desire to solve the enigma of human nature: that human beings can act like fiends from hell, but also like angels from heaven.

It seems to me that there could hardly be any scientific inquiry or findings of greater benefit to humankind than theirs. I feel sustained and uplifted by what I have learned about the results of altruism research, and it is my hope that you have been, too. I intend no blasphemy when I say I have offered this book as a kind of *gospel* of humanity, in the sense of that word's Old English roots, *god* (good) and *spell* (tale)—good tidings.

None of the altruism researchers I met in the course of writing this book is a Pollyanna, and none minimizes the potential of human beings for barbarity toward their fellows. Yet, sustained by the evidence of their own research, they are characteristically optimistic, possessed of faith in humankind and its potential for benevolence, and hopeful that that potential will some day be realized.

Is that foolish, naive, or fatuous of them? Having seen the evidence, I do not believe it is.

At a conference on altruism that I attended last year, John Darley said that Jean Piaget was once asked by an American psychologist, "Do you think, Professor Piaget, that we can advance people through your stages of intellectual development?"

"Ah," jested Piaget, "the American question!"

I take his gibe as a compliment to us. It is typically American to ask whether we can put our scientific knowledge to good use—in this case, whether we can apply what we know of human nature to move ourselves upward to higher levels of humanity. To ask the American question is to give our own answer: We believe we can, and we mean to try.

NOTES ON SOURCES

CHAPTER ONE

pp. 11–12: Arland Williams, Jr.: *The New York Times,* Jan. 14, 1982, p. 1; Jan. 15, 1982, sec. IV, p. 15; Jan. 19, 1982, p. 18; and Claire Safran, "Hero of the Frozen River," *Reader's Digest,* Sept. 1982, pp. 49–53.

p. 13: "Such is the orientation": Harriet L. Rheingold and Gena N. Emery, in Olweus, Block, and Radke-Yarrow, eds., 1986: 94.

p. 13: blood donors: National office of the American Red Cross; the precise figure is 8.8 million for the forty-eight contiguous states. Volunteers: Independent Sector, 1988.

pp. 13–14: contributions in 1988: Independent Sector, 1988; AAFRC, 1988, pp. 23–28, and *The New York Times,* June 7, 1989, p. 12, advance report on 1989 AAFRC report, "Giving U.S.A."

p. 15: Ronald DeSillers, Jr.: *The New York Times,* Mar. 9, 1988, p. A24; the $690,000 figure: *The New York Times,* Aug. 29, 1988, p. 8.

p. 15: Habitat for Humanity: *The New York Times,* "Long Island Weekly," July 10, 1988, p. 3, and Habitat for Humanity's New York office, direct communication.

pp. 15–16: Reginald Andrews: *Time,* Jan. 3, 1983, p. 53.

p. 16: Durkheim's hypothesis: cited in Oliner and Oliner, 1988: 5.

pp. 16–17: Lester Ward: quoted in Wispé, 1978: 307.

p. 17: doctors' misgivings about living organ donors: Sadler, cited in Fellner and Schwartz, 1971.

p. 18: Macaulay-Berkowitz definition: Jacqueline R. Macaulay and Leonard Berkowitz, in Macaulay and Berkowitz, eds., 1970: 3.

p. 19: money-raising efforts: Churcher, 1988. Potlatch: Perry, 1985–1986.

p. 19: tax benefits and altruism: Kennett, 1980(b): 340. Institutional altruism: Merton, 1960; Merton and Gieryn, 1978: 319–320.

pp. 19–20: Samaritania: *The New York Times,* Dec. 14, 1986, sec. 1, p. 66.

pp. 21–22: the good Samaritan: Luke 10:30–37.

p. 23: It is the dominant view: Batson, 1987: 66.

p. 23: Julie Leirich: *People,* Mar. 16, 1987, p. 31.

p. 23: the Lincoln anecdote: Batson, Bolen, et al., 1986: 212.

p. 24: the stolen bassoon: *The New York Times,* Sept. 5, 1988, p. 26.

pp. 24–25: Georgia Advocacy, Alice Smith: *People,* Mar. 17, 1987, p. 29.

p. 25: The Samaritans of New York: *The New York Times,* June 29, 1988, sec. B, p.1; and June Mann, personal communication.

p. 25: Theroux: Paul Theroux, in Viorst, ed., 1986: 83; on the feelings of Peace Corps volunteers in general, Stein, 1966: 42–44.

pp. 25–26: an Italian priest: Oliner and Oliner, 1988: 77–78.

p. 26: altruistic suicide by grenade: Blake, 1978: 53–58.

p. 27: Smith: Smith, 1966: 1.

p. 27: Comte: Comte, 1875 [orig. publ. 1851]: I, 556.

pp. 27–28: on the early decades of psychology: Koch and Leary, 1985, passim; Hothersall, 1984, chaps. 4, 9, 10.

pp. 28–29: early history of social psychology: Hunt, 1985, chap. 4; Jones, 1985.

p. 29: Bar-Tal: Bar-Tal, in Staub, Bar-Tal, et al., eds., 1984, pp. 15–16.

p. 30: total number of altruism studies: for 1970, Krebs, 1970: 292–302; for 1982, Dovidio, 1984: 362; the current estimate, John Dovidio, personal communication.

p. 33: the rat on the platform: Rice and Gainer, cited in Krebs, 1970: 261. Hungry chimpanzee: Nissen and Crawford, cited by J. Philippe Rushton and Richard M. Sorrentino, in Rushton and Sorrentino, eds., 1981: 7.

pp. 33–34: twin studies: Rushton et al., 1986.

p. 34: altruism in toddlers: Zahn-Waxler and Radke-Yarrow, 1982.

p. 34: accidents of various kinds: Latané and Darley, 1970, chap. 7. Subway car experiments: Piliavin, Rodin, and Piliavin, 1969; Piliavin and Piliavin, 1972.

p. 34: flat tire: Hurley and Allen, 1974; Krebs, 1970: 268–269.

pp. 34–35: Dropped wallets: Diener et al., 1973.

p. 35: Istanbul and Ankara: Charles Korte, in Staub et al., eds., 1984: 327–329.

p. 35: mood and altruism: Underwood et al., 1977; Salovey and Rosenhan, 1983. Rescuers and nonrescuers of Jews: Oliner and Oliner, 1988, passim.

CHAPTER TWO

p. 41: bird warnings: Gleitman, 1981, p. 446; Wilson, 1979: 157; Trivers, 1971: 43–45.

p. 42: vervets: Gould and Marler, 1987: 80; Robert Plutchik, in Eisenberg and Strayer, eds., 1987: 40.

p. 42: soldiers of social insects: Wilson, 1979: 157–159; Campbell, 1975.

pp. 42–43: slime mold: Wilson, 1975: 126–128.

p. 43: "Zoologists do not": Mark Ridley and Richard Dawkins, in Rushton and Sorrentino, eds., 1981: 19–20; ellipses not indicated.

p. 44: The soldier is sterile: Wilson, 1975:13,33; Donald T. Campbell, in Bridgeman, ed., 1983:17–20.

p. 44: vervet calls: Gould and Marler, 1987:80; Robert Plutchik, in Eisenberg and Strayer, eds., 1987:40.

pp. 44–45: the rat experiment: R. M. Church, 1959, cited in Lucke and Batson, 1980:216.

p. 45: "Their concern is for themselves": Lucke and Batson, 1980.

p. 45: wolves, elephants: Carolyn Zahn-Waxler, in Zahn-Waxler, Cummings, and Iannotti, eds., 1986:321.

p. 46: Chimpanzee food-giving: Wilson, 1979:30.

p. 46: Washoe and Cindy: Goodall, 1986:378.

pp. 46–47: far greater than their similarities: R. B. Cairns, in Zahn-Waxler, Cummings, and Iannotti, eds., 1986:68.

p. 48: Genie: Curtiss, et al., 1975.

pp. 49–50: Zahn-Waxler: The study is formally described in Zahn-Waxler, Radke-Yarrow, and King, 1979:321.

pp. 50–51: newborns' empathic crying: Hoffman, 1981:130; other sources cited in Eisenberg and Strayer, eds., 1987:125–126.

p. 51: unconscious mimicry: Hoffman, 1981:130. Countries as dissimilar as: Harriet L. Rheingold and Gena M. Emery, in Olweus, Block, and Radke-Yarrow, eds., 1986:94.

pp. 51–52: LaMere: Carnegie Hero Fund Commission, 1986:21.

p. 52: average response time: Hoffman, 1981:126–127.

pp. 52–53: Jim Lewis and Jim Springer: Powledge, 1983:26; *Time,* Jan. 12, 1987, p. 63.

pp. 53–54: differences in height: Nancy Segal, quoted in Rosen, 1987: 40, and personal communication.

p. 54: 40 percent . . . 60 percent: Plomin and Daniels, 1987:5; Loehlin, 1986.

p. 54: 50 percent of the variance: Segal, personal communication; Bouchard, 1986; Tellegen et al., in press. "The evidence is now so overwhelming": Bouchard, 1986:430.

p. 57: "If altruism is defined": Krebs, 1987:83. Darwin: *On the Origin of Species,* quoted in Krebs, 1987:83.

pp. 57–58: the grouper and the wrasse: Trivers, 1971:40.

p. 58: "It seems likely": R. L. Trivers, in Bridgeman, ed., 1983:44–45.

p. 58: the survival value of reciprocal altruism: Hardin, 1977:117–118. Critics of his theory: Krebs, 1987:86.

p. 59: group selection: Krebs, 1987:89–90; on the seabirds, Robert A.

Hinde, in Olweus, Block, and Radke-Yarrow, eds., 1986:15. Ergo: Ibid., and see Mark Ridley and Richard Dawkins, in Rushton and Sorrentino, eds., 1981:22.

p. 59: Such analyses have caused: Krebs, 1987:90; Mark Ridley and Richard Dawkins, in Rushton and Sorrentino, eds., 1981:22. Haldane: Reiss, 1984:119.

pp. 59–60: kin selection theory: Wilson, 1975:116–119

p. 60: Mark Ridley and Richard Dawkins, in Rushton and Sorrentino, eds., 1981:25.

p. 60: Trivers's comment: R. L. Trivers, in Bridgeman, ed., 1983:43. Wilson's suggestion: Wilson, 1979:160. Rushton goes further: Rushton, Russell, et al., 1984.

pp. 60–61: the Yanomamö: Chagnon and Bugos, cited in Mark Ridley and Richard Dawkins, in Rushton and Sorrentino, eds., 1981:35.

p. 61: "Humans may devise": Gould, 1986:49.

pp. 61–62: "It implies": Carolyn Zahn-Waxler, in Zahn-Waxler, Cummings, and Iannotti, eds., 1986:320.

p. 62: The capacity for empathy: Martin Hoffman, in Rushton and Sorrentino, eds., 1981:44.

p. 62: And altruism: Campbell, 1975:1115–1118; Dennis Krebs, in Bridgeman, ed., 1983:62–68; and Ervin Staub, in Zahn-Waxler, Cummings, and Iannotti, eds., 1986:136.

CHAPTER THREE

pp. 63–66: Details of !Kung life are from Thomas, 1958; Lee, 1979; and Shostak, 1983.

p. 65: explained to Richard Borshay Lee: Lee, 1979:336.

p. 66: ≠Tomazho's explanation: Lee, 1979:246.

pp. 66–69: Details of Ik life are from Turnbull, 1972.

p. 69: "superficial luxuries": Turnbull, 1972:32,289.

p. 70: Bar-Tal on Israel: personal communication.

p. 70: Staub on the Swedes and English: personal communication.

pp. 70–71: studies by Bar-Tal and others: Bar-Tal, 1976; Bar-Tal, Raviv, and Shavit, 1981; and Bar-Tal, personal communication.

p. 71: Chinese psychologist Hing-Keung Ma: Ma, 1985a, 1985c. In Philadelphia and in Madras: L'Armand and Pepitone, 1975.

p. 71: middle-class and working-class men in England: Leonard Berkowitz, cited by Durganand Sinha, in Staub et al., 1984:447.

pp. 71–72: The wallet-dropping experiment: Diener et al., 1973.

p. 72: Ankara and Istanbul: Charles Korte, in Staub, Bar-Tal, et al., eds., 1984.

p. 73: "olive tree": Barzini, 1965:336–337.

pp. 74–75: details of life in Ambéli: du Boulay, 1974:74–76.

pp. 75–76: Boston, Paris, Athens: Feldman, 1968.

pp. 77: The most important norms of altruism: Krebs and Miller, in Lindsey and Aronson, eds., 1985; Dovidio, 1984:377–382.

p. 78: pressure to conform: Reykowski, 1980.

p. 78: the Bulgarian graduate student's study: Reykowski, 1980.

p. 78: What looked like helpfulness . . . largely conformity: Reykowski, 1980.

pp. 79–80: Blood donors: Jane Piliavin, personal communication.

pp. 80–82: details of and quotes about the Good Samaritan experiment: Darley and Batson, 1973; Batson, personal communication.

pp. 83–85: details of and quotes about the prison experiment: Zimbardo et al., 1974.

pp. 85–86: Auschwitz details: Levi, 1986, passim; the quotation: Levi, 1986:159–160.

p. 86: resource dilemmas ("commons dilemmas"): Edney and Bell, 1983, 1984, 1987; Kramer, McClintock, and Messick, 1986; Axelrod, 1984.

p. 87: mandatory rationing: *The New York Times,* May 1, 1988, sec. I, p. 37.

p. 87: Wherever they draw the line: Miller and Brewer, 1986:209; Hornstein, 1976:8–9.

p. 87: the incident reported by Cohen: Cohen, 1972:39.

p. 88: the siege of Jerusalem: Raymond of Agiles, quoted in H. O. Taylor, *The Medieval Mind* (London: Koming, 1927), vol. I, p. 551.

pp. 88–89: Wilson's statement: Wilson, 1979:122–123.

p. 89: thereby strengthening the ingroup: Staub, 1985:66–71. Reassuring, exhilarating, etc.: Hornstein, 1976:16–18. Prefer others who are . . . similar: Krebs, 1987:100–101; Harris and Bauden, 1973; Harris and Bays, 1973; Harris and Klingbeil, 1976; Hardin, 1977.

p. 90: Mohammed Ali Jinnah's statement: quoted in J. G. Stoessinger, *Why Nations Go to War* (New York: St. Martin's Press, 1982):121.

pp. 90–91: Benvenisti's statements: Benvenisti, 1988.

p. 91: Tajfel experiment: Tajfel, et al., 1971, cited in Tajfel and Billig, 1974.

pp. 91–92: Adults exhibit the same propensity: Staub, 1978a:322,324; Hornstein, 1976:26–30; Gaertner and Dovidio, 1977.

p. 92: Greek torturers: Gibson and Haritos-Fatouros, 1986.

p. 92: Hans Frank's statement: Lifton, 1987:79.

p. 92: Polish indifference: Tec, 1984:115–116; Tec, 1986a:301–302,307. Only 10 percent: Tec, 1986:11.

p. 93: Danish rescue of Jews: Goldberger, 1987:5,49,51.

p. 93: school desegregation: Miller, Brewer, and Edwards, 1985:64.

p. 94: Sherif's experiments with boys in summer camp: Sherif et al., 1961.

p. 94: interracial sports teams: Slavin and Madden, cited by Samuel L. Gaertner and John F. Dovidio, in Dovidio and Gaertner, eds., 1986:325. Token or proportional allotment: Miller, Brewer, and Edwards, 1985: 66–68.

pp. 94–95: cooperative learning experiments: cited in Miller, Brewer, and Edwards, 1985:64.

p. 95: Even seating arrangements: Samuel L. Gaertner and John F. Dovidio, in Dovidio and Gaertner, eds., 1986:326–329.

CHAPTER FOUR

p. 97: Joyce M. Black: *The New York Times,* Jan. 31, 1988, sec. A, p. 48.

p. 97: Reginald Andrews: *Time,* Jan. 3, 1983, p.53.

pp. 98–101: Details of Nightingale's life are from Woodham-Smith, 1950.

pp. 102–103: Piaget's stage theory of mental development: Piaget, 1960; Piaget and Inhelder, 1969; Flavell, 1963.

pp. 103–104: Kohlberg's moral stages: Kohlberg, 1984:640.

p. 104: Eisenberg's critique: Eisenberg, 1986:126.

p. 105: Some children progress . . . faster: Carolyn Zahn-Waxler, personal communication; E. Mark Cummings, et al., in Zahn-Waxler, Cummings, and Iannotti, eds., 1986:177. The same course of development: Dovidio, 1984:367–382.

p. 105: By ten to fourteen months: Marian Radke-Yarrow and Carolyn Zahn-Waxler, in Staub, Bar-Tal, et al., eds., 1984:88.

p. 105: From fourteen months on: Marian Radke-Yarrow and Carolyn Zahn-Waxler, in Staub, Bar-Tal, et al., eds., 1984:89.

pp. 105–106: Beyond eighteen months and Jennie quote: Marian Radke-Yarrow and Carolyn Zahn-Waxler, in Staub, Bar-Tal, et al., eds., 1984:89.

p. 106: By two to two and a half years: Marian Radke-Yarrow and Carolyn Zahn-Waxler, in Staub, Bar-Tal, et al., eds., 1984:90.

p. 106: David and Michael: Joan Grusec, in Eisenberg, ed., 1982: 141.

pp. 106–107: Staub's kindergarten experiment: Staub, 1969, 1970; Staub, personal communication.

p. 107: Bar-Tal's experiments: Bar-Tal, Raviv, and Leiser, 1980; Bar-Tal, personal communication.

p. 107: Ervin Staub, for one, found a drop: Staub, 1970.

p. 108: Mary: Eisenberg-Berg and Hand, 1979:358.

p. 108: Eisenberg's major findings: Eisenberg, 1986:135–145. Eisenberg et al.'s five stages: Eisenberg, 1986:144. (For a somewhat different, though related, four-stage schema, see Hoffman, 1988:4–6.)

p. 109: essential to normal emotional development: Kagan, Kearsley, and Zelazo, 1978: chap. 3, passim. "The similarity of others' distress": Ervin Staub, in Zahn-Waxler, Cummings, and Iannotti, eds., 1986:142. Four-year-old boys: Ruth Sharabany, in Staub, Bar-Tal, et al., eds., 1984: 206, citing a study by Rutherford and Mussen. Ten-year-old boys: Ruth Sharabany, in Staub, Bar-Tal, et al., eds., 1984:206, citing a study by Hoffman. Rosenhan's study: David Rosenhan, in Macaulay and Berkowitz, eds., 1970:251–268.

p. 109: maltreated or abused preschoolers: Howes and Eldredge, 1985. Delinquents: Hott, 1979, summarizing others' research. Nazi SS men: Dicks, 1972.

p. 110: When children see someone: Marian Radke-Yarrow and Carolyn Zahn-Waxler, in Olweus, Block, and Radke-Yarrow, eds., 1986:214. The various donation experiments: Bryan, 1970; Bryan and Walbeck, 1970; Joan Grusec, in Rushton and Sorrentino, eds., 1981:69–70; Joan Grusec, in Eisenberg, ed., 1982:155–156; and for the greater impact of modeling on younger children, Peterson, 1982.

p. 110: the flat-tire experiments: Bryan and Test, cited in Krebs, 1970: 268–269.

p. 110: sidewalk donations: Hurley and Allen, 1974; Krebs, 1970: 268–269.

pp. 110–111: Effect of hearing news stories: Holloway, Tucker, and Hornstein, 1977.

p. 111: effects of TV on children: Pearl, 1984.

p. 111: the Annenberg project: Pearl, 1984.

p. 112: Hoffman and Saltzstein's study: Hoffman and Saltzstein, 1967; Hoffman, 1983:249–250; for similar findings see Ervin Staub, in Zahn-Waxler, Cummings, and Iannotti, eds., 1986:150–151; Joan Grusec and Theodore Dix, in the same, 224–226; Zahn-Waxler, 1987:17.

p. 112: children's response to reasoning apart from content: Ervin Staub, in Rushton and Sorrentino, eds., 1981:116.

p. 112: preachments or direct injunctions: Eisenberg-Berg and Geisheker, 1979; Carolyn Zahn-Waxler, personal communication. Labeling: Ervin Staub, in Rushton and Sorrentino, eds., 1981.

p. 113: Grusec et al.'s experiments: Joan Grusec, in Rushton and Sorrentino, eds., 1981:81–82.

pp. 113–114: Learning by doing: Ervin Staub, in Zahn-Waxler, Cummings, and Iannotti, eds., 1986:154–155. Cairns: Zahn-Waxler, Cummings, and Iannotti, eds., 1986:73. Staub's statement: personal communication.

p. 114: The Staub study: Staub, 1979, chap. 6.

p. 114: Exposure to other kinds of children: Eisenberg, 1986:103; James Youniss, in Zahn-Waxler, Cummings, and Iannotti, eds., 1986:95. Norm of reciprocity: James Youniss, in Zahn-Waxler, Cummings, and Iannotti, eds., 1986:97. They gradually acquire a repertoire: Backman, 1985:15, quoting

J. Garfinkel, "Studies of the Routine Grounds of Everyday Activities," *Social Problems,* 11:225–250, (1964).

p. 115: effects of internalization of norms: Eisenberg, 1982:140; Kurtines and Gewirtz, 1984:120–123.

p. 115: Twenty years ago: Krebs, 1970:286; Maccoby and Jacklin, 1974:354.

p. 115: Nursery-school children: Feshbach, 1978; Hoffman and Levine, 1976.

p. 115: boys more aggressive: E. Mark Cummings, Barbara Hollenback, et al., in Zahn-Waxler, Cummings, and Iannotti, eds., 1986:167–168; Eisenberg, Bartlett, and Haake, 1983.

pp. 115–116 Fifth- and sixth-grade children: Staub, 1978a:254.

p. 116: By adulthood the sexes show: Piliavin et al., 1981:199–202; Melson and Fogel, 1988; Maccoby and Jacklin, 1974:354.

p. 116: males and females differ relatively little: Piliavin, Dovidio, et al., 1981:199–202; Eisenberg, personal communication.

p. 116: "self-socialization": Staub, 1979:127–136, 151–153.

pp. 116–117: Pappenheim: Karpe, 1961.

pp. 117–118: Nansen: Shackleton, 1959: chap. XVII; Ladas, 1932: chap. XVII; *Encyclopaedia Britannica,* 1980 (15th ed.), Macropaedia, vol. 12.

pp. 118–119: Schindler: Wundheiler, 1985–1986; Keneally, 1982; Staub, 1989b, p. 380.

p. 120: the foot-in-the-door experiment: Freedman and Fraser, 1966.

p. 121: Schwartz's experiment: Schwartz, personal communication: Schwartz and Gottlieb, 1980c.

p. 122: Timothy Carroll: Rice, 1986:49.

p. 122: A 1986 report: Rice, 1986:46–47.

pp. 122–123: blood donor development: Piliavin, Evans, and Callero, 1984:481.

p. 123: "addicted": Piliavin, Callero, and Evans, 1982:1212–1213.

pp. 123–124: In the early years of altruism research: J. Philippe Rushton, in Rushton and Sorrentino, eds., 1981:251; Eisenberg, 1982:7.

p. 124: Freudian hypotheses: Eisenberg, 1986:15–16; McWilliams, 1984:194; Shalom Schwartz, in Staub, Bar-Tal, et al., eds., 1984:245.

p. 124: General mood: Strayer, 1980. Empathy: Staub, 1978a:54–55; Martin Hoffman, in Eisenberg, ed., 1982:218–231; Nancy Eisenberg and Paul Miller, in Eisenberg and Strayer, eds., 1987:292–316.

p. 124: Emotional expressiveness: Hampson, 1981:104.

pp. 124–125: Popularity: Hampson, 1981, 1984.

p. 125: Self-esteem: Ervin Staub, in Zahn-Waxler, Cummings, and Iannotti, eds., 1986:144–147.

p. 125: Attitude toward other human beings: Ervin Staub in Zahn-Waxler, Cummings, and Iannotti, 1986:138.

p. 125: Some early studies of altruism: J. Philippe Rushton, in Rushton and Sorrentino, eds., 1981:251–258.

pp. 125–126: Schwartz's bone marrow donor studies: Schwartz, 1973, 1975, 1977.

p. 126: volunteers: J. Philippe Rushton, in Staub, Bar-Tal, et al., eds., 1984:280.

p. 126: Tec on rescuers: Tec, 1986c:191. The conclusion to be drawn: Kurtines and Gewirtz, 1984:265, 280. Rushton's statement: J. Philippe Rushton, in Staub, Bar-Tal, et al., eds., 1984:275.

CHAPTER FIVE

pp. 128–129: details of the Genovese murder: *The New York Times*, Mar. 27, 1964, p. 1; Apr. 3, 1964, p. 24; and Rosenthal, 1964.

pp. 129–131: details of the Mosher-Mashoon rescue: Timothy Mosher, personal communication; Carnegie, 1987:25.

p. 132: reactions to the Genovese murder: Rosenthal, 1964; Latané and Darley, 1970:2–3.

pp. 132–133: Latané and Darley collaboration: Latané, personal communication.

pp. 133–134: design of the experiment: Darley and Latané, 1968; Latané and Darley, 1970:93–97.

p. 134: The results were electrifying: Darley and Latané, 1968; Latané and Darley, 1970:93–97.

p. 134: three hypothetical processes: Bibb Latané, in Grunberg et al., eds., 1987:75.

pp. 134–135: "The results of our experiments": Latané and Darley, 1970:127.

p. 135: data on the fifty-six studies: Bibb Latané, Steve A. Nida, and David W. Wilson, in Rushton and Sorrentino, eds., 1981:290–296.

p. 136: People in cities: Charles Korte, in Rushton and Sorrentino, eds., 1981:326.

p. 136: they are more easily influenced: Hansson, Slade, and Slade, 1978.

p. 136: Even in large cities: Hackler, Ho, and Urquhart-Ross, 1974.

p. 137: A study in the Netherlands: Charles Korte, in Rushton and Sorrentino, eds., 1981:326.

p. 137: The Latané and Darley statement: Latané and Darley, 1970:6.

pp. 138–148: The categorization of external influences into those that promote and those that inhibit altruistic responses is adapted from Piliavin et al., 1981:5–7, who divide responses into the "orienting" (leading to action) and the "defensive" (leading to inaction or even escape). Although they are concerned with emergency intervention, they say the distinction applies to other levels of helping behavior.

pp. 138–139: the AP story: Quoted in Shotland, 1985.

p. 139: the Clark and Word "electrocution" experiment: Cited in Piliavin et al. 1981:64–65.

p. 139: the rape experiment cited by Shotland: Shotland, 1985. The Cialdini quote: Cialdini, 1985:115.

pp. 140–141: the roadside experiments: Mason and Allen, 1972.

p. 141: Cialdini's advice: Cialdini, 1985:117–118.

pp. 141–142: Cialdini's personal experience: Cialdini, 1985:118.

pp. 142–144: Fear of looking foolish versus fear of looking bad: The experiments in this section are cited in: Bibb Latané, Steve A. Nida, and David W. Wilson, in Rushton and Sorrentino, eds., 1981:298; Piliavin, Dovidio, et al., 1981:139–142; Schwartz and Gottlieb, 1980a; Latané and Rodin, 1969; Latané and Darley, 1970:106–107; Rutkowski, Gruder, and Romer, 1983; Dovidio, 1984:401.

p. 144: the bumper sticker experiment: Ehlert, Ehlert, and Merrens, 1973, cited in Piliavin et al., 1981:149.

p. 144: effects of kinship or similarity on helping: Piliavin et al., 1981:144–150; Dovidio, 1984:404–409.

p. 145: racial differences and helping: Dovidio, 1984:405, 408–409; Piliavin et al., 1981:150–151; Gaertner and Dovidio, 1977.

pp. 145–146: the plastic surgery experiment: Kurtsburg, Safar, and Cavior, 1968.

pp. 146–148: the subway experiments: I. Piliavin, J. Rodin, and J. Piliavin, 1969; J. Piliavin and I. Piliavin, 1972.

p. 148: A regrettable finding: Pomazol and Clore, 1973; Cialdini, 1985:144–145.

p. 148: when a stranger is in serious need: Staub, 1979:8–10.

p. 149: the kindergartners: Staub, 1969.

pp. 149–150: the cafeteria and beach experiments: Moriarty, 1975.

p. 150: when a bystander has reason to believe: Krebs and Miller, 1985:47; Ervin Staub, in Zahn-Waxler, Cummings, and Iannotti, eds., 1986:144.

pp. 150–151: Kaplan's fantasy: John Kaplan, in Wispé, ed., 1978: 291–292.

p. 151: Good Samaritan laws in the U.S.: Geis, in press.

p. 151: Good Samaritan laws in other countries: Geis, in press; John Kaplan, in Wispé, ed., 1978:295.

p. 152: Kaplan's misgivings: John Kaplan, in Wispé, ed., 1978:299. Geis's prediction: Geis, in press.

p. 153: the clarity of the situation: Piliavin, Dovidio, et al., 1984: 163–173.

p. 153: narrow the bystander's focus of attention: Piliavin, Dovidio, et al., 1984:174.

pp. 153–154: Ervin Staub argues: Staub, 1978a, pp. 114–116, 239–240; personal communication.

pp. 154–156: the three heroic rescues: Carnegie, 1987; Carnegie Hero Fund Commission press release of March 3, 1988; Carnegie Hero Fund Commission press release of April 28, 1988.

p. 156: Goode on heroism: Goode, 1977:344–345. Wispé's comments: Lauren Wispé, in Wispé, ed., 1978:306.

pp. 156–157: the Geis and Huston study: Geis and Huston, 1980; Huston et al., 1976b; Huston et al., 1981.

p. 157: Geis's hopeful comment: Geis, 1981.

CHAPTER SIX

pp. 159–160: Marion van Binsbergen Pritchard's story: Rittner and Myers, 1986:28–33.

p. 160: the kidney donors: Carl H. Fellner and John R. Marshall, in Rushton and Sorrentino, eds., 1981:357.

p. 161: This is characteristic . . . of all cognitive activity: Nisbett and Wilson, 1977; Nisbett and Ross, 1980, passim. This relegation of most "overlearned" material: Hunt, 1982: 253, 276–277.

p. 162: the three-consonant experiment: Peterson, 1966.

pp. 162–163: the various models: My composite portrait is based on: Y. Bar-Tal and D. Bar-Tal, in press; Eisenberg, 1986:190–193; Piliavin et al., 1981:240–244; Ervin Staub, in Staub, Bar-Tal, et al., eds., 1984:29–49; and Shalom Schwartz and Judith Howard, in Rushton and Sorrentino, eds., 1981:189–211.

p. 164: the two kinds are thoroughly interwoven: Eisenberg, 1986:2–5; Janusz Reykowski, in Staub, Bar-Tal, et al., eds., 1984:53,71.

p. 164: The more noise, the less altruism: Mathews and Canon, 1975. "stimulus overload": Sherrod and Downs, 1974.

pp. 164–165: Milgram's hypothesis and the Netherlands experiments: Milgram, 1970; Charles Korte, in Rushton and Sorrentino, eds., 1981: 319–323.

p. 165: résumé of mood experiments: Robert Cialdini, Douglas Kenrick, and Donald Baumann, in Eisenberg, ed., 1982:352–355. Explanations of good mood effect: Shaffer, 1985–1986. Explanations of negative mood effect: Krebs and Miller, 1985:59–60.

pp. 165–166: effect of moods on attention: Salovey and Rosenhan, 1989; Carlson and Miller, 1987.

pp. 166–170: Several factors determine: Dovidio, 1984:367–374.

pp. 167–168: functions and effects of role-taking: Dennis Krebs and Cristine Russell, in Rushton and Sorrentino, eds., 1981:152; Salovey and Rosenhan, 1989:19–20; Eisenberg, 1986:106.

p. 168: Graebe: Rittner and Myers, 1986:40–42.

p. 169: This is a puzzling phenomenon: Eisenberg, 1986:31; Nancy Eisenberg and Janet Strayer, in Eisenberg and Strayer, eds., 1987:3–4; Martin Hoffman, in Eisenberg and Strayer, eds., 1987:48.

p. 169: methods of measuring empathic arousal: Eisenberg, 1986:36.

pp. 169–170: in search of more objective evidence: Robert F. Marcus, in Eisenberg and Strayer, eds., 1987; Nancy Eisenberg, Richard A. Fabes, et al., in Eisenberg and Strayer, eds., 1987; and for perspiration (skin conductance), Eisenberg, personal communication.

p. 170: minutes, days . . . fraction of a second: Batson, 1987:88, n. 1.

p. 170: by bringing to bear our accumulated knowledge: Pomazal and Jaccard, 1976.

pp. 170–171: The question, "Should someone try to help?": Bar-Tal, Korenfeld, and Raviv, 1985.

p. 172: social consequences calculations: Archer, 1987; Archer, Diaz-Loving, et al., 1981. Influence of personal norms: Shalom Schwartz and Judith Howard, in Rushton and Sorrentino, eds., 1981:199–201; Schlenker, Hallam, and McCown, 1983.

pp. 173–174: guilt as the motivation for altruism: David Rosenhan, Peter Salovey, et al., in Rushton and Sorrentino, eds., 1981:237. Induced guilt in volunteers: Hoffman, 1982; Krebs, 1982c:281–287.

p. 174: Anna Freud: Freud, 1946.

p. 174: self-esteem: Eisenberg. 1986:201–203; Elizabeth Midlarsky, in Staub, Bar-Tal, et al., eds., 1984:294,299,305. Most altruism researchers prefer: Hatfield, Walster, and Piliavin, 1978.

p. 175: When we see someone in distress: C. Daniel Batson, Jim Fultz, and Patricia A. Schoenrade, in Eisenberg and Strayer, eds., 1987; Nancy Eisenberg and Paul Miller, in Eisenberg and Strayer, eds., 1987; Carolyn Zahn-Waxler, in Zahn-Waxler, Cummings, and Iannotti, eds., 1986:312; Cialdini and Kenrick, 1976; Cialdini et al., 1987; Bar-Tal, 1976; Piliavin et al., 1981; and many others.

p. 175: the first subway study, and the Cost-Reward model: I. M. Piliavin, J. Rodin, and J. A. Piliavin, 1969.

p. 176: The Negative State Relief model: Schaller and Cialdini, in press.

pp. 176–177: Cialdini's strongest evidence: Manucia, Baumann, and Cialdini, 1984. Other Cialdini experiments bearing on the matter: Baumann, Cialdini, and Kenrick, 1981; Baumann, Cialdini, and Kenrick, 1983; Cialdini, Darby, and Vincent, 1973; Cialdini and Kenrick, 1976; Cialdini et al., in press.

p. 177: Hoffman: Hoffman, 1981.

p. 177: the Coke-Batson experiment: Coke, Batson, and McDavis, 1978.

p. 178: Batson's formal statement: Batson, 1987:93.

pp. 178–180: Batson's major experiment: Batson, Duncan, et al., 1981. Other Batson experiments bearing on the matter: Batson, Bolen, et al., 1986; Batson and Coke, 1981; Batson, Fultz, and Schoenrade, 1987; Batson, O'Quin, et al., 1983; Fultz et al., 1986.

p. 180: Cialdini and Batson mean different things: Eisenberg, 1986:42–43; Hoffman, 1975b; Hoffman, 1981; and Krebs, 1987.

p. 180: other researchers call it: Batson, 1987:93. Transformation of empathy into sympathy: Hoffman, 1981, 1982.

p. 182: we perform a kind of problem-solving: Piliavin et al., 1981: 236–253; Shalom Schwartz and Judith Howard, in Staub, Bar-Tal et al., eds., 1984:235–236; Eisenberg, 1986:34–35, 198–199.

p. 182: we reckon the costs and rewards: Dovidio, 1984:383–389.

p. 182: mental defenses against helping: Latané and Darley, 1970: 79–83; Shalom Schwartz and Judith Howard, in Rushton and Sorrentino, eds., 1981:203–208; Schwartz and Howard, 1980; Hoffman, 1988; Staub, 1978a:151–154; Piliavin et al., 1981:114–115.

p. 183: when we are motivated primarily by concern for the other person: Batson, 1987. Most kidney donors: Abram and Buchanan, 1976; Carl H. Fellner and John R. Marshall, in Rushton and Sorrentino, eds., 1981.

p. 183: negative effect of tangible rewards: Romer, Gruder, and Lizzardo, 1986.

CHAPTER SEVEN

pp. 186–205: The account of Oliner's life up to 1971 is taken from Oliner, 1986 [1979], passim, and Oliner, personal communication; from 1971 on, interview with Oliner. (The Nazi edict cited on p. 188: Tec, 1986c, 30.)

p. 192: fifty thousand such rescuers, who saved two hundred thousand Jews: Baron, 1985–86. London's study: London, 1970; Oliner, 1982.

p. 193: London's hypotheses: London, 1970: 245.

p. 194: Slawson's letter: Slawson to the Littauer Foundation, March 31, 1983; in the files of Selma Hirsh, American Jewish Committee.

p. 195: the account of Slawson's selection of Oliner: Selma Hirsh, Slawson's long-time assistant at the American Jewish Committee, personal communication.

p. 197: size of the final sample: Oliner and Oliner, 1988: 2–4, 261–64.

p. 201: Staub's appraisal: Staub, 1988b.

p. 205: relation of specific attitudes to specific behaviors: Ajzen and Fishbein, 1972, 1980.

p. 206: changes in behavior brought about by clocks, etc.: Boorstin, 1983, passim; Bronowksi, 1973, passim.

pp. 206–207: the Schwartz experiment: Schwartz, personal communication; Schwartz and Gottlieb, 1980c.

pp. 207–208: the study by Beaman and colleagues: Beaman et al., 1978.

pp. 208–209: the Piliavin et al. statement: Piliavin et al., 1981:254.

p. 210: children given concrete rewards: Joan Grusec, in Rushton and Sorrentino, eds., 1981. The reward undermines their incentive: ibid. But one kind of reward: Ervin Staub, in Rushton and Sorrentino, eds., 1981.

p. 211: The effect of such parental modeling: Radke-Yarrow, Scott, and Zahn-Waxler, 1973. The Radke-Yarrow et al. study, and statement: Radke-Yarrow, Scott, and Zahn-Waxler, 1973.

p. 212: Says Ervin Staub: Ervin Staub, in Zahn-Waxler, Cummings, and Iannotti, eds., 1986:154–155.

pp. 215–216: Data about the American Institute for Character Education come from its brochures and other publications, and from personal communications from its president, Dr. Young Jay Mulkey.

pp. 216–217: the decline and revival of moral/character education: Henry C. Johnson, Jr., in Kurtines and Gewirtz, [eds.], 1984; Pearl Oliner, 1985–1986; Rachel Hertz-Lazarowitz and Shlomo Sharan, in Staub, Bar-Tal, et al., eds., 1984.

p. 217: Rushton's statement: Rushton, 1982.

p. 217: In the 1970s, the first: Goldstein and Michaels, 1985:219. By 1987 a Gallup survey: *The Wall Street Journal,* Sept. 26, 1988, p. 33.

p. 218: the AICE survey data: Mulkey, 1983. But comparable results . . . many other sources: Ervin Staub, in Rushton and Sorrentino, eds., 1981; Brown, 1979; Feshbach, 1979; Seymour Feshbach and Norma Deitch Feshbach, in Zahn-Waxler, Cummings, and Iannotti, eds., 1986; Berndt, McCartney, et al., 1983–1984; Rachel Hertz-Lazarowitz and Shlomo Sharan, in Staub et al., eds., 1984; Spivak and Shure, 1984. Several dozen programs of empathy-training: Goldstein and Michaels, 1985:224–225. Group discussions . . . Kohlbergian moral dilemmas: Berndt, et al., 1983–1984. Cooperative learning techniques: Rachel Hertz-Lazarowitz and Shlomo Sharan, in Staub et al., eds., 1984. For a noteworthy demonstration project using many of the foregoing techniques (in San Ramon, CA), see Solomon et al., 1987; Solomon et al., 1987; Battistich, Solomon, and Watson, 1987.

pp. 218–219: college courses in philanthropy: Gurin, 1987.

p. 219: societies of physicians: Merton and Gieryn, 1978.

p. 220: In 1987 total giving: AAFRC Trust for Philanthropy, 1988:13.

p. 220: citizen crime reporting programs: Leonard Bickman, in Staub, Bar-Tal, et al., eds., 1984.

p. 221: Kennett's statement: Kennett, 1980b. "I have never known much good done": Cited in Kennett, 1980b.

p. 221: cause-related marketing and Gurin's statement: letter by Maurice G. Gurin in *The New York Times,* July 4, 1986.

p. 222: Less than 15 percent: Kaplan, 1984.

p. 222: Yet as long ago as 1968: Sadler and Sadler, 1984.

p. 222: Medical ethicists and others have suggested: Caplan, 1984.

pp. 222–223: Over a thousand articles . . . effects of TV: Leonard D. Eron and L. Rowell Huesman, in Olweus, Block, and Radke-Yarrow, eds., 1986.

BIBLIOGRAPHY

AAFRC Trust for Philanthropy, 1988. *The Annual Report on Philanthropy for the Year 1987*. New York: American Association of Fund-Raising Counsel.

Abram, Harry S., and Buchanan, Denton C., 1976–1977. "The Gift of Life: A Review of the Psychological Aspects of Kidney Transplantation." *Internat. Jour. of Psychiatry in Med.*, 7, 2:153–164.

Abrams, Samuel, 1986. "Disposition and the Environment." In Peter B. Neubauer and Albert J. Solnit, eds., *The Psychoanalytic Study of the Child*, 41:41–60.

Aderman, David, and Berkowitz, Leonard, 1983. "Self-concern and the Unwillingness to Be Helpful." *Soc. Psychol. Quarterly*, 46, 4:291–301.

Ajzen, I., and Fishbein, M., 1972. "Attitudinal and Normative Variables as Predictors of Specific Behaviors." *Jour. of Personality and Soc. Psychol.*, 27:1–9.

————, 1980. *Understanding Attitudes and Predicting Social Behaviors*. Englewood Cliffs, NJ: Prentice-Hall.

Allen, Bem P., 1978. *Social Behavior: Facts and Falsehoods About Common Sense, Hypnotism, Obedience, Altruism, Beauty, Racism, and Sexism*. Chicago: Nelson Hall.

Allison, Scott T., and Messick, David M., 1985. "Effects of Experience on Performance in a Replenishable Resource Trap." *Jour. of Personality and Soc. Psychol.*, 49, 4:943–948.

————, and Samuelson, Charles D., 1985. "Effects of Soliciting Opinions on Contributions to a Public Good." *Jour. of Applied Soc. Psychol.*, 15, 3:201–206.

Annas, Julia, 1977. "Plato and Aristotle on Friendship and Altruism." *Mind*, 86, 344:532–554.

Archer, Richard L., 1984. "The Farmer and the Cowman Should Be Friends: An Attempt at Reconciliation with Batson, Coke, and Pych." *Jour. of Personality and Soc. Psychol.*, 46, 3:709–711.

————, 1987. "Social Evaluation as an Egoistic Alternative to the Empathy-Altruism Hypothesis." Paper presented at the meeting of the Society of Experimental Social Psychology October 1987, Charlottesville, VA.

———— et al., 1981. "The Role of Dispositional Empathy and Social Evaluation in the Empathic Mediation of Helping." *Jour. of Personality and Soc. Psychol.*, 40, 4:786–796.

Ascherson, Neal, 1987. "The Death Doctors" (review of four books on Auschwitz). *The New York Review,* May 28: 29–34.

Astin, Alexander W., and Green, Kenneth C., 1987. *The American Freshman: Twenty Year Trends, 1966–1985.* Los Angeles: Higher Education Research Institute, UCLA.

————; Schalit, Marilynn; and Korn, William S., 1987. *The American Freshman: National Norms for Fall 1986.* Los Angeles: Higher Education Research Institute, UCLA.

————, 1988. *The American Freshman: National Norms for Fall 1987.* Los Angeles: Higher Education Research Institute, UCLA.

Axelrod, Robert, 1984. *The Evolution of Cooperation.* New York: Basic Books.

Babbs, Ken, 1988. "15 Self-made Heroes." *American Health,* March.

Backman, Carl W., 1985. "Identity, Self-Presentation, and the Resolution of Moral Dilemmas: Towards a Social Psychological Theory of Moral Behavior." In Barry R. Schlenker, ed., 1985.

Barash, D., 1979. *The Whisperings Within.* New York: Harper & Row.

Barnett, M. A.; King, L. M.; and Howard, G. A., 1979. "Inducing Affect About Self or Other: Effects of Generosity on Children." *Developmental Psychol.,* 15:164–167.

Baron, Lawrence, 1985–1986. "The Holocaust and Human Decency: A Review of Research on the Rescue of Jews in Nazi-Occupied Europe." *Humboldt Jour. of Soc. Relations,* 13, 1–2:237–251.

Barrett, D. E., and Radke-Yarrow, M., 1977. "Prosocial Behavior, Social Inferential Ability, and Assertiveness in Young Children." *Child Development,* 48:475–481.

Bar-Tal, Daniel, 1976. *Prosocial Behavior: Theory and Research.* New York: Hemisphere Publishing Corp.

————, 1982. "Sequential Development of Helping Behavior: A Cognitive-Learning Model." *Developmental Rev.,* 2:101–124.

————; Korenfeld, David; and Raviv, Alona, 1985. "Relationships Between the Development of Helping Behavior and the Development of Cognition, Social Perspective, and Moral Judgment." *Genetic, Social, and General Psychol. Monographs,* 111, 1:23–40.

Bar-Tal, Daniel; Nadler, A.; and Blechman, N., 1980. "The Relationship Between Children's Perception of Parents' Socialization Practices and Helping Behavior." *Jour. of Soc. Psychol.,* 111:159–167.

Bar-Tal, Daniel, and Raviv, Amram, 1982. "A Cognitive-Learning Model of Helping Behavior Development: Possible Implications and Applications." In Nancy Eisenberg, ed., 1982b.

————, and Leiser, T., 1980. "The Development of Altruistic Behavior: Empirical Evidence." *Developmental Psychol.,* 16:516–525.

————, and Shavit, M., 1981. "Motives for Helping Behavior Expressed by Kindergarten and School Children in Kibbutz and City." *Developmental Psychol.,* 17:766–772.

Bar-Tal, Yoram, and Bar-Tal, Daniel, in press. "Performance of Helping Behavior: Process and Contents." In W. M. Kurtines and J. L. Gewirtz, eds., *Moral Behavior and Development* (Hillsdale, NJ: Lawrence Erlbaum Associates).

Barzini, Luigi, 1965. *The Italians.* New York: Atheneum.

Batson, C. Daniel, 1987. "Prosocial Motivation: Is It Ever Truly Altruistic?" *Advances in Experimental Soc. Psychol.,* 20:65–122.

———— et al., 1986. "Where Is the Altruism in the Altruistic Personality?" *Jour. of Personality and Soc. Psychol.,* 50, 1:212–220.

Batson, C. Daniel, and Coke, Jay S., 1981. "Empathic Motivation of Helping Behavior." In J. Philippe Rushton and Richard M. Sorrentino, eds., 1981.

Batson, C. Daniel et al., 1981. "Is Empathic Emotion a Source of Altruistic Motivation?" *Jour. of Personality and Soc. Psychol.,* 40:290–302.

Batson, C. Daniel; Fultz, Jim; and Schoenrade, Patricia A., 1987. "Distress and Empathy: Two Qualitatively Distinct Emotions with Different Motivational Consequences." *Jour. of Personality,* 55, 1:19–39.

Batson, C. Daniel et al., 1983. "Influence of Self-Reported Distress and Empathy on Egoistic Versus Altruistic Motivation to Help." *Jour. of Personality and Soc. Psychol.,* 45, 3:706–718.

Battistich, Victor; Solomon, Daniel; and Watson, Marilyn, 1987. "Effects of an Elementary School Program to Enhance Prosocial Behavior on Children's Social Problem-Solving Skills and Strategies." San Ramon, CA: Developmental Studies Center.

Baumann, Donald J.; Cialdini, Robert B.; and Kenrick, Douglas T., 1981. "Altruism as Hedonism: Helping and Self-Gratification as Equivalent Responses." *Jour. of Personality and Soc. Psychol.,* 40, 6:1039–1046.

————, 1983. "Mood and Sex Differences in the Development of Altruism as Hedonism." *Academic Psychol. Bull.,* 5, 2:299–307.

Beaman, Arthur L. et al., 1978. "Increasing Helping Rates Through Information Dissemination: Teaching Pays." *Personality and Soc. Psychol. Bull.,* 4, 3:406–411.

Beaman, Arthur L. et al., 1983a. "Fifteen Years of Foot-in-the-Door Research: A Meta-Analysis." *Personality and Soc. Psychol. Bull.,* 9, 2:181–196.

Beaman, Arthur L. et al., 1983b. "The Importance of Reinforcement Schedules on the Development and Maintenance of Altruistic Behaviors." *Academic Psychol. Bull.,* 5:309–317.

Benvenisti, Meron, 1988. "Growing Up in Jerusalem." *New York Times Magazine,* October 16:34–37.

Berkowitz, Leonard, 1972. "Social Norms, Feelings, and Other Factors

Affecting Helping and Altruism." *Advances in Experimental Soc. Psychol.*, 6:63–108.

————, 1973. "Reactance and the Unwillingness to Help." *Psychol. Bull.*, 79:310–317.

————, 1978. "Decreased Helpfulness with Increased Group Size Through Lessening the Effects of the Needy Individual's Dependency." *Jour. of Personality*, 46:299–310.

————, 1983. "Some Thoughts About Research on Reactions to Help." In Jeffrey D. Fisher et al., eds., *New Directions in Helping* (New York: Academic Press).

————, 1986. "Helpfulness and Altruism." In Leonard Berkowitz, *A Survey of Social Psychology*, 3rd ed. (New York: Holt, Rinehart & Winston).

Berndt, Thomas et al., 1983–1984. "The Effects of Group Discussions on Children's Moral Decisions." *Soc. Cognition*, 2, 4:343–359.

Bickman, Leonard, 1971. "The Effect of Another Bystander's Ability to Help on Bystander Intervention in an Emergency." *Jour. of Experimental Soc. Psychol.*, 7:367–379.

Bierman, John, 1981. *Righteous Gentile: The Story of Raoul Wallenberg, Missing Hero of the Holocaust.* New York: Viking.

Bihm, Elson; Gaudet, Irby; and Sale, Owen, 1979. "Altruistic Responses Under Conditions of Anonymity." *Jour. of Soc. Psychol.*, 109, 1:25–30.

Blake, Joseph A., 1978. "Death by Hand Grenade: Altruistic Suicide in Combat." *Suicide and Life-Threatening Behavior*, 8, 1:46–59.

Boorman, Scott A., and Levitt, Paul R., 1980. *The Genetics of Altruism.* New York: Academic Press.

Boorstin, Daniel, 1983. *The Discoverers.* New York: Random House.

Bouchard, Thomas J., Jr., 1986. "Diversity, Development and Determinism: A Report on Identical Twins Reared Apart." In Manfred Amelang, ed., *Bericht über den 35. Kongress der Deutschen Gesellschaft für Psychologie in Heidelberg 1986.* Göttingen: Verlag für Psychologie, 417–435.

Brabazon, James, 1975. *Albert Schweitzer: A Biography.* New York: G. P. Putnam's Sons.

Brewer, Marilyn, 1979. "Ingroup Bias in the Minimal Intergroup Situation: A Cognitive-Motivational Analysis." *Psychol. Bull.*, 86:307–324.

Bridgeman, Diane L., ed., 1983. *The Nature of Prosocial Development.* New York, Academic Press.

Briggs, Nathaniel C. et al., 1986. "On Willingness to be a Bone Marrow Donor." *Transfusion*, 26, 4:324–330

Bronowski, J., 1973. *The Ascent of Man.* Boston: Little, Brown.

Brown, Dyke, 1979. "Progress Report on Childhood Inquiry." Mimeo. Orinda, CA: Developmental Studies Center of San Ramon, CA.

Bryan, James H., 1966. "Helping and Hitchhiking." Unpub. paper, Northwestern University.

————, 1970. "Children's Reactions to Helpers: Their Money Isn't Where

Their Mouths Are." In Jacqueline R. Macaulay and Leonard Berkowitz, eds., 1970.

————; Redfield, Joel; and Mader, Sandra, 1971. "Words and Deeds About Altruism and the Subsequent Reinforcement Power of the Model." *Child Development*, 42:1501–1508.

Bryan, James H., and Walbek, Nancy, 1970. "The Impact of Words and Deeds Concerning Altruism upon Children." *Child Development*, 41:747–757.

Bryant, Brenda, and Crockenberg, S., 1980. "Correlates and Dimensions of Prosocial Behavior." *Child Development*, 51:529–544.

Budd, Louis J., 1956. "Altruism Arrives in America." *Amer. Quarterly*, 8:40–52.

Burley, J., and Stiller, C. R., 1985. "Emotionally Related Donors and Renal Transplantation." *Transplantation Proc.*, 17, 6, suppl. 3:123–127.

Bushman, Brad J., 1984. "Perceived Symbols of Authority and Their Influence on Compliance." *Jour. of Applied Soc. Psychol.*, 14, 6:501–508.

Callero, Peter L., 1985–1986. "Putting the Social in Prosocial Behavior: An Interactionist Approach to Altruism." *Humboldt Jour. of Soc. Relations*, 13, 1–2:15–32.

————, and Piliavin, Jane Allyn, 1983. "Developing a Commitment to Blood Donation: The Impact of One's First Experience." *Jour. of Applied Soc. Psychol.*, 13, 1:1–16.

Campbell, Donald T., 1972. "On the Genetics of Altruism and the Counter-Hedonic Components in Human Culture." *Jour. of Social Issues*, 28, 3:21–37.

————, 1975. "On the Conflicts Between Biological and Social Evolution and Between Psychology and Moral Tradition." *American Psychologist*, 30:1103–1126.

Carcopino, Jérôme, 1940. *Daily Life in Ancient Rome*. New Haven: Yale University Press.

Carlson, Michael, and Miller, Norman, 1987. "Explanation of the Relation Between Negative Mood and Helping." *Psychol. Bull.*, 102, 1:91–108.

Carnegie Hero Fund Commission, 1984. *Annual Report, 1984*. Pittsburgh, PA: Carnegie Hero Fund Commission.

————, 1985. *Annual Report, 1985*. Pittsburgh, PA: Carnegie Hero Fund Commission.

————, 1986. *Annual Report, 1986*. Pittsburgh, PA: Carnegie Hero Fund Commission.

————, 1987. *Annual Report, 1987*. Pittsburgh, PA: Carnegie Hero Fund Commission.

Carter, Lillian, and Spann, Gloria Carter, 1977. *Away from Home: Letters to My Family*. New York: Simon & Schuster.

Chagnon, Napoleon, 1984. *Yanomamö: The Fierce People*. New York: Holt, Rinehart & Winston.

Churcher, Sharon, 1988. "Making It by Doing Good." *New York Times Magazine,* July 3:16ff.

Cialdini, Robert B., 1985. *Influence: Science and Practice.* Glenview, IL: Scott, Foresman & Company.

———; Darby, B. L.; and Vincent, J. E., 1973. "Transgression and Altruism: A Case of Hedonism." *Jour. of Experimental Soc. Psychol.,* 9:502–516.

Cialdini, Robert B., and Kenrick, Douglas T., 1976. "Altruism as Hedonism: A Social Development Perspective on the Relationship of Negative Mood State and Helping." *Jour. of Personality and Soc. Psychol.,* 34:907–914.

———, and Baumann, Donald J., 1982. "Effects of Mood on Prosocial Behavior in Children and Adults." In Nancy Eisenberg, ed., 1982b.

Cialdini, Robert B. et al., 1987. "Empathy-Based Helping: Is It Selflessly or Selfishly Motivated?" *Jour. of Personality and Soc. Psych.,* 52, 4:749–758.

Clark, Russell D, and Word, Larry E., 1972. "Why Don't Bystanders Help? Because of Ambiguity?" *Jour. of Personality and Soc. Psychol.,* 24, 3:392–400.

———, 1974. "Where Is the Apathetic Bystander? Situational Characteristics of the Emergency." *Jour. of Personality and Soc. Psychol.,* 29:279–287.

Clary, E. Gil, and Miller, Jude, 1986. "Socialization and Situational Influences on Sustained Altruism." *Child Development,* 57:1358–1369.

Cohen, Ronald, 1972. "Altruism: Human, Cultural, or What?" *Jour. of Social Issues.,* 28, 3:39–57.

Coke, Jay S.; Batson, C, Daniel; and McDavis, K., 1978. "Empathic Mediation of Helping: A Two-Stage Model." *Jour. of Personality and Soc. Psychol.,* 36:752–766.

Colaizzi, Antoinette; Williams, Kim J.; and Kayson, Wesley, A., 1984. "When Will People Help? The Effects of Gender, Urgency, and Location on Altruism." *Psychol. Reports,* 55, 1:139–142.

Comte, Auguste, [1851] 1875. *System of Positive Polity.* London: Longmans Green.

Cummings, E. Mark, 1987. "Coping with Background Anger in Early Childhood." *Child Development,* 58:976–984.

———; Iannotti, Ronald J.; and Zahn-Waxler, Carolyn, 1985. "Influence of Conflict Between Adults on the Emotions and Aggression of Young Children." *Developmental Psychol.,* 21, 3:495–507.

Cunningham, Michael R., 1985–1986. "Levites and Brother's Keepers: A Sociobiological Perspective on Prosocial Behavior." *Humboldt Jour. of Soc. Relations,* 13, 1–2:35–67.

Curtiss, S. et al., 1975. "An Update on the Linguistic Development of Genie." In D. P. Data, ed., *Georgetown University Roundtable in Language and Linguistics* (Washington, D.C.: Georgetown University Press).

Darley, John, and Batson, C. Daniel. 1973. "From Jerusalem to Jericho." *Jour. of Personality and Soc. Psychol.* 27, 1:100–108.

Darley, John, and Latané, Bibb, 1968. "Bystander Intervention in Emergencies: Diffusion of Responsibility." *Jour. of Personality and Soc. Psychol.*, 8, 4:377–383.

Davis, Mark H., 1983. "Measuring Individual Differences in Empathy: Evidence for a Multidimensional Approach." *Jour. of Personality and Soc. Psychol.*, 44, 1:113–126.

Dawes, Robyn M.; McTavish, J.; and Shaklee, H., 1977. "Behavior, Communication, and Assumptions About Other People's Behavior in a Commons Dilemma Situation." *Jour. of Personality and Soc. Psychol.*, 35:1–11.

Dawes, Robyn M. et al., 1986. "Organizing Groups for Collective Action." *Amer. Polit. Sci. Rev.*, 80, 4:1171–1185.

Dawes, Robyn M. et al., 1987. "Not Me or Thee but We: The Importance of Group Identity in Eliciting Cooperation in Dilemma Situations: Experimental Manipulations." Paper presented at 11th Research Conference on Subjective Probability, August 1987, Cambridge, Eng.

Derlega, V. J., and Grzelak, J., eds. 1982. *Cooperation and Helping Behavior: Theories and Research.* New York: Academic Press.

Developmental Studies Center, n.d. *Child Development Project.* San Ramon, CA: The Child Development Project.

Dicks, H. V., 1972. *Licensed Mass Murder: A Sociological Study of Some SS Killers.* New York: Basic Books.

Diener, Edward et al., 1973. "Selected Demographic Variables in Altruism." *Psychol. Reports,* 33:226.

Dovidio, John F., 1984. "Helping Behavior and Altruism: An Empirical and Conceptual Overview." *Advances in Experimental Soc. Psychol.* 17:361–427.

———, and Campbell, John B., 1983. "Waiting to Help? Attention and Helping Behavior." *Academic Psychol. Bull.,* 5:229–236.

Dovidio, John F., and Gaertner, Samuel L., 1981. "The Effects of Race, Status, and Ability on Helping Behavior." *Soc. Psychol. Quarterly,* 44, 3:192–203.

———, 1983a. "The Effects of Sex, Status, and Ability on Helping Behavior." *Jour. of Applied Soc. Psychol.,* 13, 3:191–205.

———, 1983b. "Race Normative Structure, and Help-Seeking." In Jeffrey D. Fisher et al., eds., *New Directions in Helping* (New York: Academic Press).

———, eds., 1986. *Prejudice, Discrimination, and Racism.* Orlando, FL: Academic Press.

Dovidio, John F., and Schroeder, David A., 1987. "Negative Affect and the Empathy-Altruism Hypothesis: A Second Look." Paper presented at the 1987 meeting of the Society for Experimental Social Psychology, October 1987, Charlottesville, VA.

du Boulay, Juliet, 1974. *Portrait of a Greek Mountain Village.* Oxford: Clarendon Press.

Durant, Will, 1944. *Caesar and Christ.* New York: Simon & Schuster.

Eaves, L. J., and Last, K. A., 1980. "Assessing Empathy in Twins from Their Mutual Perception of Social Attitudes." *Personality and Individual Differences,* 1:172–176.

Eber, Milton, and Kunz, Lyle B., 1984. "The Desire to Help Others." *Bull. of the Menninger Clinic,* 48, 2:125–140.

Edney, Julian J., and Bell, Paul A., 1983. The Commons Dilemma: Comparing Altruism, the Golden Rule, Perfect Equality of Outcomes, and Territoriality." *Soc. Science Jour.,* 20, 4:23–33.

———, 1984. "Sharing Scarce Resources: Group-Outcome Orientation, External Disaster, and Stealing in a Simulated Commons." *Small Group Behavior,* 15, 1:87–108.

———, 1987. "Freedom and Equality in a Simulated Commons." *Political Psychol.,* 8, 2:229–243.

Eisenberg, Nancy, 1982a. "Prosocial Moral Reasoning Stories: Procedures." Mimeo.

———, ed., 1982b. *The Development of Prosocial Behavior.* New York: Academic Press.

———, 1983. "The Relation Between Empathy and Altruism." *Academic Psychol. Bull.,* 5:195–207.

———, 1986. *Altruistic Emotion, Cognition, and Behavior.* Hillsdale, NJ: Lawrence Erlbaum Associates.

———; Bartlett, Kim; and Haake, Robert, 1983. "The Effects of Nonverbal Cues Concerning Possession of a Toy on Children's Proprietary and Sharing Behaviors." *Jour. of Genetic Psychol.,* 143:79–85.

Eisenberg, Nancy et al., 1985a. "The Development of Prosocial Behavior and Cognitions in German Children." *Jour. of Cross-Cultural Psychol.,* 16, 1:69–82.

Eisenberg, Nancy; Lennon, Randy; and Roth, Karlsson, 1983. "Prosocial Development: A Longitudinal Study." *Developmental Psychol.* 19, 6:846–855.

Eisenberg, Nancy et al., 1985b. "Children's Justification for Their Adult and Peer-Directed Compliant (Prosocial and Nonprosocial) Behaviors." *Developmental Psychol.,* 21, 2:325–331.

Eisenberg, Nancy, and Miller, Paul, 1987. "The Relation of Empathy to Prosocial and Related Behaviors." *Psychol. Bull.,* 101:91–119.

Eisenberg, Nancy; Reykowski, Janusz; and Staub, Ervin, eds., 1988. *Social and Moral Values: Individual and Societal Perspectives.* Hillsdale, NJ: Lawrence Erlbaum Associates.

Eisenberg, Nancy, and Strayer, Janet, eds., 1987. *Empathy and Its Development.* Cambridge: Cambridge University Press.

Eisenberg-Berg, Nancy, 1979. "Development of Children's Prosocial Moral Judgment." *Developmental Psychol.,* 15, 2:128–137.

———, and Geisheker, E., 1979. "Content and Preachings of the Model

Preacher: The Effect on Children's Generosity." *Developmental Psychol.*, 15, 2:168–175.

Eisenberg-Berg, Nancy, and Hand, Michael, 1979. "The Relationship of Preschoolers' Reasoning About Prosocial Moral Conflicts to Prosocial Behavior." *Child Development*, 50:356–363.

———, n.d. Untitled; protocol of stories for use in altruism research with younger children.

Eisenberg-Berg, Nancy, and Neal, C., 1979. "Children's Moral Reasoning About Their Own Prosocial Behavior." *Developmental Psychol.*, 16:102–107.

Feinman, Saul, 1979. "Trusting a Stranger: Effects of City Size, Sex, and Appearance of Stranger." Paper presented at the meeting of the Southwestern Sociological Association, March 28–31, Fort Worth, TX.

Fellner, Carl H., and Schwartz, Shalom H., 1971. "Altruism in Disrepute: Medical Versus Public Attitudes Toward the Living Organ Donor." *New England Jour. of Med.*, 284, 11:582–585.

Feshbach, Norma Deitch, 1978. "Studies of Empathic Behavior in Children." In B. A. Maher, ed., *Progress in Experimental Personality Research* (New York: Academic Press), 8:1–47.

———, 1979. "Empathy Training: A Field Study in Affective Education." In S. Feshbach and A. Fraczek, eds., *Aggression and Behavior Change* (New York: Praeger).

———, 1982. "Sex Differences in Empathy and Social Behavior in Children." In Nancy Eisenberg, ed., 1982b.

——— et al., 1983. *Learning to Care: Classroom Activities for Social and Affective Development.* Glenview, IL: Scott, Foresman & Company.

Flavell, J. H., 1963. *The Developmental Psychology of Jean Piaget.* Princeton, NJ: D. Van Nostrand.

Foehl, Jack C., and Goldman, Morton, 1983. "Increasing Altruism by Using Compliance Techniques." *Jour. of Soc. Psychol.*, 119, 1:21–29.

Fogelman, Eva, and Wiener, Valerie Lewis, 1985. "The Few, the Brave, the Noble." *Psychol. Today*, August:60–65.

Freedman, D. G., 1979. *Human Sociobiology.* New York: Free Press.

Freedman, Jonathan L., and Fraser, Scott C., 1966. "Compliance Without Pressure: The Foot-in-the-door Technique." *Jour. of Personality and Soc. Psychol.*, 4:195–203.

Freud, Anna, 1946. "A Form of Altruism." In Anna Freud, ed., *The Ego and the Mechanism of Defense* (New York: International Universities Press).

Fried, Rona, and Berkowitz, Leonard, 1979. "Music Hath Charms . . . and Can Influence Helpfulness." *Jour. of Applied Soc. Psychol.*, 9, 3:199–208.

Froming, William J.; Allen, Leticia; and Jensen, Richard, 1985. "Altruism, Role-Taking, and Self-Awareness: The Acquisition of Norms Governing Altruistic Behavior." *Child Development*, 56:1223–1228.

Fromm, Erich, 1947. *Man for Himself.* New York: Rinehart.

Fuchs, Ina et al., 1986a. "Kibbutz, Israeli City, and American Children's Moral Reasoning About Prosocial Moral Conflicts." *Merrill-Palmer Quarterly*, 32, 1:37–50.

Fultz, Jim et al., 1986b. "Social Evaluation and the Empathy-Altruism Hypothesis." *Jour. of Personality and Soc. Psychol.*, 50, 4:761–769.

Gaertner, Samuel L., and Dovidio, John F., 1977. "The Subtlety of White Racism, Arousal, and Helping Behavior." *Jour. of Personality and Soc. Psychol.*, 35, 10:691–707.

———, 1986. "Problems, Progress, and Promise." In John F. Dovidio and Samuel L. Gaertner, eds., 1986.

Gallagher, Winifred, 1987. "To the Manner Born." *Rolling Stone*, November 19:56ff.

Geis, Gilbert, 1981. "The Crime Intervenor: Samaritan or Superman?" Distinguished Faculty Lecture, University of California, Irvine.

———, in press. "Sanctioning the Selfish: Applying the Bad Samaritan Law in Portugal."

———, and Huston, Ted L., 1980. "Altruism, Risk-Taking, and Self-Destructiveness: A Study of Interveners into Violent Criminal Events." In Norman L. Farberow, ed., *The Many Faces of Suicide: Indirect Self-Destructive Behavior* (New York: McGraw-Hill).

Gergen, Kenneth et al., 1972. "Individual Orientations to Prosocial Behavior," *Jour. of Social Issues*, 8:105–130.

Ghiselin, Michael T., 1974. *The Economy of Nature and the Evolution of Sex.* Berkeley: University of California Press.

Gibbs, John C., 1987. "Social Processes in Delinquency: The Need to Facilitate Empathy as Well as Sociomoral Reasoning." In W. M. Kurtines and J. L. Gewirtz, eds., *Moral Development Through Social Interaction* (New York: John Wiley & Sons).

———, and Schnell, Steven V., 1985. "Moral Development 'Versus' Socialization." *Amer. Psychologist*, 40, 10:1071–1080.

Gibson, Janice T., and Haritos-Fatouros, Mika, 1986. "The Education of a Torturer." *Psychol. Today*, November: 50–58.

Gies, Miep, 1987. *Anne Frank Remembered: The Story of the Woman Who Helped to Hide the Frank Family.* New York: Simon & Schuster.

Ginsburg, Harvey J., and Miller, Shirley M., 1981. "Altruism in Children: A Naturalistic Study of Reciprocation and an Examination of the Relationship Between Social Dominance and Aid-Giving Behavior." *Ethology and Sociobiology*, 2, 2:75–83.

Glassman, Robert B., 1980. "An Evolutionary Hypothesis About Teaching and Proselytizing Behaviors." *Zygon: Jour. of Religion and Science*, 15, 2:133–154.

———; Packel, Edward W.; and Brown, Douglas L., 1986. "Green Beards and Kindred Spirits: A Preliminary Mathematical Model of Altruism Toward Nonkin Who Bear Similarities to the Giver." *Ethology and Sociobiology*, 7:107–115.

Gleitman, H., 1981. *Psychology*. New York: W. W. Norton.

Goldberger, Leo, ed., 1987. *The Rescue of the Danish Jews: Moral Courage Under Stress*. New York: New York University Press.

Goldstein, Arnold P., and Michaels, Gerald Y., 1985. *Empathy: Development, Training, and Consequences*. Hillsdale, NJ: Lawrence Erlbaum Associates.

Goodall, Jane, 1986. *The Chimpanzees of Gombe*. Cambridge: Harvard University Press.

Goode, William J., 1979. *The Celebration of Heroes*. Berkeley: University of California Press.

Gordon, Milton M., 1975. "Toward a General Theory of Racial and Ethnic Group Relations." In Nathan Glazer and D. Patrick Moynihan, eds., *Ethnicity: Theory and Practice* (Cambridge: Harvard University Press).

Gould, James L., and Marler, Peter, 1987. "Learning by Instinct," *Scientific American*, January:74–85.

Gould, Stephen Jay, 1977. "Caring Groups and Selfish Genes." *Natural History*, December:20–27.

———, 1986. "Cardboard Darwinism" (a review of three books of sociobiology). *The New York Review*, September 25:47–54.

———, 1987. "Animals and Us" (a review of four books about animals and animal psychology). *The New York Review*, June 25:20–26.

Gruder, Charles L.; Romer, Daniel; and Korth, Bruce, 1978. "Dependency and Fault as Determinants of Helping." *Jour. of Experimental Soc. Psychol.*, 14, 2:227–235.

Grunberg, Leil E. et al., eds., 1987. *A Distinctive Approach to Psychological Research: The Influence of Stanley Schachter*. Hillsdale, NJ: Lawrence Erlbaum Associates.

Gurin, Maurice C., 1987. "Courses in Philanthropy: A First in U.S. Colleges." *Fund Raising Management*, August:60–63.

Guttmann, J.; Bar-Tal, D.; and Leiser, P., 1985. "The Effect of Various Reward Situations on Children's Helping Behavior." *Educational Psychol.*, 5:65–71.

Hackler, James C.; Ho, Kwai-Yiu; and Urquhart-Ross, Carol, 1974. "The Willingness to Intervene: Differing Community Characteristics." *Social Problems*, 21, 3:328–344.

Hallie, Philip P., 1979. *Lest Innocent Blood Be Shed: The Story of the Village of Le Chambon, and How Goodness Happened There*. New York: Harper & Row.

Hamlyn, D. W., 1987. *A History of Western Philosophy*. New York: Viking.

Hampson, Robert B., 1981. "Helping Behavior in Children: Addressing the Interaction of a Person-Situation Model." *Developmental Rev.*, 1:93–112.

———, 1984. "Adolescent Prosocial Behavior: Peer-Group and Situational Factors Associated with Helping." *Jour. of Personality and Soc. Psychol.*, 46, 1:153–162.

Hansson, Robert O.; Slade, Kenneth M.; and Slade, Pamela S., 1978. "Urban-Rural Differences in Responsiveness to an Altruistic Model." *Jour. of Soc. Psychol.*, 105:99–105.

Hardin, Garrett, 1977. *The Limits of Altruism: An Ecologist's View of Survival.* Bloomington: Indiana University Press.

Hardyck, Jane Allyn; Piliavin, Irving M.; and Vadum, Arlene C., 1971. "Reactions to the Victim in a Just or Non-just World." Paper read at the meeting of the Society of Experimental Social Psychology, Bethesda, MD.

Harris, Mary B., 1972. "The Effects of Performing One Altruistic Act on the Likelihood of Performing Another." *Jour. of Soc. Psychol.,* 88, 1:65–73.

———, and Baudin, Hortensia, 1973. "The Language of Altruism: The Effects of Language, Dress, and Ethnic Group." *Jour. of Soc. Psychol.,* 91:37–41.

Harris, Mary B., and Bays, Gail, 1973. "Altruism and Sex Roles." *Psychol. Reports,* 32:1002.

Harris, Mary B., and Ho, Junghwan, 1984. "Effects of Degree, Locus, and Controllability of Dependency, and Sex of Subject on Anticipated and Actual Helping." *Jour. of Soc. Psychol.,* 122:245–255.

Harris, Mary B., and Klingbeil, Dolores R., 1976. "The Effects of the Ethnicity of Subject and Accent and Dependency of Confederate on Aggressiveness and Altruism." *Jour. of Soc. Psychol.,* 98:47–53.

Harris, Mary B., and Meyer, Fred W., 1973. "Dependency, Threat, and Helping." *Jour. of Soc. Psychol.,* 90:239–242.

Harris, Mary B., and Samerotte, George, 1975. "The Effects of Aggressive and Altruistic Modeling on Subsequent Behavior." *Jour. of Soc. Psychol.,* 95:173–182.

———, 1976. "The Effects of Actual and Attempted Theft, Need, and a Previous Favor on Altruism." *Jour. of Soc. Psychol.,* 99:193–202.

Hatfield, Elaine; Walster, G. William; and Piliavin, Jane Allyn, 1978. "Equity Theory and Helping Relationships." In Lauren Wispé, ed., 1978.

Hellman, Peter, 1980. *Avenue of the Righteous.* New York: Atheneum.

Hessing, Dick J., and Elffers, Henk, 1985. "General and Physical Self-Esteem and Altruistic Behavior." *Psychol. Reports,* 56, 3:930.

Hoffman, Martin L., 1970. "Conscience, Personality, and Socialization Techniques." *Human Development,* 13:90–126.

———, 1971a. "Father Absence and Conscience Development." *Developmental Psychol.,* 4, 3:400–406.

———, 1971b. "Identification and Conscience Development." *Child Development,* 42:1071–1082.

———, 1975a. "Altruistic Behavior and the Parent-Child Relationship." *Jour. of Personality and Soc. Psychol.,* 31, 5:937–943.

———, 1975b. "Developmental Synthesis of Affect and Cognition and Its Implications for Altruistic Motivation." *Developmental Psychol.,* 11, 5:607–622.

———, 1975c. "Sex Differences in Moral Internalization and Values." *Jour. of Personality and Soc. Psychol.,* 32, 4:720–729.

————, 1981. "Is Altruism Part of Human Nature?" *Jour. of Personality and Soc. Psychol.*, 40, 1:121–137.

————, 1982. "Development of Prosocial Motivation: Empathy and Guilt." In Nancy Eisenberg, ed., 1982b.

————, 1983. "Affective and Cognitive Processes in Moral Internalization." In E. T. Higgins, D. Ruble, and W. Hartup, eds., *Social Cognition and Social Development: A SocioCultural Perspective* (New York: Cambridge University Press).

————, 1987. "The Contribution of Empathy to Justice and Moral Development." In Nancy Eisenberg and Janet Strayer, eds., 1987.

————, 1988. "Empathy and Prosocial Activism." In Nancy Eisenberg, Janusz Reykowski, and Ervin Staub, eds., 1988.

————, and Levine, Laura E., 1976. "Early Sex Differences in Empathy." *Developmental Psychol.*, 12, 6:557–558.

Hoffman, Martin L., and Saltzstein, Herbert D., 1967. "Parent Discipline and the Child's Moral Development." *Jour. of Personality and Soc. Psychol.*, 5, 1:45–57.

Holden, Constance, 1987. "The Genetics of Personality." *Science,* 237: 598–601.

Holloway, S.; Tucker, I.; and Hornstein, I., 1977. "The Effects of Social and Nonsocial Information on Interpersonal Behavior of Males: The News Makes News." *Jour. of Personality and Soc. Psychol.*, 35:514–522.

Hornstein, Harvey A., 1976. *Cruelty and Kindness: A New Look at Aggression and Altruism.* Englewood Cliffs, NJ: Prentice-Hall.

————, 1982. "Promotive Tension: Theory and Research." In V. J. Derlega and J. Grzelak, eds., 1982.

Hothersall, David, 1984. *History of Psychology.* Philadelphia: Temple University Press.

Hott, Louis R., 1979. "The Antisocial Character." *Amer. Jour. of Psychanal.*, 39, 3:235–244.

Howard, Robert B., 1987. "The Passing of Benevolence." *Postgrad. Med.*, 81, 2:13–15.

Howell, Nancy, 1986. "Images of the Tasaday and the !Kung: Reassessing Isolated Hunter-Gatherers." Paper presented at the Indiana University African Studies Center, October 1, Bloomington, IN.

Howes, Carollee, and Eldredge, Robert, 1985. "Responses of Abused, Neglected, and Non-Maltreated Children to the Behaviors of Their Peers." *Jour. of Applied Developmental Psychol.*, 6, 2–3:261–270.

Huneke, Douglas K., 1985–1986. "The Lessons of Herman Graebe's Life: The Origins of a Moral Person." *Humboldt Jour. of Soc. Relations,* 13, 1–2:320–332.

Hunt, Morton, 1959. *The Natural History of Love.* New York: Alfred A. Knopf.

————, 1982. *The Universe Within: A New Science Explores the Human Mind.* New York: Simon & Schuster.

————, 1985. *Profiles of Social Research: The Scientific Study of Human Interactions.* New York: Russell Sage Foundation.

Hurley, Dennis, and Allen, Bem, 1974. "The Effect of the Number of People Present in a Nonemergency Situation." *Jour. of Soc. Psychol.,* 92:27–29.

Huston, Ted L.; Geis, Gilbert; and Wright, Richard, 1976. "The Angry Samaritans." *Psychol. Today,* June:61–64.

———— et al., 1976. "Good Samaritans as Crime Victims." In Emilio C. Viano, ed., *Victims and Society* (Washington, D.C.: Visage Press).

Huston Ted L. et al., 1981. "Bystander Intervention into Crime: A Study Based on Naturally Occurring Episodes." *Soc. Psychol. Quarterly,* 44, 1:14–23.

Iannotti, Ronald J., 1978. "Effect of Role-Taking Experiences on Role Taking, Empathy, Altruism, and Aggression." *Developmental Psychol.,* 14, 2:119–124.

Independent Sector, 1988. *Giving and Volunteering in the United States: Summary of Findings.* (A survey conducted by the Gallup Organization.) Washington, D.C.: Independent Sector.

Isen, Alice M., 1970. "Success, Failure, Attention, and Reaction to Others: The Warm Glow of Success." *Jour. of Personality and Soc. Psychol.,* 15, 4:294–301.

————; Horn, Nancy; and Rosenhan, D. L., 1973. "Effects of Success and Failure on Children's Generosity." *Jour. of Personality and Soc. Psychol.,* 27, 2:239–247.

Isen, Alice M., and Levin, Paula F., 1972. "Effect of Feeling Good on Helping: Cookies and Kindness." *Jour. of Personality and Soc. Psychol.,* 21, 3:384–388.

Isen, Alice M. et al., 1978. "Affect, Accessibility of Material in Memory, and Behavior: A Cognitive Loop?" *Jour. of Personality and Soc. Psychol.,* 36, 1:1–12.

Isen, Alice M., and Simmonds, Stanley F., 1978. "The Effects of Feeling Good on a Helping Task That Is Incompatible with Good Mood." *Social Psychol.,* 41, 4:346–349.

Jegstrup, Elsebet, 1985–1986. "Spontaneous Action: The Rescue of the Danish Jews from Hannah Arendt's Perspective." *Humboldt Jour. of Soc. Relations,* 13, 1–2:260–284.

Johnson, Daniel B., 1982. "Altruistic Behavior and the Development of the Self in Infants." *Merrill-Palmer Quarterly,* 28, 3:379–388.

Jones, Edward E., 1985. "Major Developments in Social Psychology Since 1930." In Gardner Lindzey and Elliot Aronson, eds., 1985.

Kagan, Jerome; Kearsley, Richard B.; and Zelazo, Philip R., 1978. *Infancy: Its Place in Human Development.* Cambridge: Harvard University Press.

Kane, Elizabeth, 1988. *Birth Mother: The Story of America's First Legal Surrogate Mother.* San Diego: Harcourt Brace Jovanovich.

Kaplan, Arthur, 1984. "Organ Procurement: It's Not in the Cards." *The Hastings Center Report,* October:9–12.

Kaplan, John, 1978. "A Legal Look at Prosocial Behavior: What Can Happen If One Tries to Help or Fails to Help Another." In Lauren Wispé, ed., 1978.

Karpe, Richard, 1961. "The Rescue Complex in Anna O's Final Identity." *The Psychoanalytic Quarterly,* 30:1–27.

Katz, Joseph, 1972. "Altruism and Sympathy: Their History in Philosophy and Some Implications for Psychology." *Jour. of Social Issues,* 28, 3:59–69.

Kelley, Harold H., and Michela, John L., 1980. "Attribution Theory and Research." *Ann. Rev. of Psychol.,* 31:457–501.

Keneally, Thomas, 1983. *Schindler's List.* New York: Penguin Books.

Kennett, David A., 1980a. "Altruism and Economic Behavior, I: Developments in the Theory of Public and Private Redistribution." *Amer. Jour. of Econ. and Sociol.,* 39, 2:183–198.

———, 1980b. "Altruism and Economic Behavior, II: Private Charity and Public Policy." *Amer. Jour. of Econ. and Sociol.,* 39, 4:337–354.

Kenrick, Douglas T., 1987. "Gender, Genes, and the Social Environment." In P. C. Shaver and C. Hendrick, eds., *Review of Personality and Social Psychology,* 8:14–43.

———, and Funder, David C., in press. "Profiting from Controversy: Lessons from the Person-Situation Debate." *Amer. Psychologist.*

Kerber, Kenneth W., 1984. "The Perception of Nonemergency Helping Situations: Costs, Rewards, and the Altruistic Personality." *Jour. of Personality,* 52, 2:177–187.

Kidd, R. F., and Marshall, L., 1982. "Self-Reflection, Mood, and Helpful Behavior." *Jour. of Research in Personality,* 16:319–334.

Knight, George P., and Kagan, Spencer, 1977. "Development of Prosocial and Competitive Behaviors in Anglo-American and Mexican-American Children." *Child Development,* 48, 4:1385–1394.

Koch, Sigmund, and Leary, David E., eds., 1985. *A Century of Psychology as a Science.* New York: McGraw-Hill.

Kohlberg, Lawrence, 1984. *The Psychology of Moral Development.* San Francisco: Harper & Row.

Kramer, Heinrich, and Sprenger, James, [1486] 1971. *The Malleus Maleficarum.* New York: Dover Publications.

Kramer, Roderick M., and Brewer, Marilyn B., 1984. "The Effects of Group Identity on Resource Use in a Simulated Commons Dilemma." *Jour. of Personality and Soc. Psychol.,* 46:1044–1057.

Kramer, Roderick M.; McClintock, Charles G.; and Messick, David M., 1986. "Social Values and Cooperative Response to a Simulated Resource Conservation Crisis." *Jour. of Personality,* 54, 3:576–592.

Krebs, Dennis L., 1970. "Altruism—An Examination of the Concept and a Review of the Literature." *Psychol. Bull.,* 73:258–302.

———, 1982a. "Helping in Emergencies: The Construction and Disintegration of a Model" (review of Piliavin, Dovidio, Gaertner, and Clark, 1981). *Contemp. Psychol.*, 27, 10:775–778.

———, 1982b. "Altruism—A Rational Approach." In Nancy Eisenberg, ed., 1982b.

———, 1982c. "Prosocial Behavior, Equity, and Justice." In Jerald Greenberg and Ronald Cohen, eds., *Equity and Justice in Social Behavior* (New York: Academic Press).

———, 1982d. "Psychological Approaches to Altruism: An Evaluation." *Ethics*, 92, 3:447–458.

———, 1983a. "Commentary and Critique: Applied Approaches to Prosocial Development." In Diane L. Bridgeman, ed., 1983.

———, 1983b. "Commentary and Critique: Cross-Cultural Approaches to Prosocial Development." In Diane L. Bridgeman, ed., 1983.

———, 1983c. "Commentary and Critique: Psychological and Philosophical Approaches to Prosocial Development." In Diane L. Bridgeman, ed., 1983.

———, 1983d. "Commentary and Critique: Sociobiological Approaches to Prosocial Development." In Diane L. Bridgeman, ed., 1983.

———, 1987. "The Challenge of Altruism in Biology and Psychology." In C. Crawford, M. Smith, and D. Krebs, eds., *Sociobiology and Psychology: Ideas, Issues, and Findings* (Hillsdale, NJ: Lawrence Erlbaum Associates).

———, and Miller, Dale T., 1985. "Altruism and Aggression." In Gardner Lindzey and Elliot Aronson, eds., 1985.

Krebs, Dennis; Schroder, Marianne; and Denton, Kathy, 1987. "On the Corruption of Pure Reason in the Moral Domain." Paper given at the symposium "From moral judgment to action and back again," Harvard University, January, Cambridge, MA.

Kunda, Ziva, and Schwartz, Shalom H., 1983. "Undermining Intrinsic Moral Motivation: External Reward and Self-Presentation." *Jour. of Personality and Soc. Psychol.*, 45, 4:763–771.

Kurtines, William M., and Gewirtz, Jacob L., eds., 1984. *Morality, Moral Behavior, and Moral Development.* New York: John Wiley & Sons.

Kurtzburg, R. L.; Safar, H.; and Carior, N., 1968. "Surgical and Social Rehabilitation of Adult Offenders." *Proc. of the 76th Annual Convention of the Amer. Psychol. Assoc.*, 3:649–650.

Ladas, Stephen P., 1932. *The Exchange of Minorities: Bulgaria, Greece, and Turkey.* New York: Macmillan.

Landes, William M., and Posner, Richard A., 1978. "Salvors, Finders, Good Samaritans, and Other Rescuers." *Jour. of Legal Studies*, 7, 1:83–128.

Lang, John S., 1987. "How Genes Shape Personality." *U.S. News & World Report*, April 13.

L'Armand, Kathleen, and Pepitone, Albert, 1975. "Helping to Reward

Another Person: A Cross-cultural Analysis." *Jour. of Personality and Soc. Psychol.*, 31, 2:189–198.

Latané, Bibb, 1981. "The Psychology of Social Impact." *Amer. Psychologist,* 36, 4:343–356.

———, and Darley, John, 1968. "Group Inhibition of Bystander Intervention in Emergencies." *Jour. of Personality and Soc. Psychol.*, 10, 3:215–221.

———, 1970. *The Unresponsive Bystander: Why Doesn't He Help?* Englewood Cliffs, NJ: Prentice-Hall.

Latané, Bibb, and Nida, Steve, 1981. "Ten Years of Research on Group Size and Helping." *Psychol. Bull.*, 89, 2:308–324.

Latané, Bibb, and Rodin, Judith, 1969. "A Lady in Distress: Inhibiting Effects of Friends and Strangers on Bystander Intervention." *Jour. of Experimental Soc. Psychol.*, 5:189–202.

Lee, Richard Borshay, 1979. *The !Kung San: Men, Women, and Work in a Foraging Society.* Cambridge: Cambridge University Press.

Lennon, Randy; Eisenberg, Nancy; and Carroll, James, 1986. "The Relation Between Nonverbal Indices of Empathy and Preschoolers' Prosocial Behavior." *Jour. of Applied Developmental Psychol.*, 7:219–224.

Lennon, Randy, and Eisenberg, Nancy, 1987. "Emotional Displays Associated with Preschoolers' Prosocial Behavior." *Child Development,* 58:992–1000.

Levi, Primo, 1986. *Survival in Auschwitz and the Reawakening: Two Memoirs.* New York: Summit Books.

Levin, Paula F., and Isen, Alice M., 1975. "Further Studies on the Effect of Feeling Good on Helping." *Sociometry,* 38, 1:141–147.

Lewontin, R. C.; Rose, Steven; and Kamin, Leon J., 1984. *Not in Our Genes: Biology, Ideology, and Human Nature.* New York: Pantheon Books.

Liberman, Kenneth, 1985–1986. "The Tibetan Cultural Praxis: Bodhicitta Thought Training." *Humboldt Jour. of Soc. Relations,* 13, 1–2:113–126.

Liebrand, Wim B. G., and van Run, Godfried J., 1985. "The Effects of Social Motives on Behavior in Social Dilemmas in Two Cultures." *Jour. of Experimental Soc. Psychol.*, 21:86–102.

Liebrand, Wim B. G. et al., 1986. "Value Orientation and Conformity." *Jour. of Conflict Resolution,* 30, 1:77–97.

Lifton, Robert Jay, 1986. *The Nazi Doctors.* New York: Basic Books.

———, 1987. *The Future of Immortality.* New York: Basic Books.

Lindzey, Gardner, and Aronson, Elliot, eds., 1969. *Handbook of Social Psychology,* 2nd ed. Reading, MA: Addison-Wesley.

———, eds., 1985. *Handbook of Social Psychology,* 3rd ed. Reading, MA: Addison-Wesley.

Loehlin, John C., 1982. "Are Personality Traits Differentially Heritable?" *Behavior Genetics,* 12, 4:417–428.

———, 1985. "Fitting Heredity-Environment Models Jointly to Twin and

Adoption Data from the California Psychological Inventory." *Behavior Genetics,* 15, 3:199–221.

———, 1986. "Heredity, Environment, and the Thurstone Temperament Schedule." *Behavior Genetics,* 16, 1:61–73.

———; Horn, Joseph M.; and Willerman, Lee, 1981. "Personality Resemblance in Adoptive Families." *Behavior Genetics,* 11, 4:309–330.

———, 1985. "Personality Resemblances in Adoptive Families When the Children Are Late-Adolescent or Adult." *Jour. of Personality and Soc. Psychol.,* 48, 2:376–392.

———, 1987. "Personality Resemblance in Adoptive Families." *Jour. of Personality and Soc. Psychol.,* 53, 5:961–969.

London, Perry, 1970. "The Rescuers: Motivational Hypotheses About Christians Who Saved Jews from the Nazis." In Jacqueline R. Macaulay and Leonard Berkowitz, eds., 1970.

Lucke, Joseph F., and Batson, C. Daniel, 1980. "Response Suppression to a Distressed Conspecific: Are Laboratory Rats Altruistic?" *Jour. of Experimental Soc. Psychol.,* 16, 3:214–227.

Ma, Hing-keung, 1985a. "Cross-cultural Study of Altruism." *Psychol. Reports,* 57, 1:337–338.

———, 1985b. "Cross-cultural Study of the Hierarchical Structure of Human Relationships," *Psychol. Reports,* 57, 3, pt. 2:1079–1083.

———, 1985c. "A Cross-cultural Study of Sex Differences in Human Relationships." *Psychol. Reports,* 56, 3:799–802.

Macaulay, Jacqueline R., and Berkowitz, Leonard, eds., 1970. *Altruism and Helping Behavior.* New York: Academic Press.

Maccoby, Eleanor Emmons, and Jacklin, Carol Nagy, 1974. *The Psychology of Sex Differences.* Palo Alto: Stanford University Press.

McWilliams, Nancy, 1984. "The Psychology of the Altruist." *Psychoanalytic Psychol.,* 1, 3:193–213.

Main, Mary, and George, C., 1985. "Responses of Abused and Disadvantaged Toddlers to Distress in Agemates: A Study in the Day Care Setting." *Developmental Psychol.,* 21, 3:407–412.

Manucia, Gloria K.; Baumann, Donald J.; and Cialdini, Robert B., 1984. "Mood Influences on Helping: Direct Effects or Side Effects?" *Jour. of Personality and Soc. Psychol.,* 46, 2:357–364.

Marcus, Robert F., 1980. "Empathy and Popularity of Preschool Children." *Child Study Journal,* 10, 3:133–145.

Mason, David, and Allen, Bem, 1972. "The Bystander Effect as a Function of Ambiguity and Emergency Character." *Jour. of Soc. Psychol.,* 100:145–146.

Mathews, K. E., and Canon, L. K., 1975. "Environmental Noise Level as a Determinant of Helping Behavior." *Jour. of Personality and Soc. Psychol.,* 32:571–577.

Maybury-Lewis, David, 1965. *The Savage and the Innocent.* Cleveland: World.

Melson, Gail F., and Fogel, Alan, 1988. "Learning to Care." *Psychol. Today,* January:39–45.

Merton, Robert K., 1960. "Some Thoughts on the Professions in American Society." *Brown University Papers XXXVII.*

———, 1987. "Three Fragments from a Sociologist's Notebooks." *Ann. Rev. of Sociol.,* 13:1–28.

———, and Gieryn, Thomas F., 1978. "Institutionalized Altruism: The Case of the Professions." In T. Lynn Smith, and Man Singh Das, eds., *Sociocultural Change Since 1950* (New Delhi, India: Vikas Publishing House).

Messick, David M., 1984. "Solving Social Dilemmas: Individual and Collective Approaches." *Representative Research in Soc. Psychol.,* 14:72–87.

——— et al., 1983. "Individual Adaptations and Structural Change as Solutions to Social Dilemmas." *Jour. of Personality and Soc. Psychol.,* 44, 2:294–309.

Midlarsky, Elizabeth; Kahana, Eva; and Corley, Robin, 1985–1986. "Personal and Situational Influences on Late Life Helping." *Humboldt Jour. of Soc. Relations,* 13, 1–2:217–233.

Milgram, Stanley, 1970. "The Experience of Living in Cities." *Science,* 167:1461–1468.

Miller, Dale T., 1977. "Altruism and Threat to a Belief in a Just World." *Jour. of Experimental Soc. Psychol.,* 13, 2:1–13.

Miller, Norman, and Brewer, Marilynn B., 1986. "Categorization Effects on Ingroup and Outgroup Perception." In John F. Dovidio and Samuel L. Gaertner, eds., 1986.

———, and Edwards, Keith, 1985. "Cooperative Action in Desegregated Settings: A Laboratory Analogue." *Jour. of Social Issues,* 41, 3:63–79.

Misavage, Robert, and Richardson, James T., 1974. "The Focusing of Responsibility: An Alternative Hypothesis in Help-Demanding Situations." *Eur. Jour. of Soc. Psychol.,* 4, 1:5–15.

Morgan, Charles J., 1985. "Natural Selection for Altruism in Structured Populations." *Ethol. and Sociobiol.,* 6, 4:211–218.

Morgan, Ted, 1987. "The Barbie File." *New York Times Magazine,* May 10:19–28.

Moriarty, T., 1975. "Crime, Commitment, and the Responsive Bystander: Two Field Experiments." *Jour. of Personality and Soc. Psychol.,* 31:370–376.

Mulkey, Young Jay, 1983. *The Character Education Curriculum: An Evaluation with Principals and Teachers.* San Antonio: American Institute for Character Education.

Mullis, Ronald L.; Smith, David W.; and Vollmers, Kenneth E., 1983. "Prosocial Behaviors in Young Children and Parental Guidance." *Child Study Journal,* 13, 1:13–21.

Mussen, Paul H., 1982. "Personality Development and Liberal Sociopolitical Attitudes." In Nancy Eisenberg, ed., 1982b.

———— et al., eds., 1983. *Handbook of Child Psychology.* 4th ed. New York: John Wiley & Sons.

Nadler, A.; Bar-Tal, D.; and Drukman, D., 1982. "Density Does not Help: Help Giving, Help Seeking, and Help Reciprocating of Residents of High and Low Student Dormitories." *Population and Environment,* 5:26–42.

Nagel, Thomas, 1979. *The Possibility of Altruism.* Princeton: Princeton University Press.

Nisbett, Richard E., and Ross, Lee, 1980. *Human Inference: Strategies and Shortcomings of Social Judgment.* Englewood Cliffs, NJ: Prentice-Hall.

Nisbett, Richard E., and Wilson, T. D., 1977. "Telling More Than We Can Know: Verbal Reports on Mental Processes." *Psychol. Rev.,* 84:231–259.

Nissen, H. W., and Crawford, M. P., 1936. "A Preliminary Study of Food-Sharing Behavior in Young Chimpanzees." *Jour. of Comparative Psychol.,* 22:383–419.

O'Connell, Brian, ed., 1983. *America's Voluntary Spirit: A Book of Readings.* New York: The Foundation Center.

O'Donohue, Joseph, and O'Donohue, Mary Ann, 1987. "The Peace Corps Experience: Its Lifetime Impact on U.S. Volunteers." Paper presented at the annual convention of the American Psychological Association, September, New York, NY.

Oliner, Pearl, 1985–1986. "Legitimating and Implementing Prosocial Education." *Humboldt Jour. of Soc. Relations,* 13, 1–2:389–408.

Oliner, Samuel P., 1976. "Sorokin's Contribution to American Sociology." *Nationalities Papers,* 4, 2:125–147.

————, 1982. "The Need to Recognize the Heroes of the Nazi Era." *Reconstructionist,* June:24–27.

————, 1984. "The Unsung Heroes in Nazi-Occupied Europe: The Antidote for Evil." *Nationalities Papers,* 12, 1:28–30.

————, [1979] 1986. *Restless Memories: Recollections of the Holocaust Years.* Berkeley, CA: Judah L. Magnes Museum.

————, and Hallum, Ken, 1978. "Minority Contempt for Oppressors: A Comparative Analysis of Jews and Gypsies." *California Sociologist,* 1, 1:41–57.

Oliner, Samuel P., and Oliner, Pearl, 1988. *The Altruistic Personality: Rescuers of Jews in Nazi Europe.* New York: Free Press.

Olweus, Dan; Block, Jack; and Radke-Yarrow, Marian, eds., 1986. *Development of Antisocial and Prosocial Behavior: Research, Theories, and Issues.* New York: Academic Press.

Parmelee, Arthur H., 1986. "Children's Illnesses: Their Beneficial Effects on Behavioral Development." *Child Development,* 57, 1:1–10.

Peace Corps, 1986. *Peace Corps Times,* November/December 1986. Washington, D.C.: Peace Corps.

Pearl, David, 1984. "Violence and Aggression." *Society,* 21, 6:17–22.

Perry, Richard J., 1985–1986. "A Bouquet of Altruisms: Pseudo-Deductivism and the Salvaging of an Idea." *Humboldt Jour. of Soc. Relations*, 13, 1–2:68–85.

Peterson, Lloyd R., 1966. "Short-Term Memory." *Scientific American*, July: 90–95.

Peterson, Lizette, 1980. "Developmental Changes in Verbal and Behavioral Sensitivity to Cues of Social Norms of Altruism." *Child Development*, 51:830–838.

———, 1982. "An Alternative Perspective to Norm-Based Explanations of Modeling and Children's Generosity." *Merrill-Palmer Quarterly*, 28, 2:283–290.

———, 1983a. "Influence of Age, Task Competence, and Responsibility Focus on Children's Altruism." *Developmental Psychol.*, 19, 1:141–148.

———, 1983b. "Role of Donor Competence, Donor Age, and Peer Presence on Helping in an Emergency." *Developmental Psychol.*, 19, 6:873–880.

———, 1983c. "The Role of Neglected Factors in Age-Related Trends in Children's Altruism." *Academic Psychol. Bull.*, 5:273–279.

———; Hartmann, Donald; and Gelfand, Donna M., 1977. "Developmental Changes in the Effects of Dependency and Reciprocity Cues on Children's Moral Judgments and Donation Rates." *Child Development*, 48:1331–1339.

Peterson, Lizette; Reaven, Noah; and Homer, Andrew L., 1984. "Limitations Imposed by Parents on Children's Altruism." *Merrill-Palmer Quarterly*, 30, 3:269–286.

Peterson, Lizette; Ridley-Johnson, Robyn; and Carther, Cynthia, 1984. "The Supersuit: An Example of Structured Naturalistic Observation of Children's Altruism." *Jour. of General Psychol.*, 110:235–241.

Piaget, Jean, 1960. "The General Problem of the Psychobiological Development of the Child." in J. M. Tanner and B. Inhelder, eds., *Discussion on Child Development*, vol. 4, (New York: International Universities Press).

———, and Inhelder, Bärbel, 1969. *The Psychology of the Child*. New York: Basic Books.

Piliavin, Irving M.; Piliavin, Jane Allyn; and Rodin, Judith, 1975. "Costs, Diffusion, and the Stigmatized Victim." *Jour. of Personality and Soc. Psychol.*, 32, 3:429–438.

———, 1969. "Good Samaritanism: An Underground Phenomenon?" *Jour. of Personality and Soc. Psychol.*, 13, 4:289–299.

Piliavin, Jane Allyn, 1987. "Temporary Deferral and Donor Return." *Transfusion*, 27, 2:199–200.

———, and Callero, Peter, 1989. *Giving the Gift of Life to Unnamed Strangers: The Community Responsibility Blood Donor*. Baltimore: Johns Hopkins University Press.

———, and Evans, Dorcas E., 1982. "Addiction to Altruism? Opponent-

Process Theory and Habitual Blood Donation." *Jour. of Personality and Soc. Psychol.,* 43, 6:1200–1213.

Piliavin, Jane Allyn et al., 1981. *Emergency Intervention.* New York: Academic Press.

———, 1982. "Responsive Bystanders: The Process of Intervention." In V. J. Derlega and J. Grzelak, eds., 1982.

Piliavin, Jane Allyn; Evans, Dorcas, E.; and Callero, Peter, 1984. "Learning to 'Give to Unnamed Strangers.' " In Ervin Staub et al., eds., 1984.

Piliavin, Jane Allyn, and Piliavin, Irving M., 1972. "Effect of Blood on Reactions to a Victim." *Jour. of Personality and Soc. Psychol.,* 23, 3:353–361.

———, and Broll, Lorraine, 1976. "Time of Arrival at an Emergency and Likelihood of Helping." *Personality and Soc. Psychol. Bull.,* 2, 3:273–276.

Plomin, Robert, and Daniels, Denise, 1987. "Why Are Children in the Same Family So Different from One Another?" *Behavioral and Brain Sciences,* 10:1–60.

Pomazal, Richard J., 1977. "The Effects of Models on Donations as a Function of the Legitimacy of the Cause." *Representative Research in Soc. Psychol.,* 8:23–32.

———, and Clore, Gerald L., 1973. "Helping on the Highway: The Effects of Dependency and Sex." *Jour. of Applied Soc. Psychol.,* 3, 2:150–164.

Pomazal, Richard J., and Jaccard, James J., 1976. "An Informational Approach to Altruistic Behavior." *Jour. of Personality and Soc. Psychol.,* 33, 3:317–326.

Posner, Gerald, and Ware, John, 1986. *Mengele: The Complete Story.* New York: McGraw-Hill.

Powledge, Tabitha, 1983. "The Importance of Being Twins." *Psychol. Today,* July: 21–27.

Puka, Bill, 1983. "Altruism and Moral Development." In Diane L. Bridgeman, ed., 1983.

Radke-Yarrow, Marian; Scott, Phyllis M.; and Zahn-Waxler, Carolyn, 1973. "Learning Concern for Others." *Developmental Psychol.,* 8, 2:240–260.

Raviv, A.; Bar-Tal, D.; and Levin-Lewis, T., 1980. "Motivations for Donation Behavior by Boys of Three Different Ages." *Child Development,* 51:610–613.

Reiss, Michael J., 1984. "Human Sociobiology." *Zygon: Jour. of Religion and Science,* 19, 2:117–140.

Reykowski, Janusz, 1980. "Origin of Prosocial Motivation: Heterogeneity of Personality Development." *Studia Psychologica,* 22, 2:91–106.

———, 1982a. "Social Motivation," *Ann. Rev. of Psychol.,* 33:132–154.

———, 1982b. "Development of Prosocial Motivation: A Dialectic Process." In Nancy Eisenberg, ed., 1982b.

———, and Smolenska, Zuzanna, 1982. "Psychological Space and Regulation of Social Behavior." *Eur. Jour. of Soc. Psychol.,* 12:353–366.

Rice, Gerard T., 1986. *Peace Corps in the 80's.* Washington, D.C.: Peace Corps.

Rimland, Bernard, 1984. "The Altruism Paradox." *Southern Psychologist,* 2, 1:8–9.

Rittner, Carol, and Myers, Sandra, eds., 1986. *The Courage to Care.* New York: New York University Press.

Romer, Daniel; Gruder, Charles; and Lizzadro, Terri, 1986. "A Person-Situation Approach to Altruistic Behavior." *Jour. of Personality and Soc. Psychol.,* 51, 5: 1001–1012.

Rosen, Clare Mead, 1987. "The Eerie World of Reunited Twins." *Discover,* September: 36–46.

Rosenbaum, Max, and Muroff, Melvin, eds., 1984. *Anna O.: Fourteen Contemporary Reinterpretations.* New York: Free Press.

Rosenhan, David L., 1978. "Toward Resolving the Altruism Paradox: Affect, Self-Reinforcement, and Cognition." In Lauren G. Wispé, ed., 1978.

———; Salovey, Peter; and Hargis, Kenneth, 1981. "The Joys of Helping: Focus of Attention Mediates the Impact of Positive Affect on Altruism." *Jour. of Personality and Soc. Psychol.,* 40, 5:899–905.

Rosenhan, David L. et al., 1981. "Emotion and Altruism." In J. Philippe Rushton and Richard M. Sorrentino, eds., 1981.

Rosenthal, A. M., 1964. "Study of the Sickness Called Apathy." *New York Times Magazine,* May 3.

Rubenstein, Daniel I., and Wrangham, Richard W., 1980. "Why Is Altruism Towards Kin So Rare?" *Zeitschr. für Tierpsychol.,* 54, 4:381–387.

Rubin, Zick, and Peplau, Anne, 1973. "Belief in a Just World and Reactions to Another's Lot: A Study of Participants in the National Draft Lottery." *Jour. of Social Issues,* 29, 4:73–93.

———, 1975. "Who Believes in a Just World?" *Jour. of Social Issues,* 31, 3:65–89.

Rushton, J. Philippe, 1975. "Generosity in Children: Immediate and Long-Term Effects of Modeling, Preaching, and Moral Judgment." *Jour. of Personality and Soc. Psychol.,* 31, 3:459–466.

———, 1976. "Socialization and the Altruistic Behavior of Children." *Psychol. Bull.,* 83:898–913.

———, 1978. "Urban Density and Altruism: Helping Strangers in a Canadian City, Suburb, and Small Town." *Psychol. Reports,* 43:987–990.

———, 1982. "Altruism and Society: A Social Learning Perspective." *Ethics,* 92:425–446.

———, 1984. "The Altruistic Personality: Evidence from Laboratory, Naturalistic, and Self-Report Perspectives." In Ervin Staub et al., eds., 1984.

———; Chrisjohn, Roland D.; and Fekken, G. Cynthia, 1981. "The Altruistic Personality and the Self-Report Altruism Scale." *Personality and Individual Differences,* 2:293–302.

Rushton, J. Philippe et al., 1986. "Altruism and Aggression: The Heritability of Individual Differences." *Jour. of Personality and Soc. Psychol.*, 50, 6:1192–1198.

Rushton, J. Philippe; Littlefield, Christine H.; and Lumsden, Charles J., 1986. "Gene-Culture Coevolution of Complex Social Behavior: Human Altruism and Mate Choice." *Proc. of the National Acad. of Sci., USA*, 83:7340–7343.

Rushton, J. Philippe; Russell, Robin J. H.; and Wells, Pamela A., 1984. "Genetic Similarity Theory: Beyond Kin Selection." *Behavior Genetics*, 14, 3:179–193.

Rushton, J. Philippe, and Russell, Robin J. H., 1985. "Genetic Similarity Theory: A Reply to Mealey and New Evidence." *Behavior Genetics*, 15, 6:575–582.

Rushton, J. Philippe, and Sorrentino, Richard M., eds., 1981. *Altruism and Helping Behavior: Social, Personality, and Developmental Perspectives.* Hillsdale, NJ: Lawrence Erlbaum Associates.

Rushton, J. Philippe, and Wiener, Janet, 1975. "Altruism and Cognitive Development in Children." *Brit. Jour. of Soc. and Clin. Psychol.*, 14, 4:341–349.

Rutkowski, Gregory K; Gruder, Charles; and Romer, Daniel, 1983. "Group Cohesiveness, Social Norms, and Bystander Intervention." *Jour. of Personality and Soc. Psychol.*, 44, 3: 545–552.

Rutte, Christel G.; Wilke, Henk A. M.; and Messick, David M., 1987a. "The Effects of Framing Social Dilemmas as Give-Some or Take-Some Games." *British Jour. of Soc. Psychol.*, 26:103–108.

———, 1987b. "Scarcity or Abundance Caused by People or the Environments as Determinants of Behavior in the Resource Dilemma." *Jour. of Experimental Soc. Psychol.*, 23:208–216.

Sadler, Alfred M., and Sadler, Blair L., 1984. "A Community of Givers, Not Takers." *The Hastings Center Report*, October.

Sagi, Abraham, and Hoffman, Martin L., 1976. "Empathic Distress in the Newborn." *Jour. of Developmental Psychol.*, 12, 2:175–176.

Salovey, Peter, and Rosenhan, David L., 1983. "Effects of Joy, Attention, and Recipient's Status on Helpfulness." Paper presented at the annual meeting of the American Psychological Association, Anaheim, CA.

———, 1989. "Mood States and Prosocial Behavior." In H. L. Wagner and A. S. R. Manstead, eds., *Handbook of Social Psychophysiology* (Chichester, England: John Wiley & Sons).

Samerotte, George, and Harris, Mary B., 1976. "Some Factors Influencing Helping: The Effects of a Handicap, Responsibility, and Requesting Help." *Jour. of Soc. Psychol.*, 98:39–45.

Samuelson, Charles D., and Messick, David M., 1986. "Alternative Structural Solutions to Resource Dilemmas." *Organizational Behavior and Human Decision Processes*, 37:139–155.

Sauvage, Pierre, 1985–1986. "Ten Things I Would Like to Know About Righteous Conduct in Le Chambon and Elsewhere During the Holocaust." *Humboldt Jour. of Soc. Relations,* 13, 1–2:252–259.

Scarr, Sandra, and McCartney, Kathleen, 1983. "How People Make Their Own Environments: A Theory of Genotype → Environment Effects." *Child Development,* 54:424–435.

Schaller, Mark, and Cialdini, Robert B., in press. "The Economics of Empathic Helping: Support for a Mood Management Motive." *Jour. of Experimental Soc. Psychol.*

Schaps, Eric; Solomon, Daniel; and Watson, Marilyn, 1985–1986. "A Program That Combines Character Development and Academic Achievement." *Educational Leadership,* December/January: 32–35.

Schlenker, Barry R., ed. 1985. *The Self and Social Life.* New York: McGraw-Hill.

———; Hallam, John R.; and McCown, Nancy E., 1983. "Motives and Social Evaluation: Actor-Observer Differences in the Delineation of Motives for a Beneficial Act." *Jour. of Experimental Soc. Psychol.,* 19:254–273.

Schroeder, David A. et al., in press. "Empathic Concern and Helping Behavior: Egoism or Altruism?" *Jour. of Experimental Soc. Psychol.*

Schulweis, Harold M., 1986. "They Were Our Brothers' Keepers." *Moment,* May: 47–50.

———, n.d. "Using History to Restore a Sense of Balance." *Baltimore Jewish Times.*

Schwartz, Shalom H., 1968. "Awareness of Consequences and the Influence of Moral Norms on Interpersonal Behavior." *Sociometry,* 31, 4:355–369.

———, 1970a. "Elicitation of Moral Obligation and Self-Sacrificing Behavior: An Experimental Study of Volunteering to Be a Bone Marrow Donor." *Jour. of Personality and Soc. Psychol.,* 15, 4:283–293.

———, 1970b. "Moral Decision Making and Behavior." In Jacqueline R. Macaulay and Leonard Berkowitz, eds., 1970.

———, 1973. "Normative Explanations of Helping Behavior: A Critique, Proposal, and Empirical Test." *Jour. of Experimental Soc. Psychol.,* 9:349–364.

———, 1975. "The Justice of Need and the Activation of Humanitarian Norms." *Jour. of Social Issues,* 31, 3:111–136.

———, 1977. "Normative Influences on Altruism." *Advances in Experimental Soc. Psychol.,* 10:221–279.

———, 1986. "Altruism and Aggression." In H. A. Michener, J. D. Delamater, and S. H. Schwartz, *Social Psychology* (San Diego: Harcourt Brace Jovanovich.

———, and Ben-David, A., 1976. "Responsibility and Helping in an Emergency: Effects of Blame, Ability, and Denial of Responsibility." *Sociometry,* 39:406–415.

Schwartz, Shalom H., and Fleishman, John A., 1982. "Effects of Negative Personal Norms on Helping Behavior." *Personality and Soc. Psychol. Bull.*, 8, 1:81–86.

Schwartz, Shalom H., and Gottlieb, Avi, 1980a. "Bystander Anonymity and Reactions to Emergencies." *Jour. of Personality and Soc. Psychol.*, 39:418–430.

————, 1980b. "Participants' Postexperimental Reactions and the Ethics of Bystander Research." *Jour. of Experimental Soc. Psych.*, 17:396–407.

————, 1980c. "Participation in a Bystander Intervention Experiment and Subsequent Everyday Helping: Ethical Considerations." *Jour. of Experimental Soc. Psychol.*, 16:161–171.

Schwartz, Shalom H., and Howard, Judith A., 1980. "Explanations of the Moderation Effect of Responsibility Denial on the Personal Norm-Behavior Relationship." *Soc. Psychol. Quart.*, 43:441–446.

————, 1982. "Helping and Cooperation: A Self-Based Motivational Model." In V. J. Derlega and J. Grzelak, eds., 1982.

Schweitzer, Albert, [1933] 1949. *Out of My Life and Thought.* New York: Henry Holt and Company.

Segal, Nancy L., 1984. "Cooperation, Competition, and Altruism Within Twin Sets: A Reappraisal." *Ethol. and Sociobiol.*, 5:163–177.

————, 1985. "Holocaust Twins: Their Special Bond." *Psychol. Today*, August:52–58.

————, 1987. "Cooperation, Competition, and Altruism in Human Twinships: A Sociobiological Approach." In Kevin MacDonald, ed., *Sociobiological Perspectives on Human Development* (New York: Springer-Verlag).

Seth, Indu R., and Gupta, Prabha, 1983. "Altruism in Hindus and Muslims." *Psychol. Studies*, 28, 2:69–73.

Seyfarth, Robert M., and Cheney, Dorothy L., 1984. "Grooming, Alliances and Reciprocal Altruism in Vervet Monkeys." *Nature*, 308:541–543.

Shackleton, Edward, 1959. *Nansen the Explorer.* London: Witherby.

Shaffer, David R., 1985–1986. "Is Mood-Induced Altruism a Form of Hedonism?" *Humboldt Jour. of Soc. Relations*, 13, 1–2:195–216.

Sharabany, R., and Bar-Tal, D., 1982. "Theories of the Development of Altruism: Review, Comparison, and Integration." *Internat. Jour. of Behavioral Development*, 5:49–80.

Sherif, Muzafer et al., 1961. *Intergroup Conflict and Cooperation.* Norman, OK: University of Oklahoma Institute of Intergroup Relations.

Sherrod, Drury R., and Downs, Robin, 1974. "Environmental Determinants of Altruism: The Effects of Stimulus Overload and Perceived Control on Helping." *Jour. of Experimental Soc. Psychol.*, 10, 5:468–479.

Shostak, Marjorie, 1983. *Nisa: The Life and Words of a !Kung Woman.* New York: Vintage.

Shotland, R. Lance, 1985. "When Bystanders Just Stand By." *Psychol. Today*, June:50–55.

————, and Huston, Ted L., 1979. "Emergencies: What Are They and Do They Influence Bystanders to Intervene?" *Jour. of Personality and Soc. Psychol.*, 37, 10:1822–1834.

Simons, Caolyn W., and Piliavin, Jane Allyn, 1972. "Effect of Deception on Reactions to a Victim." *Jour. of Personality and Soc. Psychol.*, 21, 1:56–60.

Skinner, B. F., 1972. *Beyond Freedom and Dignity.* New York: Bantam/Vintage.

————, 1978. "The Ethics of Helping People." In Lauren G. Wispé, ed., 1978.

Smith, Adam, [1759] 1966. *The Theory of Moral Sentiments.* New York: A. M. Kelley.

Smith, Eric Alden, 1985. "Inuit Foraging Groups: Some Simple Models Incorporating Conflicts of Interest, Relatedness, and Central-Place Sharing." *Ethol. and Sociobiol.*, 6:27–47.

Smith, Ronald E.; Wheeler, Gregory; and Diener, Edward, 1975. "Faith Without Works: Jesus People, Resistance to Temptation, and Altruism." *Jour. of Applied Soc. Psychol.*, 5, 4:320–330.

Smithson, Michael; Amato, Paul R.; and Pearce, Philip, 1983. *Dimensions of Helping Behavior.* Oxford: Pergamon Press.

Solomon, Daniel et al., 1987a. *Promoting Prosocial Behavior in Schools: A Second Interim Report on a Five-Year Longitudinal Demonstration Project.* San Ramon, CA: Developmental Studies Center.

———— et al., 1985. "A Program to Promote Interpersonal Consideration and Cooperation in Children." In Robert Slavin et al., eds., *Learning to Cooperate, Cooperating to Learn* (New York: Plenum Publishing Corp.).

———— et al., 1987b. *Enhancing Children's Prosocial Behavior in the Classroom.* San Ramon, CA: Developmental Studies Center.

Spivak, G., and Shure, M., 1974. *Social Adjustment of Young Children.* San Francisco: Jossey-Bass.

Staub, Ervin, 1969. "A Child in Distress: The Effect of Focusing Responsibility on Children on Their Attempts to Help." *Developmental Psychology,* 2, 1:153.

————, 1970. "A Child in Distress: The Influence of Age and Number of Witnesses on Children's Attempts to Help." *Jour. of Personality and Soc. Psychol.*, 14, 2:130–140.

————, 1971a. "A Child in Distress: The Influence of Nurturance and Modeling on Children's Attempts to Help." *Developmental Psychology,* 5:123–133.

————, 1971b. "Helping a Person in Distress: The Influence of Implicit and Explicit 'Rules' of Conduct on Children and Adults." *Jour. of Personality and Soc. Psychol.*, 17, 2:137–144.

————, 1971c. "The Learning and Unlearning of Aggression." In *The Control of Aggression and Violence,* edited by Jerome Singer. New York: Academic Press, Ch. 4.

————, 1971d. "The Use of Role Playing and Induction in Children's

Learning of Helping and Sharing Behavior." *Child Development*, 42: 805–816.

———, 1974. "Helping a Distressed Person: Social, Personality, and Stimulus Determinants." *Advances in Experimental Soc. Psychol.*, 7:293–341.

———, 1975. "To Rear a Prosocial Child: Reasoning, Learning by Doing, and Learning by Teaching Others." In David J. DePalma and Jeanne M. Foley, eds., *Moral Development: Current Theory and Research* (Hillsdale, NJ: Lawrence Erlbaum Associates).

———, 1978a. *Positive Social Behavior and Morality.* Vol. 1, *Social and Personal Influences.* New York: Academic Press.

———, 1978b. "Predicting Prosocial Behavior: A Model for Specifying the Nature of Personality-Situation Interaction. In L. A. Pervin and M. Lewis, eds., *Perspectives in International Psychology* (New York: Plenum Press).

———, 1979. *Positive Social Behavior and Morality.* Vol. 2, *Socialization and Development.* New York: Academic Press.

———, 1981. "Promoting Positive Behavior in Schools, in Other Educational Settings, and in the Home." In J. Philippe Rushton and Richard Sorrentino, eds., 1981.

———, 1984. "Steps Toward a Comprehensive Theory of Moral Conduct: Goal Orientation, Social Behavior, Kindness, and Cruelty." In William M. Kurtines and Jacob L. Gewirtz, eds., 1984.

———, 1985. "The Psychology of Perpetrators and Bystanders." *Political Psychol.*, 6, 1:61–85.

———, 1986. "A Conception of the Determinants and Development of Altruism and Aggression: Motives, the Self, and the Environment." In Carolyn Zahn-Waxler, E. Mark Cummings, and Ronald J. Iannotti, eds., 1986.

———, 1988a. "The Evolution of Caring and Nonaggressive Persons and Societies." *Jour. of Social Issues,* 44, 2:81–100.

———, 1988b. "The Roots of Altruism and Heroic Rescue" (review of Oliner and Oliner, 1988). *The World and I,* July.

———, in press (a). "The Evolution of Bystanders, German Psychoanalysts, and Lessons for Today." *Political Psychol.*

———, 1989b. *The Roots of Evil: The Psychological and Cultural Origins of Genocide.* New York: Cambridge University Press.

———, in press (b). "The Psychology of Torture and Torturers." *Jour. of Social Issues.*

———, and Baer, Robert S., 1974. "Stimulus Characteristics of a Sufferer and Difficulty of Escape as Determinants of Helping." *Jour. of Personality and Soc. Psychol.*, 30, 2:279–284.

Staub, Ervin et al., eds., 1984. *The Development and Maintenance of Prosocial Behavior: International Perspectives on Positive Morality.* New York: Plenum Press.

Staub, Ervin, and Feinberg, Helene K., 1980. "Regularities in Peer Interaction, Empathy, and Sensitivity to Others." Paper presented at the meeting of the American Psychological Association, Montreal, Can.

Staub, Ervin, and Noerenberg, Henry, 1981. "Property Rights, Deservingness, Reciprocity, Friendship: The Transactional Character of Children's Sharing Behavior." *Jour. of Personality and Soc. Psychol.*, 40:271–289.

Stein, Morris I., 1966. *Volunteers for Peace: The First Group of Peace Corps Volunteers in a Rural Community Development Program in Colombia, South America.* New York: John Wiley & Sons.

Strayer, Janet, 1980. "Naturalistic Study of Empathetic Behaviors and Their Relation to Affective States and Perspective-Taking Skills in Preschool Children." *Child Development,* 51:815–822.

Tajfel, Henri, and Billig, Michael, 1974. "Familiarity and Categorization in Intergroup Behavior." *Jour. of Experimental Soc. Psychol.*, 10:159–170.

Teachman, Goody; and Orme, Michael, 1981. "Effects of Aggressive and Prosocial Film Material on Altruistic Behavior of Children." *Psychol. Reports,* 48, 3:699–702.

Tec, Nechama, 1983. "Righteous Christians in Poland." *Internat. Soc. Sci. Rev.,* Winter:12–19.

———, 1984a. "Sex Distinctions and Passing as Christians During the Holocaust." *East European Quarterly,* 18, 1:113–123.

———, 1984b. *Dry Tears: The Story of a Lost Childhood.* New York: Oxford University Press.

———, 1986a. "Polish Anti-Semitism and the Rescuing of Jews." *East European Quarterly,* 20, 3:299–315.

———, 1986b. "Polish Anti-Semites and Jewish Rescue During the Holocaust." *Proc. of the Ninth Congress of Jewish Studies,* div. B, 3:181–188.

———, 1986c. *When Light Pierced the Darkness.* New York: Oxford University Press.

Tellegen, Auke et al., in press. "Personality Similarity in Twins Reared Apart and Together. *Jour. of Personality and Soc. Psychol.*

Thomas, Elizabeth Marshall, 1958. *The Harmless People.* New York: Vintage.

Thomas, George C.; Batson, C. Daniel; and Coke, Jay S., 1981. "Do Good Samaritans Discourage Helpfulness? Self-Perceived Altruism After Exposure to Highly Helpful Others." *Jour. of Personality and Soc. Psychol.*, 40, 1:194–200.

Thompson, William C.; Cowan, Claudia L.; and Rosenhan, David L., 1980. "Focus of Attention Mediates the Impact of Negative Affect on Altruism." *Jour. of Personality and Soc. Psychol.*, 38, 2:291–300.

Titmuss, Richard M., 1971. *The Gift Relationship: From Human Blood to Social Policy.* New York: Pantheon Books.

Toi, Miho, and Batson, C. Daniel, 1982. "More Evidence That Empathy Is a Source of Altruistic Motivation." *Jour. of Personality and Soc. Psychol.*, 43, 2:281–292.

Trivers, Robert L., 1971. "The Evolution of Reciprocal Altruism." *Quarterly Rev. of Biol.*, 46:35–57.

———, 1985. *Social Evolution.* Menlo Park, CA: Benjamin/Cummings.

Turnbull, Colin, 1972. *The Mountain People.* New York: Simon & Schuster.

———, 1978. "Rethinking the Ik." In Charles D. Laughlin, Jr., and Ivan A. Brady, eds., *Extinction and Survival in Human Populations* (New York: Columbia University Press).

Underwood, Bill et al., 1977. "Attention, Negative Affect, and Altruism," *Personality and Soc. Psychol. Bull.*, 3, 1:54–58.

Underwood, Bill, and Moore, Bert S., 1982. "The Generality of Altruism in Children." In Nancy Eisenberg, ed., 1982b.

van de Kragt, Alphonse J. C.; Orbell, John M.; and Dawes, Robyn M., 1983. "The Minimal Contributing Set as a Solution to Public Goods Problems." *Amer. Polit. Sci. Rev.*, 77, 1:112–122.

van de Kragt, Alphonse J. C. et al., 1986. "Doing Well and Doing Good as Ways of Resolving Social Dilemmas." In Henk A. M. Wilke, Dave M. Messick, and Christel G. Rutte, eds., *Experimental Social Dilemmas* (Frankfurt am Main: Verlag Peter Lang).

Viorst, Milton, 1986. *Making a Difference: The Peace Corps at Twenty-Five.* New York: Weidenfeld & Nicholson.

Walster, Elaine; Berscheid, Ellen; and Walster, G. Wiliam, 1970. "The Exploited: Justice or Justification?" In Jaqueline Macaulay and Leonard Bernstein, eds., 1970.

Wexler, Mark N., 1981. "The Biology of Human Altruism." *Soc. Science*, 56, 4:195–203.

———, 1981–1982. "Sociobiology and Human Altruism: A Social Scientist's Perspective." *Humboldt Jour. of Soc. Relations*, 9, 1:32–60.

Whiting, Beatrice, and Whiting, John, 1975. *Children of Six Cultures.* Cambridge: Harvard University Press.

Whitworth, John McKelvie, 1976. *God's Blueprints: A Sociological Study of Three Utopian Sects.* London and Boston: Routledge & Kegan Paul.

Wicklund, Robert, and Gewirtzer, Peter, 1982. *Symbolic Self-Completion.* Hillsdale, NJ: Lawrence Erlbaum Associates.

Wiener, Valerie Lewis, 1987. "Psychology of Favors: Age and Gender Differences in Everyday Helping." Paper presented at the 1987 meeting of the American Psychological Association, New York, NY.

Wilson, Edward O., 1975. *Sociobiology: The New Synthesis.* Cambridge: Harvard University Press.

———, [1970] 1979. *On Human Nature.* New York: Bantam Books.

Wilson, Midge, and Dovidio, John F., 1985. "Effects of Perceived Attractiveness and Feminist Orientation on Helping Behavior." *Jour. of Soc. Psychol.*, 125, 4:415–420.

Wispé, Lauren G., ed., 1978. *Altruism, Sympathy, and Helping: Psychological and Sociological Principles.* New York: Academic Press.

Woodham-Smith, Cecil, 1950. *Florence Nightingale.* London: Constable/The Book Society.

Wundheiler, Luitgard N., 1985–1986. "Oskar Schindler's Moral Development During the Holocaust." *Humboldt Jour. of Soc. Relations,* 13, 1–2:333–356.

Zahn-Waxler, Carolyn et al., 1984. "Altruism, Aggression, and Social Interaction in Young Children with a Manic-Depressive Parent." *Child Development,* 55:112–122.

Zahn-Waxler, Carolyn; Cummings, E. Mark; and Iannotti, Ronald J., eds., 1986. *Altruism and Aggression: Social and Biological Origins.* Cambridge: Cambridge University Press.

Zahn-Waxler, Carolyn, and Kochanska, Grazyna, 1989. "The Origins of Guilt." In Ross Thompson, ed., *36th Annual Nebraska Symposium on Motivation: Socioeconomic Development* (Lincoln, NE: University of Nebraska Press).

Zahn-Waxler, Carolyn, and Radke-Yarrow, Marian, 1982. "The Development of Altruism: Alternative Research Strategies." In Nancy Eisenberg, ed., 1982b.

———, and King, Robert A., 1979. "Child Rearing and Children's Prosocial Initiations Towards Victims of Distress." *Child Development,* 50, 2:319–330.

———, 1983. "Early Altruism and Guilt." *Academic Psychol. Bull.,* 5, 2:247–259.

Zimbardo, Philip G. et al., 1974. "The Psychology of Imprisonment: Privation, Power, and Pathology." In Zick Rubin, ed., *Doing Unto Others* (Englewood Cliffs, NJ: Prentice-Hall).

ACKNOWLEDGMENTS

I am grateful to the many people who, in various ways, made this book possible.

My first and principal thanks go to the researchers and scholars who provided me with background information, guidance, reprints, unpublished manuscripts, and original documents (and especially to those who gave generously of their time in the form of interviews): Bem Allen, Western Illinois University; Richard L. Archer, Southwest Texas State University; Daniel Bar-Tal, Tel Aviv University; C. Daniel Batson, University of Kansas; Donald Baumann, University of Montana; Arthur L. Beaman, University of Montana; Leonard Berkowitz, University of Wisconsin—Madison; Joseph A. Blake, Indiana University East; James H. Bryan, Northwestern University; Linnda R. Caporael, Rensselaer Polytechnic Institute; Robert Cialdini, Arizona State University; E. Mark Cummings, National Institute of Mental Health; John Darley, Princeton University; Robyn M. Dawes, Carnegie-Mellon University; John Dovidio, Colgate University; Julian J. Edney, Colorado State University; Nancy Eisenberg, Arizona State University; Norma Deitch Feshbach and Seymour Feshbach, both of the University of California, Los Angeles; William J. Froming, University of Florida; Jim Fultz, Northern Illinois University; Gilbert Geis, University of California, Irvine; John Gibbs, Ohio State University; Robert B. Glassman, Lake Forest College; William J. Goode, Harvard University; Charles Gruder, University of Illinois, Chicago; Robert B. Hampson, Southern

Methodist University; Mary B. Harris, University of New Mexico; Selma G. Hirsh, The American Jewish Committee; Martin L. Hoffman, New York University; Nancy Howell, University of Toronto; Carollee Howes, University of California, Los Angeles; Ted Huston, University of Texas, Austin; Alice Isen, University of Maryland, Baltimore County; David A. Kennett, Vassar College; Douglas T. Kenrick, Arizona State University; Dennis Krebs, Simon Fraser University; Bibb Latané, University of North Carolina; Wim Liebrand, University of Groningen, Netherlands; John Loehlin, University of Texas, Austin; Mary Main, University of California, Berkeley; Robert E. Marcus, University of Maryland Institute for Child Study; Robert K. Merton, Columbia University; David Messick, University of California, Santa Barbara; Norman Miller, University of Southern California; Young Jay Mulkey, American Institute for Character Education; Paul Mussen, University of California, Berkeley; Samuel P. Oliner and Pearl M. Oliner, both of Humboldt State University; Lizette Peterson, University of Missouri, Columbia; Jane Allyn Piliavin, University of Wisconsin–Madison; Robert Plomin, Pennsylvania State University; Richard J. Pomazal, University of Pittsburgh; Janusz Reykowski, Polska Akademia Nauk, Poland; Carol Rittner, United States Holocaust Memorial Council; Daniel Romer, University of Illinois, Chicago; David L. Rosenhan, Stanford University; Zick Rubin, Brandeis University; J. Philippe Rushton, University of Western Ontario; Sandra Scarr, University of Virginia; Rabbi Harold Schulweis, Temple Valley Beth Shalom, Encino, California; Shalom Schwartz, The Hebrew University of Jerusalem; Nancy L. Segal, University of Minnesota; Daniel Solomon, Developmental Studies Center, San Ramon, California; Ervin Staub, University of Massachusetts, Amherst; Morris I. Stein, New York University; Nechama Tec, University of Connecticut, Stamford; Goody Teachman, Ontario Institute for Studies in Education; George C. Thomas, University of Kansas, Lawrence; Robert Trivers, University of California, Santa Cruz; Mark N. Wexler, Simon Fraser University; and Carolyn Zahn-Waxler, National Institute of Mental Health.

Special thanks are due to C. Joseph Martin, superintendent of Burlington, New Jersey, city public schools, and William McNamara, principal of the Elias Boudinot School, for making my visit to the Boudinot School possible.

I also thank the Carnegie Hero Fund Commission for its help and Timothy Mosher, one of its honorees, for recounting his story;

the Peace Corps; Claudia Sawicki, director of East End Hope for Hospice; and Marjorie Judge and Esther Taylor, both of Southampton, New York, who told me of their work as hospice volunteers.

I am indebted most of all to Ervin Staub, already named above, a fountain of information, who in addition to all else read this book in manuscript and gave me many valuable corrections. It is, of course, not his fault or anyone else's but mine if errors still remain.

Connie Roosevelt, my editor, believed in this project from the beginning and gave me much creative criticism along the way. Bernice Hunt, my wife, read the manuscript in both its first and its final forms, and offered countless valuable editorial suggestions.

I gratefully acknowledge permission to reprint the following passages:

On p. 46: from *The Chimpanzees of Gombe* by Jane Goodall (Harvard University Press, copyright © 1986), p. 378; by permission of the publisher;

On p. 73: from *The Italians* by Luigi Barzini (Atheneum Publishers, copyright © 1964), pp. 336–337; by permission of the publisher;

On pp. 74–75: from *Portrait of a Greek Mountain Village* by Juliet du Boulay (Oxford University Press, copyright © 1972), pp. 38–39, 74, and 76; by permission of the author;

On pp. 83–85: from "The Psychology of Imprisonment, Privation, Power, and Pathology," by Philip G. Zimbardo et al., in *Doing Unto Others,* edited by Zick Rubin (Prentice-Hall, copyright © 1974), pp. 63–64, 67, and 70–72; by permission of Philip G. Zimbardo;

On pp. 139 and 141–142: from *Influence: Science and Practice* by Robert B. Cialdini (Scott, Foresman and Company, copyright © 1988), pp. 129 and 131–132; by permission of the publisher and the author;

On pp. 159–160 and 168: from *The Courage to Care,* edited by Carol Rittner and Sondra Myers (New York University Press, copyright © 1986), pp. 28, 33, and 40–42; by permission of the publisher.

INDEX

Abused children, 13
  bystander effect and, 138
Adulthood, development of altruism in
      (self-socialization), 116–120, 124–126
  bystander effect and, 120–121
  Nansen, 117–118
  Pappenheim, 116–117
  Peace Corps return volunteers, 121–122
  Schindler, 119
Africa
  the Ik tribe, 66–69
  the !Kung tribe, 63–66, 92
  relief aid for starvation victims in, 14
Aggression, 29
Aiding (norm of altruism), 77
AIDS research, raising funds for, 13
Air Florida plane crash (1982), heroic altruism
      during, 11–12, 184
Albanians, We-They hatred between Serbs and,
      90
Allen, Ben P., 141
Altruism
  cost-reward calculations of, 148, 175, 177
  creating social supports for, 219–224
    bystander laws, 220
    citizen crime-reporting program, 220
    committed leadership, 224
    control over TV programming, 222–223
    incentives, 219–220
    intergroup activities, 223–224
    organ donation request systems, 222
    public recognition of corporate altruism,
      221–222
  in the curriculum, 212–219
  definitions of, 17–21, 195
  developmental research on determining roots
      of, 104–108
  due to heredity, 99, 105
  egoistic theory of, 175–177

empathy-altruism hypothesis, 178–181, 182
as form of hedonism, 175–176
genetic contributions to, 48–62, 96
Good Samaritan parable, 21–22, 184
hereditary versus learned, 33–34
heroic, 11–12, 51–52, 97
  impulsive or spontaneous helping and,
      153–154
  of Mosher, 129–131, 132, 137
  during natural catastrophes, 86
  of Williams, 11–12, 184
human altruism compared with animal
      altruism, 47, 62–63
hybrid form of, 19–20, 178
institutional, 19
knowledge-created awareness of, 205–209
as learned behavior, 47
mutually enforced, 86–87
natural history of, 102–108
natural selection puzzle, 57–62
norms of, 77
Oliner's definition of, 195
as outcome of various motivations, 181
paradox of, 224
perplexities of, 12–13
power of visual variables and, 145–148
present-day examples of, 13–16
as prosocial behavior, 18
pseudoaltruism, 19–20, 178
reciprocal, 57–59, 62
scientific study of, 26–36
self-sacrificing, 16, 154
self-socialization and, 116–120, 124–126
societal values and norms responsible for,
      72–80
"trait" of, 126
true, 21–26, 181
working definition of, 21
Altruism in animals, 31, 41–47

ABOUT THE AUTHOR

MORTON HUNT writes about the behavioral and social sciences. He attended Temple University and the University of Pennsylvania, worked briefly on the staffs of two magazines, and has been a free-lance writer since 1949. He has written seventeen books, as well as over 400 magazine articles for the *New York Times Magazine*, *The New Yorker*, and other periodicals, and has won a number of prestigious science-writing awards.